Looking to London

Also by Cynthia Cockburn:

Anti-militarism: Political and Gender Dynamics of Peace Movements

From Where We Stand: War, Women's Activism and Feminist Analysis

The Line: Women, Partition and the Gender Order in Cyprus

The Postwar Moment: Militaries, Masculinities and International Peacekeeping
(co-edited with Dubravka Zarkov)

The Space Between Us: Negotiating Gender and National Identities in Conflict

Bringing Technology Home: Gender and Technology in a Changing Europe
(co-edited with Ruza Fürst-Dilić)

Gender and Technology in the Making (co-authored with Susan Ormrod)

In the Way of Women: Men's Resistance to Sex Equality in Organizations

Two-Track Training: Sex Inequalities and the Youth Training Scheme

Machinery of Dominance: Women, Men and Technical Know-how

Brothers: Male Dominance and Technological Change

The Local State: Management of Cities and People

Looking to London

Stories of War, Escape and Asylum

Cynthia Cockburn

First published 2017 by Pluto Press
345 Archway Road, London N6 5AA

www.plutobooks.com

British Library Cataloguing in Publication Data
A catalogue record for this book is available from the British Library

ISBN   978 0 7453 9922 5   Hardback
ISBN   978 0 7453 9921 8   Paperback
ISBN   978 1 7868 0126 5   PDF eBook
ISBN   978 1 7868 0128 9   Kindle eBook
ISBN   978 1 7868 0127 2   EPUB eBook

This book is printed on paper suitable for recycling and made from fully
managed and sustained forest sources. Logging, pulping and manufacturing
processes are expected to conform to the environmental standards of the
country of origin.

Typeset by Stanford DTP Services, Northampton, England

Simultaneously printed in the United Kingdom and United States of America

For Charles,
with whom I became a Londoner.

Contents

Acknowledgements

I wish to thank very warmly all who have supported me in researching and writing this book. Each chapter ends with a footnote, naming and thanking the many people who generously spent time helping me with it. Midway through the project I was unexpectedly hospitalized twice for cancer surgery and received memorable NHS care at University College London Hospital (UCLH), and afterwards at Heathgrove Lodge nursing home in the London Borough of Barnet. Special thanks go to the community of NHS surgeons, doctors, nurses, physios, care workers, cleaners and others from whose skill and kindliness I benefited in those months. I continued my study of London's demography from my UCLH hospital bed: of the first 56 staff of all grades I encountered on the ward, I estimate that only 12 per cent were white British, while 88 per cent were migrants originating in 22 different countries. Here was London's celebrated diversity expressed within the walls of a single workplace, a clear parallel to the place-based communities I was writing about in the localities 'out there'. While recovering the strength I needed to cope with buses and tubes, I often called on the services of a local cab company, Prime Cars, and would like to thank Kamrul and other helpful drivers for enlivening journeys in rain and shine.

My greatest joy in life is the company of my daughters, Claudia Cockburn and Jess Coburn, and my beloved grand-daughters, Elsa Maria, Josie and Deniel. I know you know what your never-failing love and encouragement means to me. Many friends, too, supported me in getting home and back to work. Thanks to you all, but most particularly to you, Liz (Khan) and Sue (Finch), who gave so much time to my needs.

Finally, my publishers. It's been a great pleasure to return to Pluto Press, who trusted me enough back in the 1970s to publish my first book, and several subsequently. It was good to find them surviving and thriving after many setbacks, and as supportive as ever. My special thanks to Anne Beech, Pluto's perceptive and positive-minded

Editor-in-Chief, who encouraged me to persist with the book despite setbacks, and guided me gently through the final stages of writing and editing. Thanks also to Emily Orford, Neda Tehrani, Melanie Patrick, Robert Webb and other Pluto staff who helped in so many ways to get the book into print. *Looking to London* has many failings, this I know. But all of them are down to me, and in spite of the best efforts of all the many people I name and thank.

Introduction

This book is a celebration of London, but a cautious one. It celebrates the city's famous cultural diversity. It celebrates the generations of migrants who have made it what it is. And it celebrates the courage of today's many refugees from war, who are helping make a reality of their belief that London welcomes newcomers. The celebration has to be cautious, however, because London is a profoundly unequal place, of obscene wealth and profound poverty, building sky-high palaces while homeless people, among them many refugees, sleep rough on the streets below. We need to remember, too, that today London is a financial centre fostering capitalist exploitation worldwide, and yesterday was the capital of an empire that created the conditions giving rise to wars in Asia and Africa today.

Nonetheless, I have my own reason to value London. I arrived here 63 years ago, as a labour migrant, an ill-informed 19-year-old from the socially conservative, class-ridden and almost wholly white British industrial East Midlands in which I was born. Travelling to the capital in search of a shorthand-typist's pay packet changed the trajectory of my life, entirely for the better. I kept a diary in those days. It tells me that on Saturday, 29 August 1953, my father brought me to London and deposited me and my suitcase in a hostel housing 300 women. That Monday, 31 August, early in the morning I went out onto the pavement and, asking my way from people around me, located my workplace. I was shown to a desk and sat down at the typewriter – one of those heavy manual machines we used in those days. The people with whom, morning and evening, I packed into London's red buses absorbed my attention. Many were, I discovered, labour migrants like myself, but from further afield. Quite a few were Caribbean and Asian, from the Commonwealth.

My first move out of hostel accommodation was into a small flat in Victoria, shared with other women. Next, I lived for a while in a rented room, which I had to myself. My job was in the clerical grades of government service, and when I reached the age of 21 I became liable to a foreign 'posting'. They sent me to Bangkok, Thailand, to be the secretary of the British Information Officer in the UK Embassy. There, I began to register facts about the wider world of which till then I'd been ignorant. Thailand, one of the few countries in Asia that avoided colonization, taught me what 'imperialism' had meant elsewhere. I had a lesson in 'revolution' too. At the back of a cupboard in the office I found an extraordinarily beautiful photographic portrait of Ho Chi Minh. Who was this man? Learning about North Vietnam directed my gaze towards Mao Tse Tung, and I began to read about the 'long march' of the communists which, only eight years previously, had culminated in the creation of the People's Republic of China. I wanted to go there. I wanted to see for myself. But when the British Embassy learned that I was seeking a Chinese visa, the Chargé d'Affaires stood me on the mat and said 'No way! Not while you're an employee of the British state. Are you defecting or something?' So I resigned my job, got the visa and travelled in China. Those weeks were an important addition to my erratic education. And with a tale to tell, I found I could write.

Back in London in 1958, now with a partner, I settled down in a small rented flat in Primrose Hill. I made a living from freelance journalism while he studied architecture at North London Polytechnic. Behaving, as so many did in those days, in a socially endorsed and orderly manner, we got married (in church, no less) and a few years later had our first child. It was at that point, in 1966, we moved from our flat in Primrose Hill to an address in Kentish Town. Property was cheap in those days, and with only modest help from our families we were able to buy the freehold of a nineteenth-century terrace house. This house became a truly felt 'home' and would, as it turned out, remain my home till the present day, half a century on. I often dwell on this relationship of mine to the concept of home, the comfort, security and longevity that define it. It's what makes me pay such close attention to refugee women as they speak of the homes they have been forced to abandon, and their feelings about the places – tents, bed-and-breakfast lodgings, rented rooms – they've inhabited on their way to achieving a new one.

Wars and refuge from wars began to take on significance for me as my partner and I explored our borough, Camden. We found ourselves among two large migrant communities, Greek Cypriot and Irish. I remember so well the little Cypriot shop in Inverness Street where we would go for olives and *pitta* bread. Each weekend there would be a wedding in the Greek Orthodox Church at the end of our street. Cyprus was still a British colony then, and many of the older Camden Cypriots had come here as economic migrants. But now some were coming in flight from the fierce anti-imperialist war on the island (remember EOKA?). When independence was won in 1969, refugees continued to arrive, displaced now by the continuing conflict between the ascendant Greek Cypriots and the Turkish Cypriot minority, supported by Turkey, which would eventually result in the division of the island. Around us in Camden we often heard Irish accents too. Of course London had been home to many Irish for decades, indeed centuries. The island of Ireland lies only 20 miles away at the closest point, and was Britain's first colony. But in the late 1960s the Irish Catholic insurgency in British-ruled and predominantly Protestant Northern Ireland, 'the Troubles' as it was called, was getting under way, impelling more Irish across the water.

So, settled in Camden, we were alert to two anti-colonial struggles being lived out in our neighbourhood. However, it has to be said, the main political preoccupation for us in the late 1960s and 1970s was the Cold War, the stand-off between the rival capitalist and communist power blocs that had emerged from the Second World War, both now armed with the 'Atom Bomb'. What got us on to the streets was the menace of the 'nuclear arms race'. The first major march of protest to Aldermaston, in Berkshire, the centre of nuclear weapons development in Britain, took place at Easter 1958. A revived feminist movement had transformed our consciousness during the 1970s, and in the early 1980s feminism found expression within the anti-nuclear movement. Women set up a peace camp at the gates of the Royal Air Force base at Greenham Common in Berkshire, as it prepared to receive US cruise missiles and warheads. The long-lived Greenham women's camp drew thousands to its blockades and demonstrations. As Londoners, we formed local 'Greenham support groups' – the Sirens, the Common Singers – and went at weekends to join the campers, cut the fence and invade the base. And we 'carried Greenham home' to the streets of London.

At this time, and in subsequent decades, I was enabled by help from many encouraging individuals and generous grant-giving bodies to start writing in a different mode, building a sustainable career in academic 'action-research'. I began with a study of local government and its complex relationship with 'community', a concern renewed in this present study in the focus on London's borough councils.[1] The field of gender studies was flourishing in the 1980s. In that decade my theme was men and masculinity in relation to technology, organization and power.[2] But in the 1990s I began to research and write about women anti-war activists and peace-makers (such as we had ourselves been at Greenham Common), and to seek an understanding of the part played by gender differentiation and inequality in militarism and war. The countries I chose for fieldwork on this theme included, naturally enough, those to which life in London had earlier alerted me. Ireland was one of the first. Cyprus soon after. Bosnia, Israel/Palestine, Uganda, Colombia, the Korean peninsula and the Japanese island of Okinawa were among the others.[3]

Seeing the effects of armed conflict on individual lives, and the social movements for peace and justice that arise in response, was what made me so conscious of the presence of asylum seekers and refugees among the diverse communities around me at home. I began to distinguish the war-traumatized minority among London's minorities. And among them, particularly, I noticed women, affected so specifically and profoundly by the militarization of their societies, by masculine violence on every scale, and by displacement. That's why, in mid-2014, I set out with my free pensioner's bus pass to meet the generation of women not long-since arrived here in flight from oppression, injustice and war. I wanted to learn more about the conflicts they'd fled, about their journeys, the reception they received here and what's involved in resettlement. The process, this time, was not research in academic mode, but what I would term 'engaged documentary'.

THE STRUCTURE OF THE BOOK

So here's the way the book is organized. Chapter 1 is about London's magnetic attraction for migrants from overseas. Well over one in three of resident Londoners today was born in some other country, migrated here, settled – and maybe raised a family. There's scarcely a country in the world without its representative Londoners. Even Antarctica contributes 13. So I look at how waves of incomers were drawn to the capital as it grew from a fortified Roman town to a late nineteenth-century industrial capital. Immigration control began in 1905, with racist selective intention. After the Second World War, new controls sought to deter black- and brown-skinned migrants from former colonies, while continuing to admit white Commonwealth citizens. We see how the challenge to the UK border changed markedly in the 1980s and 1990s, with a rapid growth in the numbers seeking asylum from oppression and conflict. A sequence of immigration acts sought to stem the flow by reducing right of entry and creating deterrent reception conditions. As 'terror' became an issue in the following decade, surveillance and security legislation cast asylum seekers as a threat. Affecting London particularly was the introduction in 2000 of compulsory dispersal of incomers to selected regions to take the pressure off the capital. The chapter ends with a look at London's continuing appeal for refugees, local authorities' responsibilities of care towards them, and the strategies of integration and cohesion the boroughs apply.

Next comes the first of four chapters in which I drop to the local level, to look more closely at the experience of a particular London borough and one of its notable minority communities – one that has substantial numbers who have arrived there as refugees in flight from war. Thus, Chapter 2 takes us to the north-east Inner London Borough of Hackney and its well-established community of Kurds. It introduces the Kurds as a people, one that has lived for millennia in a region which today spans the borders of four nation states: Iran, Iraq, Syria and Turkey. In particular we look at the story of those Kurds living in south-east Turkey and their struggle for recognition and minority rights, which since the 1980s has involved an intermittent armed resistance by the Kurdistan Workers' Party (the PKK) against the oppression of the Turkish state. I go on to tell of the flight of Kurdish refugees to the UK and the choice made by many to settle and re-home in Hackney and neighbouring boroughs. In Hackney I meet officers, councillors and some Kurdish community organizations, before tracing the important role played by women and feminism in the Kurdish movement in Turkey and in the thought and writings of the imprisoned Kurdish leader, Abdullah Öcalan. I introduce three Kurdish women, now Londoners. The first is Suna, who tells of her imprisonment and torture for Kurdish activism in Istanbul, and her escape to London. Second is Bercem, who as a child arrived with her parents, stowaways on a Channel ferry. And then comes Turkan, who has continued to pay a price for her commitment to the Kurdish movement, which the UK government deems a terror organization.

Next, to one of the four poorest countries in the world, Somalia, where 73 per cent of the population live in poverty, people are deeply riven by clan, failed governments and armed conflict have prevailed since the early 1990s and, in the last decade, the terror group Al-Shabaab have been a continuing source of violence. Chapter 3 opens with a brief history, follows with an account of recent strife, and then looks at the position of women in Somali society in the past and today. I trace the internal displacement of population, the flight of refugees across the border to camps in Kenya, and beyond to a worldwide Somali diaspora. In the peak year of 1999, Somalis comprised 11 per cent of refugees arriving in the UK. Many followed the steps of early seafaring Somali migrants and settled near the docks in London's East End. I focus in on the London Borough of Tower Hamlets and learn of council policies in relation to their sizeable Somalilander community today. At a Somali cultural event I meet Hinda and Ubah, two young women who experienced war, escaped to the UK in the 1990s, and are now raising families in Tower Hamlets. Illustrating the activism of many refugee Londoners, I introduce Dahabo, who has been prompted by her asylum-seeking experience to become a feminist advocate for women's rights, and is the founder of Voices of Somali Women in London.

The entry point in Chapter 4 is the bitter conflict between the Sinhalese Buddhist majority of Sri Lanka, dominant in the institutions of the post-colonial state, and the Tamil Hindu population dwelling mainly in the north and east of the island. State discrimination against the Tamil minority gave rise to resistance and eventually an armed movement, the Liberation Tigers of Tamil Eelam (LTTE, or the Tamil Tigers), seeking an independent state. An exceedingly violent civil war culminated in 2009 in the defeat of the Tigers. Many Tamils fled the country – the UK a favoured destination. I look at the numbers seeking asylum here, and the UK government's resistance to granting it. I home in on a Tamil community in the Outer London Borough of Hounslow, in West London. I explore the council's strategies towards this and its other minorities, and go on to tell the story of Thavarani

(Rani) Nagulendram, founder of the Tamil Community Centre in Hounslow, who experienced the early years of the conflict and came to London in 1991. Now, 27 years on, Rani thinks of London as her permanent home. But some Tamil women are not so permitted. They are imprisoned by the Home Office, awaiting the result of asylum appeals. I draw on critical feminist investigations into Yarl's Wood Immigration Removal Centre, and end the chapter with the stories of Veena and Srisivakumar, two Tamil women who recently experienced its un-homely regime, anticipating forced deportation to Colombo where both had reason to fear a renewal of imprisonment and torture.

The fourth borough case study brings us back to north-central London and simultaneously returns us to Africa. Chapter 5 looks at refugees from the Sudan in Camden – the story begins when the Sudan was a single country, though already deeply conflictual. The country is dominated politically by the relatively pale-skinned, Arabic-speaking, Muslim Sudanese of the northern Nile region, who have sought to impose Islamic belief and law on the entire polity. Their despising and repression of the black-skinned 'African' peoples of the south, many of them Christians, led to a prolonged war and, in 2011, the creation of a separate state of South Sudan, where war has continued. Before and since separation, the 'Arab' regime in Khartoum has also engaged in brutal repression of rebellions by Darfuris in the north-west and the 'African' people of the Nuba Mountains in the south-east. We see the effect of these wars on women, in particular the prevalence of rape and other sexualized violence. I introduce Grace, a southern woman who fled the south–north conflict as a refugee in 2000, reaching London with the help of a people smuggler, and settled in the London Borough of Camden, where I got to know her in a Sudanese women's community project. After looking at Camden's policy and practice towards its incoming minority communities, I introduce 'Fatima' and 'Amina', the first of Darfuri origin, the second an inhabitant of Khartoum who was arrested and tortured by the regime for her activism in support of Darfuris. Finally we hear the story of Marwa, daughter of Nuban parents relocated to the capital, where all were active against the regime. A Londoner for ten years now, she remains a Nuban activist.

In early 2017, approaching the end of this documentation of war, flight and resettlement, my narrative in Chapter 6 steps abruptly into the here and now, where I'm living in a city that is challenged by a surging demand for asylum and deeply divided about how to respond. The eastern Mediterranean region has been experiencing the biggest flow of refugees occurring anywhere since the Second World War. Most are fleeing the current civil war in Syria, while others are driven by prolonged conflicts in other countries – Iraq, Afghanistan, Somalia, Eritrea. The chapter opens with the historic causes of the Syrian war, including the part Britain played in laying the groundwork for today's conflict. I trace a trajectory from the popular uprising of 2011 to outright war today, the involvement of international and regional powers, and the impact on women. We move on to the 'migration crisis', and the inability of the states on whose national borders the refugees are clustered to gain the agreement of the European Union countries, and the rest of the world, on a fair and feasible way of 'sharing the burden'. I track the UK's foot-dragging response and miserly resettlement quota. The years 2014 to 2017 have seen, fostered by the movement Citizens UK, the growth of an energetic expression of 'Refugees Welcome', but within a climate of increasing hostility to immigrants of all kinds, manifest in the outcome of the referendum on EU membership and the associated 'Brexit' movement. Then follows an account of a positive initiative of Syrian refugee support and resettlement in the London Borough of Lambeth, involving an energetic partnership between the community activists of Lambeth Citizens (including diverse faith groups working together), local schools and a hands-on charity, working closely with officers and elected members of the local authority. The book closes with the story of a newly arrived Syrian family.

1

London: Magnet for Migrants

Two things are special about London: its sheer size, and its cultural diversity. With more than eight million inhabitants at the 2011 census, London is eight times more populous than the next biggest UK city, Birmingham, and at least twice as large as the biggest in Europe, Berlin, which has little more than three and a half million. It rivals New York, the most populous city in the USA, a country with five times our national population. London's growth over the last two centuries has been spectacular. Starting with around a million inhabitants in 1801, Greater London had reached three million by 1861, six million by 1901 and by 1931 was almost its present size. It lost a little during the Second World War, but remained fairly steady at between seven and eight million during the remainder of the century, until a notable 14 per cent hike in the first decade after the millennium.[1]

The other famed feature of London's demography is the number and variety of Londoners' countries of origin, generating an extraordinary and inspiring range of distinctive looks, life trajectories and cultures in the streets and neighbourhoods of the capital. The census of 2011, the latest we have on going to press, tells us that almost three million (37 per cent) of Greater London's 8.2 million inhabitants are first-generation migrants, individuals who were born in some country other than the UK and have come here during their lifetime. Of this migrant population just over half (52 per cent) are women. A language other than English is the main language of more than one in five Londoners.[2] In four of Greater London's 32 boroughs, those who are foreign-born make up more than half of the census population. These boroughs are Brent, Kensington and Chelsea, Newham and Westminster. Eighteen of the world's countries have populations of more than 50,000 in London. Six have 100,000 or more – they are Bangladesh, India, Republic of Ireland, Nigeria, Pakistan and Poland.

Bear in mind, besides, that a subsequent generation, children born to these adults since they arrived in the UK, do not feature in the census at all. They may well double the size of these communities.[3]

Any capital city, or, let us say, any town as it grows to become a capital, inevitably attracts inward migration from near and far. Some is individual, some comes in waves from particular directions, bringing distinctive cultures. In *The Peopling of London*, Nick Merriman reminds us that, situated as we are at the far western edge of the continent, attached to it by a land bridge during ice ages, cut off by sea during periods of warming, 'It is possible to argue that, from early immigrants to the refugees of today, everyone living in London is descended, however distantly, from people who have come from abroad.'[4] Some stone-age arrivals left their knapped flints and animal bones on the shores of the proto-Thames. When the Romans invaded in 43 CE and founded the walled town of London, they brought with them as soldiers, administrators and slaves people not only from their Italian homeland but from all over the Roman Empire – Greece, Anatolia, Africa. Merchants accompanied them. No doubt many Celts, the island's predecessor-people, lived within the walls of Roman London too, and in the half millennium between the Roman withdrawal and the Norman Conquest, there came Angles, Saxons, Jutes, Frisians and eventually Vikings, from across the North Sea. The historian Bede, writing in the eighth century CE, describes London as 'a trading centre for many nations who visit it by land and sea'.[5] The Norman Conquest in 1066 brought French lords and lackeys to the capital. Some of these 'French' were Jews, who played a crucial role financing the Exchequer and the ruling class, but were already subject to discrimination, being forbidden to own land, carry arms or employ Christians. In 1290 they were expelled from London, indeed from Britain, altogether. Was this the moment Britain put into effect a state-regulated border, as 'racially' motivated then as it would be 700 years later?

As the capital's population grew in the second millennium of the Christian era, it was mainly by inland migration from the provinces and peripheries. But people were still coming from across the Channel too. Merchants from Italy, Spain, Germany, France and Holland were characteristic inhabitants of London throughout the mediaeval period. Merriman tells of an incident on May Day in 1517 when a mob took to the streets attacking foreigners and destroying their homes and workshops. The rioters were put down, as no doubt they would have been today, by armed officers of the state.[6] By the early 1570s the 'recent overseas' communities are estimated to have been between 5 and 10 per cent of London's 100,000 population. The proportion was increased yet further by the influx during the seventeenth and eighteenth centuries of religious refugees from the Continent. Possibly 50,000 French Protestants – the Huguenots – persecuted by the Catholic church and state, came here in search of safety. Several thousand settled in Spitalfields and other parts of East London, making the place famous for wool and silk weaving. In the middle of the nineteenth century thousands of mainland Europeans, many of them radicals and revolutionaries, crossed the Channel in flight from the nation-building turmoil on the Continent around 1848, sometimes termed the 'People's Spring'.[7] At this point in time Britain still had no governmental provision for the exclusion or expulsion of refugees. There was even a sense of compassion and justice among some locals. Witness the author of an article in the *Times* of 28 February 1853: 'Every civilized people on the face of the earth must be fully aware that this country is the asylum of nations, and that it will defend the asylum to the last ounce of its treasure and the last drop of its blood.'[8]

TWENTIETH CENTURY: SELECTIVE IMMIGRATION

When an argument for immigration control gathered momentum in the late nineteenth century it was in response to an influx of Jews fleeing pogroms in Tsarist Russia and Prussia, large numbers of whom headed for Britain, many settling in London. One motivation for control was fear of cheap migrant labour competing for English workers' jobs – the Trades Union Congress (TUC) supported border-keeping. Another driving factor, however, was anti-Semitic prejudice. The outcome was the Aliens Act of 1905. The Act tactfully avoided actual mention of Jews however. Those it termed 'undesirable immigrants' were cast as those unable to demonstrate that they could support themselves, who would thus be obliged to have 'recourse to public funds' and thereby become 'a burden on the state' and 'a detriment to the public'. Curiously, exception was made in the case of applicants seeking admission 'solely to avoid persecution or punishment on religious or political grounds' (who were in the main Jewish). This may sound compassionate, but in practice it was not allowed to impede the Act's anti-Semitic implementation. Astonishingly few applicants were admitted into the country under the Act – only 505 in the first year of operation and no more than 50 in any year thereafter. What's more, some given entry may well have been thrown out again, for the courts could condemn to deportation any alien who within a year of entry was found to be 'wandering', 'living under insanitary conditions' or in receipt of parochial relief. Further alien restriction laws in 1914 and 1919 responded to various threats perceived in the context of the First World War, such as infiltration of German spies and incursions of refugees. These acts led to a new raft of border-controlling state employees that would morph into the Aliens Branch, the UK Border Agency and, since 2013, UK Visas and Immigration.[9]

The authors of the Runnymede Trust guide to British immigration control, on whom I draw in the paragraph above, stress that 'immigration control in Britain has *never* been a question of a rational and coherent policy affecting everyone who wanted to settle in the UK, but has *always* been a matter of keeping out *some* people who were regarded as undesirable for whatever reason'.[10] This is borne out by the next phase of control enactment, which was intimately linked to laws from the mid-twentieth century redefining 'nationality', as the British Empire was obliged to cede independence to more and more of its colonies. The British Nationality and Status of Aliens Act of 1914 had accorded the status of 'British subject' to everyone inhabiting the world-spanning British Empire. The fear of UK governments now was the potential for a huge influx of people of brown- and black-skin phenotype from far afield.[11] Certainly the labour shortage following the Second World War had to be addressed, and for this reason the arrival of many hundreds of thousands of Irish, Poles, Ukrainians and other white Europeans was not resented. But a careful redrawing of British nationality rules was set in train for the purpose of preventing large-scale coloured immigration. To this end, the British Commonwealth, as the UK, together with present and ex-colonies had long been known, was reshaped. In 1949 a declaration from London scrubbed the word 'British' from its title, renaming it the Commonwealth of Nations. Hegemonic among this post-war Commonwealth were the predominantly white (or white-governed) states such as Canada and Australia, which came to be known as 'Old Commonwealth'. Newly independent countries opting to join, whose citizens were of course mainly brown or black, were distinguished as 'New Commonwealth'.

For a while after the war, the free movement of Commonwealth citizens continued. This was the situation that met the several hundred Jamaican migrants who arrived on the passenger ship *Empire Windrush* in 1948. More boatloads would follow, bearing black people from the Caribbean seeking work. Many settled in London, changing the face of the boroughs in which they clustered. A white backlash began. Reactionary Conservative MP Cyril Osborne found a ready audience when he 'spoke out for the white man in this country'. In 1958 there were anti-black riots in Notting Hill. Fascist groups such as the White Defence League and the National Front, gained adherents.[12] The political response was a successive tightening of controls on entry. A White Paper in 1965 imposed an annual quota of 8,500 from the New Commonwealth.[13] Then a far-reaching Immigration Act of 1971 gave the state total discretion over Commonwealth immigration except for a particular category now termed 'patrials', who would have a right of abode in the UK. The definition of 'patrial' and 'non-patrial' is complex. The Runnymede Trust explain, 'Roughly translated ... patrials were largely of British descent and therefore white. Non-patrial citizens of the UK and colonies were most likely to be black.'[14] In curbing migration from the 'new' Commonwealth the Act softened the blow to Canada, Australia and New Zealand of the UK's joining the European Union, which in 1972 opened wide the door to European labour. The Labour Government of 1974 to 1979 did nothing to reverse this trajectory, and Margaret Thatcher, on bringing the Conservatives back to power in the election of 1979, met little political resistance to the yet more restrictionist programme proclaimed in her manifesto. Thatcher's British Nationality Act 1981 further reclassified and narrowed down citizenship. As Zig Layton-Henry later described it, 'This landmark act ... confirmed Britain's intention to divest itself of its imperial legacy and obligations'.[15]

So what did the population of London look like in the year 1981, as the British Nationality Act clinched control of migrant flows from the former colonies? How many Londoners at that point were of the visibly black- and brown-skinned phenotypes that the immigration control measures of the last two decades had been designed to keep out? Out of a total Greater London population of 6.6 million, 144,072 were born in an African country. Adding to these the number born in Caribbean countries, gives us a total of 311,471. Thus, just under 5 per cent of the London population at that moment would have been phenotypically, that is visibly, black Londoners. In that same year, 1981, among Londoners were 139,140 born in India, 35,616 born in Pakistan, and 22,102 born in Bangladesh – a total of almost 200,000. Leaving aside other Asians, then, at least 3 per cent of Londoners were phenotypically 'brown' at that moment. To all these foreign-born people we can add their children, born since arrival.[16] These figures are not strikingly large. What would have made these communities more visible was the fact that they clustered in certain boroughs. As regards the African and Caribbean communities, the London Borough of Brent had the biggest proportion, at 13.3 per cent of its total population, or more than one person in seven. Next came Hackney and Lambeth, with one African/Caribbean person in every ten. The other boroughs with black clusters of 6 per cent or more were, in declining order, Haringey, Wandsworth, Newham, Southwark, Hammersmith and Fulham, Ealing, Lewisham and Harrow. Turning to the South Asian communities from India, Pakistan and Bangladesh, there were four boroughs in which these constituted 6 per cent or more of the population in 1981 – in descending order, Ealing with 8.9 per cent, Newham with 8.0 per cent, Brent (again) with 6.8 per cent and Hounslow with 6.6 per cent. Waltham Forest, Harrow and Redbridge all had a presence from the Indian subcontinent of between 2 and 5 per cent.

Interestingly, London went on to become still more colourful. If we look ahead another three decades to 2011, we see that these same communities continued to grow. The population census of that year showed the African and Caribbean population of Greater London had increased by almost half a million, and the Indian, Bangladeshi and Pakistani population by well over a quarter of a million. The overall growth of these selected 'visibly black and brown' citizenry in Greater London had been 146 per cent. Whereas they had been 7.7 per cent of all Londoners in 1981, by 2011 they had doubled, to become 15.3 per cent, or almost one in seven. In the long run, therefore, the racialized controls of the 1970s in no way achieved the effect the legislators sought. The city's famed mixity was flourishing.

THE 'NEW WORLD ORDER' BRINGS A SURGE OF REFUGEES

In 1981, however, what was not foreseen was that the focus of border control was about to shift – would be obliged to shift – from dealing with the effects of an imperial past to an entirely new reality: the end of the Cold War and the outbreak of deadly new conflicts. It was during the second half of the 1980s that the Cold War began to thaw. A relaxation in the Soviet stance was signalled by the *glasnost* (opening) and *perestroika* (restructuring) introduced by Mikhail Gorbachev when he became General Secretary of the Communist Party in 1985. The Berlin Wall dividing East and West Germany was brought down by popular action in 1989. In December 1991 a declaration of the Supreme Soviet of the USSR recognized the independence of the former Soviet Republics, which would shortly after associate in a Commonwealth of Independent States. The melting away of a two-bloc world greatly diminished the risk of nuclear war, but signalled a surge of ambition in Western governments. There was much talk of a 'new world order', featuring economic, political and military dominance by the remaining 'superpower', the USA. What was not foreseen was that the world was about to exchange 45 years of (largely, though not entirely) 'cold' war for an indefinite period of emphatically 'hot' conflict in diverse regions and countries. The wars of the 1990s and 2000s would cause great suffering and displacement, increasing the movement of people across national borders seeking immediate safety and, as it would turn out in many cases, long-term resettlement. Yugoslavia disintegrated in a decade of armed conflict that devastated Bosnia-Herzegovina, Croatia and Kosovo. In 1991 war broke out in the Persian Gulf, when Iraq invaded Kuwait and a coalition led by the USA hit back. In 1994 an unanticipated genocidal war flared in the Central African country of Rwanda. The world stood by and watched as up to a million died in three months, mainly Tutsi people slaughtered by ethnic Hutus. These were wars that dominated the world's news headlines, but there were deadly conflicts besides in Sri Lanka, Somalia, Sudan, Uganda, Democratic Republic of the Congo, Turkey and elsewhere. These too caused an outflow of refugees during the 1990s. The new millennium brought the Al-Qaeda aerial attack on targets in New York and Washington and the ensuing 'war on terror' launched by George W.

Bush, which would devastate Afghanistan, Iraq and other countries of the Middle East, culminating in the current war in Syria.

Let's look, then, at the trend in the numbers of people seeking asylum in the UK, year on year, from that moment back in 1981 until the present day. Figure 1 shows how, until 1988, no more than a few thousand people each year – between 2,000 and 6,000 – were making applications. Though the annual number did actually triple in those years, looking back it seems to have been a different era. The shock came towards the end of the decade. In 1989 the figure of asylum seekers tripled, to reach 16,775, and from there quadrupled to 73,400 by 1991. Between 1999 and 2002 annual applications would soar to an unprecedented 90,000 to 100,000. In the most recent ten years the annual numbers have steadied somewhat, but maintain a relatively high level of between 20,000 and 40,000.

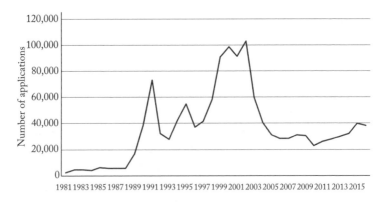

Figure 1   Asylum applications to the UK for main applicants and
dependants 1981–2016

These figures derive from Office of National Statistics, Home Office, *Asylum Statistics*, Table as_02: Asylum applications and initial decisions for main applicants and dependants, by country of nationality, http://tinyurl.com/ltzlmgg

It was not until the late 1980s, it seems, that the authorities turned their collective mind to this epochal change. The British government had, at certain moments in the past, facilitated the admission and resettlement of quotas of refugees in particular cases. For example, Britain felt obliged to accept and resettle the South Asians, mainly Indians, ejected from Uganda by edict of Idi Amin in 1972. Again, a number of Chilean refugees were accepted during this same decade, following a military coup in which the democratically elected President Salvador Allende was overthrown by General Augusto Pinochet. And in the years following the termination of the US–North Vietnam war in 1975, a quota of around 16,000 refugees were taken in from Vietnam and neighbouring countries. The asylum challenge of the 1980s, however, was of a different kind. The refugees seeking to enter the UK were now from far and wide, and a crisis-by-crisis response was not enough.

One of the first measures was the Immigration (Carriers' Liability) Act in 1987, which made airlines and shipping companies liable to fines should they bring passengers to the UK without proper documentation. A further Immigration Act the following year restricted the right of certain categories of migrant to 'family reunion'. Importantly and positively the Asylum and Immigration Appeals Act of 1993 incorporated into domestic law the international UN Refugee Convention of 1951, acknowledging our obligation to give shelter to people fleeing persecution for reasons of 'race', religion, nationality or political opinion. But together with the Asylum and Immigration Act that followed it three years later, it had the intention of curbing the numbers of asylum seekers. The 1996 Act additionally toughened the in-country regime for new asylum seekers. Those applying at the port of entry would be entitled to social security benefit (albeit less than the national rate), but those who applied after achieving entry by some other ploy were to be excluded altogether from benefit. A 'white list' of countries was introduced by this Act, that is, states to which it was allegedly 'safe' for failed asylum seekers to be forcibly returned.[17] These harsh new measures of deterrence and ejection drew fierce protests from refugee-support organizations, including the Refugee Council, and from many local authority and voluntary sector organizations.[18]

The Immigration and Asylum Act of 1999, the year in which asylum applications leaped from less than 60,000 to more than 90,000 within twelve months, was particularly significant. It created an entirely new body, the National Asylum Support Service (NASS), to administer its rigorous new programme. Steve Cohen remarks on the irony in that title: 'support' this was *not*. The Act significantly *reduced* support by removing most of the remaining non-contributory benefits, and with certain limited exceptions henceforth denied council housing and a range of non-contributory benefits to people subject to immigration controls. Most significantly for our story, most new asylum seekers would not be permitted to live in London. Henceforth, due to housing and administrative pressures on London authorities, asylum seekers, if dependent on state support, would have no choice but to accept location in a distant region designated by the Home Office. I shall return to this 'dispersal' policy and its significance for London's minority communities later in this chapter. Further, under the 1999 Act, a system of vouchers replaced cash assistance to asylum seekers awaiting their decisions. Building on the responsibility of employers to verify their employees' legality, more government personnel and private sector suppliers of services were drawn into the surveillance system. Based on coercion, the Act was, Cohen concluded, nothing short of a modern Poor Law.[19]

This raft of legislation in the course of the 1990s certainly manifested the government's dual aim of making the border harder to penetrate, while simultaneously increasing deterrence by meaner in-country provisions. Nonetheless, the outcome must have disappointed the authorities. The number of people detected trying to evade border controls rose from 3,300 in the year 1990 to over 14 times that number (over 47,000) the following year. Governmental anxiety about the relentless increase in refugees hammering on the door was only in part mitigated by a buoyant economy and a labour shortage, combined with *emigration* averaging 230,000 a year.[20]

A NEW DIMENSION: FEAR

The first millennial decade brought a new urgency to the issue of border control: security against 'terror'. The air attack on Washington and New York on 11 September 2001, by Islamist extremists, known as 9/11, followed by the US declaration of a worldwide 'war on terror', brought armed conflict to Afghanistan almost immediately, to Iraq in 2003 and soon further afield – as Al-Qaeda morphed into Islamic State/Da'esh and inspired like-minded *jihadist* organizations such as Al-Shabaab in the Horn of Africa and Boko Haram in Nigeria, Niger and Chad. Security had been a concern in the UK throughout the Irish 'Troubles'. But the Labour Government's Anti-Terrorism Crime and Security Act of 2001, sparked by 9/11, was the start of a new wave of legislation mainly addressing the perceived Islamist threat. The development was strongly criticized by human rights advocates. Liz Fekete, in a substantial publication produced by the Campaign Against Criminalising Communities (CAMPACC) and Index on Censorship, wrote, 'These are the most far-reaching anti-terrorist laws ever to be implemented in the UK: they not only deny civil liberties and erode long-cherished freedoms but, through the creation of a separate criminal justice system for foreigners, institutionalize xeno-racism.' This was 'targetting the victims of terror rather than its perpetrators.'[21]

Among the innovations of the post-millennial anti-terror legislation was the publication of a list of 'proscribed organizations'. Henceforth membership of, or even the mildest association with, one of these could see you prosecuted. We are about to meet examples – watch out for the PKK in Chapter 2, and the Tamil Tigers in Chapter 4. Frances Webber, in the CAMPACC publication cited above, pointed out that support for liberation struggle is the foundation for most asylum claims. So, it had become 'a case of "damned if you do; damned if you don't" – an asylum seeker who claims support or membership of a listed group risks arrest, and one who disavows support for the group will have the claim rejected on the ground that he or she is not persecuted at home.'[22]

London experienced its 9/11 on 7 July 2005, when multiple terror attacks killed 52 people and injured more than 700. Further acts and orders addressing terrorism came apace – in 2005, 2006, 2008, 2009, 2010 and beyond. At the same time, in parallel, immigration legislation showed increasing concern with security. Fran Cetti notes of this period that 'the image of the terrorist has ... intensified the perception of the threatening nature of the alien/outsider at the border ... transforming highly vulnerable individuals into a collective force of danger.'[23] Support would be withheld from asylum seekers, even if destitute, if they had evaded control at the port of entry, claiming asylum only later, when already (illegally) in the UK. There would be, besides, new powers to detain (that is, to incarcerate) asylum seekers at any time during their pursuit of 'leave to remain' in the country. The Asylum and Immigration (Treatment of Claimants) Act that followed in 2004, was designed primarily to limit the role of the courts of justice in immigration appeals, placing decisions in the hands of bureaucrats in a single-tier immigration tribunal. This

Act made it a punishable offence to arrive in the UK without a valid travel document. An Immigration, Asylum and Nationality Act of 2006 cross-referenced the new terror laws by introducing a clause refusing asylum to anyone who had carried out or encouraged others to 'commit, prepare or instigate terrorism'. A Borders, Citizenship and Immigration Act of 2009 was notable for extending the number of years it would take migrants to progress to 'naturalization' and full citizenship. The most recent pieces of legislation, the immigration acts of 2014 and 2016, have made it simpler and quicker to remove from the country immigrants illegally accessing and 'abusing' public services and wrongfully taking employment. Asylum seekers' access to bank accounts and driving licences has been restricted. Individuals liable to deportation may now be flown out prior to appeal, unless they can convince the authorities that in their home country they would be subject to 'serious irreversible harm' (that is, tortured or killed). This condition bears particularly hard on women, for the phrase 'serious irreversible harm' specifically excludes harm that might occur in the family or private life. That the asylum seeker might be returned to the circumstances of an abusive marriage or domestic slavery is considered no reason to refrain from deportation.[24]

A significant feature of the legislation of the last decade has been the shifting of the UK national border away from the immigration desks located in ports and airports, outward into the cities, towns and villages of the UK, where surveillance and control of asylum seekers has been made the responsibility of more and more categories of ordinary citizens going about their daily life. Landlords must examine the documentation of their tenants, employers that of each job applicant. Benefits personnel must scrutinize those of every claimant, university registrars of every enrolling student, to verify that no 'migrant' is an 'illegal'. The fines for failing to report suspected transgressors go higher with every new act of parliament. Simultaneously, the scope of the social roles enlisted extends ever wider – if you are asked to register a civil marriage you must now report any suspicion you may have that it is a 'marriage of convenience' designed to thwart Home Office border law. A group of concerned researchers has been prompted to make a film, *Everyday Borders*, asking what it will mean for us as individuals to be burdened with this border-guard role, and how it may bear on Britain as a convivial pluralist society.[25] It seems we are entering a new reality in which the noun 'the border' calls for a complementary verb, 'to border'. Don Flynn, director of the Migrants Rights Network, believes that:

> We should understand borders as the product of an active political and social process of 'bordering' which is present in the lines which people must cross as they move between the realms of the private and the public, or as they move through the terrains in which civil society is obliged to enact its accountability to the state ... The border is never safely crossed once and for all.[26]

Meantime, while the new mobility and unpredictability of the national border was ratcheting up anxiety and apprehension around incomers and all who had to deal with them, the UK government's counter-terrorism strategy, known as 'Contest', was creating a comparable sense of unease in and among already established minority communities. Contest was a creation of the New Labour administration in 2003, revised in 2006, after the London bombings of 7 July 2005, and several times subsequently.[27] It had four 'work streams', known as the 'four Ps': Pursue, Prevent, Protect and Prepare. Of these, it was Prevent, measures to *stop people becoming* terrorists or supporters of terrorism, that bore most palpably on ordinary people in their daily lives. This was because its intention was intrusive – to watch for processes of radicalization in everyday life, especially in the young, and to intervene to stop them. The authorities must seek out and engage with parents, with Muslim teachers and pupils in schools and colleges, and with cultural projects such as theatre groups, youth clubs and women's organizations as well as religious centres and activities.[28] For this reason Prevent has given rise to considerable criticism, even distress and anger. Its focus has been almost exclusively on Muslim-majority communities, implying that *only* Muslims and *all* Muslims are liable to become security threats. This is borne out by the fact that local authorities are funded to carry out their Prevent work directly in proportion to the number of Muslim residents in their areas. There is understandably a feeling in Muslim communities that Prevent is being used to spy on them.

Local councils and other local authorities, including the police, inevitably incurred a great deal of the responsibility for implementing counter-terrorism measures. This was because, as Councillor Simon

Blackburn, Chair of the Safer and Stronger Communities Board, wrote: 'It is clear that our position at the heart of our communities gives us a unique reach'.[29] The role was especially significant in London, where terror attacks were most likely. But many individuals, whether elected councillors or local authority employees, tasked with implementing Prevent measures in schools, mosques and other centres of local life, felt a profound contradiction between the role of service and care that had drawn them to their work, and this new responsibility for surveillance. Civil society organizations were critical too. An Open Society Justice Initiative report of October 2016, entitled *Eroding Trust*, investigated 17 cases and concluded that the Prevent strategy 'suffers from multiple, mutually reinforcing structural flaws, the foreseeable consequence of which is a serious risk of human rights violations'. It called on the government at a minimum to place the health and education systems outside its remit.[30] However, the criticism, rather than causing the government to curtail its counter-radicalization strategy, led to a recent announcement that it would 'be strengthened, not undermined'.[31]

'DISPERSAL': THE PERSISTENT PULL OF LONDON

One provision of the 1999 Immigration and Asylum Act was particularly significant for London. The pressure from new asylum arrivals was bearing hardest on the capital, and some London borough councils were creating schemes to relocate their 'surplus' incomers to other authorities outside the capital where housing was marginally more available and less costly. In 1998 the Local Government Association and the Home Office worked together to rationalize and organize this process in a 'voluntary dispersal scheme'. However, few local authorities stepped forward to offer themselves as reception locations, and asylum seekers themselves were resistant to the idea of living anywhere but London. So the 1999 Act took matters in hand and introduced an element of compulsion, a 'no-choice' policy for asylum seekers lacking independent resources. In future, free accommodation and support would be conditional on their 'dispersal' to designated regions in the Midlands and the North.[32]

Implementation of the dispersal policy was the principal task of that newly created National Asylum Support System (NASS). The destination cities and towns, mainly in the Midlands and Northern counties of England, were chosen as already having a multiethnic population and it was believed they would have the potential for developing adequate voluntary and community sector support for the incomers. But the Home Office was clear that a primary criterion was the availability of housing. This meant the chosen locations were going to be areas of economic decline and urban poverty. A Chartered Institute of Housing report bore this out, stating that the Home Office's 'cluster areas' overlapped closely with the 88 local authority areas identified as having the highest levels of 'social exclusion' in the country.[33] The Home Office established a network of regional consortia of local authorities, services and organizations that would between them provide the full range of services needed by the incoming asylum seekers. It was estimated that NASS would need to find 37,120 units of affordable accommodation in the first year of the policy. The plan was that each consortium would contract out for the provision of dwellings with its local authorities, which would in turn form partnerships with private landlords, housing associations (registered social landlords) and refugee community associations in their region. The scheme proved difficult to implement however. Participating local authorities quickly complained that it was costing them considerably more than NASS was reimbursing (£30 million in the first year).[34]

In theory, then, from the year 2000 London borough councils had the asylum reception problem crossed off their 'to do' list. Asylum seeker arrivals would be someone else's problem. But that was not the reality the councils experienced. In the first place, a great many asylum seekers and refugees were already living in the capital. Although the statistics are impossible to verify, a trustworthy guesstimate by the London Research Centre was that between 240,000 and 280,000 asylum seekers and refugees were living in London shortly before the 1999 Act was put into effect – over 85 per cent of the national total. They would continue to need support of many kinds from London's local authorities. Many were in unsuitable accommodation. In September 1999, just over a quarter of the 23,507 destitute asylum-seeker households supported by London borough councils under the National Assistance Act of 1948 were living in bed-and-breakfast accommodation.[35] Not a few were among the Londoners sleeping rough, under bridges, in parks, in doorways. Even now, a decade and a half after dispersal became the rule, there are believed to be between 2,000 and 3,000 asylum seekers in Greater London awaiting decisions on their case, and a far greater number of individuals with the between-worlds status of 'refugee'.[36]

Then, in the ensuing years there were the non-stop arrivals, due to London's magnetic attraction. The ports of arrival – Heathrow, Gatwick, Dover – were close to the capital, but under the NASS regime those asylum seekers allowed through were heading, like it or lump it, for 'dispersal'. However, rather few of the incomers were enthusiastic about going to Cardiff or Glasgow. They had travelled with London in mind. The luckiest came with some resources of their own and were able to find private rented accommodation somewhere in the capital. Others had friends or family already established here, into whose rooms or apartments they could squeeze (and they could do this without losing their right to subsistence support). The chief executive of the Refugee Council, in a highly critical article in the *Guardian*, had admonished the government on the dispersal policy, which he called a 'stairway to hell'. You wait and see, he wrote, 'Many, if not a majority, will drift back to London'.[37] And so they did, making their way back south as soon as they could escape the attentions of the authorities. They were drawn by existing London communities from their country of origin, by friendships, by the many here who spoke their language. Some were seeking the services of the immigration-specialist advice centres and law firms that cluster in the capital. We have to remember too that when a war breaks out in their country many people who are in the UK quite legally, on tourist or student visas, are fearful to return, and join the ranks of those seeking asylum. A high proportion of these are in London, so a considerable task of care for asylum seekers has, contrary to official intention, remained with the London borough councils.

In the first place, to them falls full responsibility under the 1989 Children's Act for the care of destitute lone youngsters under the age of 18. In the case of any unaccompanied asylum-seeking child (UASC) turning up in the borough, the council must assess the child's needs and write a care plan. It might involve finding a foster home for her or him, a place in a children's home or, in the case of a teenager, a hostel, and deploying the entire range of services including schooling. When the so-called 'Jungle' camp in Calais, where many of the refugees were under 18, was emptied by the French authorities in October 2016, London borough councils offered to take in a quota. Eighty were brought over under the scheme, and a further 67 turned up as 'in-borough presentations' – children found sleeping rough after finding their own way across the Channel, some hidden in lorries. London boroughs were estimated to be looking after 1,440 UASCs in 2016, no less than one-third of the total in the UK. They were granted £650–£800 a week in government funding per child for housing, education, health and social care. But the following month they had to seek £70 million more to cover the full cost.[38] The London Asylum Seekers Consortium is a pan-London support group assisting the councils in handling this demanding task of care for UASCs.

The London boroughs, besides, have to respond to the needs of asylum seekers following a decision on their application. Many of those who are refused asylum go into hiding to escape deportation. Some of them head south, seeking the anonymity of London. Those granted asylum are reclassified as 'refugees', and enter a different relationship with the system. Imagine, for example, a woman arriving at the UK border from Eritrea. Let's call her Selam. She is 'illegal', with no valid documentation. She has no relatives here. She is pregnant. NASS 'disperse' her to Glasgow, where she lives, accommodated by the regional consortium, housed and supported by the state during the weeks or months it takes for her application for asylum to be processed. Asylum is granted, and Selam is informed that she has five years' 'leave to remain', during which time she may continue to seek British citizenship. But at this moment she's told that after 28 days her entitlement to state support will cease, and during this four-week 'grace period' she must achieve self-sufficiency. Wishing to join the strong Eritrean community she knows to exist in London, she heads off south, trusting in the renowned National Health Service to see her through imminent childbirth. A study by the Refugee Council found that a very small proportion of 'new refugees' in fact succeed in independently finding a home and a livelihood in this 'grace period'.[39]

In the coming months and years it is to the various London authorities that Selam, as thousands like her before and since, will turn for help with many aspects of her life. The Greater London Authority has an overview of the needs of asylum seekers and refugees, but no practical responsibility for the care of individuals. The London borough councils will have the principal role, together with various public services, but it is their policy to seek the partnership of voluntary sector organizations and particularly refugee community organizations. Selam's priority needs will be help in negotiating benefit rights, and support in accessing maternity services and in caring for her newborn child. Eventually she will need guidance into the schools system (and with obtaining free school meals), and help with job search and training, language courses and accessing legal advice. All this is an extra burden for a local government system drastically hit by government spending cuts. Figures published in the Local Government Finance Settlement for 2016/17 signalled an average cut of nearly 30 per cent to London councils' core funding over the next four years, on top of a cut of almost 50 per cent since 2010.[40]

To return to Selam, her greatest, and unending, problem will be housing. The nationwide housing shortage is felt with particular severity in London. The shortage is partly due to the much higher average cost of dwellings in the capital than elsewhere, and its rapid increase. Between 1995 and 2016 the average price of a dwelling rose more than 500 per cent, from £107,514 to £658,674.[41] Conversely, the unsatisfied demand is one of the factors pushing up the prices. Between the census years of 2001 and 2011 only 200,000 new dwellings were built for an increase in Greater London's population of 800,000. Meanwhile, in the same ten years, the number of families in London living in shared homes almost doubled.[42] In 2015 there were more than a quarter of a million Londoners on waiting lists for council housing.[43] It is estimated that London needs 40,000 new homes every year for 20 years to deal with the anticipated population increase, and an additional 9,000 a year to deal with the deficit. At present scarcely more than half that number is being built annually.[44] Housing, therefore, is a never-ending headache for London's borough councils. A council must manage its own supply of 'council housing', and consider applications for tenancies by resident asylum seekers, refugees and other migrants. Even if such a one is lucky enough to be accepted on to the council's 'waiting list', there will be many years during which she or he will need advice and help accessing private rented accommodation or social housing. Councils seek support in this from voluntary sector organizations, relying on them to help individuals find private landlords advertising rooms and flats, apply for Housing Benefit, or seek a loan if a deposit is required.

It appears that two decades ago, when new immigration control legislation was coming thick and fast, local authorities, and in particular London borough councils, were being slow to get their act together on policy and practice for refugees and asylum seekers. After the 1996 Immigration Act, the British Refugee Council and the Association of London Government advised London local authorities that they needed to make improvements to their practices concerning refugees and asylum seekers. They should recognize them as a distinct target group – vulnerable and disadvantaged. Each authority should establish a multi-agency forum to coordinate council strategy for them, and ensure that it become central to the running of the council, reporting to a full committee. It should establish programmes of action for this target group in key service areas, and refugee community organizations should be closely involved as partners.[45] Then, a decade later, in 2008 the London Asylum Seekers Consortium conducted research that found the majority of London borough councils consulted felt that even now they needed much better information about the numbers and needs of asylum seekers and refugees in their borough, and improved planning and consultation mechanisms with other London authorities in providing for them.[46] In my travels around London boroughs between late 2015 and early 2017, recounted in Chapters 2 to 6, I found little evidence of either a London-wide system, or clearly signposted services in individual councils.

BEYOND THE INDIVIDUAL: THE QUALITY OF COMMUNITY

Meanwhile, in addition to this ongoing responsibility of care that London borough councils bear for individual asylum seekers and refugees, they have a very particular task with regard to whole communities of ethnic minorities, the communities that the individual incomers join as they are given 'leave to remain' and eventually obtain citizenship. They acquired this responsibility, called 'cohesion and integration', early in the millennium. It was a policy development following from a series of outbreaks of violence in the north of England. One after another, in the months of May, June and July 2001, the towns of Oldham, Burnley and Bradford experienced rioting on the streets that left hundreds injured. What sparked it off was not immediately clear, although 'drug gangs' featured in the reports. What caused most concern was that the animosity was clearly racialized. The fights were between local men of the white British community and South Asian men of Pakistani, Bangladeshi and Indian origin of which there were sizeable established minorities in these towns, many of them third- and fourth-generation labour migrants. Investigations were speedily carried out in the three locations. The government set up a Ministerial Group on Public Order that produced its own report, often referred to as the 'Denham Report' after its author John Denham,[47] and then established an Independent Review Team, which later in 2001 produced a further analysis, *Community Cohesion*, subsequently known as the 'Cantle Report' after Chairman of the Team, Ted Cantle.[48] Cantle reported a great 'depth of polarization' existing in the three towns, around segregated communities living 'parallel lives'. Fear was growing from ignorance of each other, and was being exploited by extremists. He argued that further violence would follow unless purposeful steps were taken to improve 'cohesion'. The report proposed measures to foster contact and mixing among ethnic minorities and majorities, the promotion of 'a meaningful concept of citizenship', and improved 'community policing'.

'Integration and cohesion' thenceforth became a much-touted catchphrase at all levels of governance. The government published a White Paper on 'integration with diversity in modern Britain' in 2001,[49] and the following year set up a dedicated Cohesion Unit in the Home Office. Taken together, the deployment of the concepts 'integration' and 'cohesion' represented a paradigm shift in policy, challenging the widely used notion of 'multiculturalism', that is to say, the side-by-side coexistence of many ethnicities in a given area, a celebration of 'difference' that was coming to be seen as naively ignorant of tension and animosity. Moving beyond 'multiculturalism', however, should not mean disrespectfully seeking to homogenize cultures by 'assimilation' of minority groups into the majority. 'Integration' became the preferred term. The theory and practice involved in adopting the two terms was further elaborated by the Commission on Integration and Cohesion set up by the government in 2006. In its report, *Our Shared Future*, the commission distinguished the one concept from the other, while embracing both: 'Cohesion is principally the process that must happen in all communities to ensure different groups of people get on well together; while integration is principally the process that ensures new residents and existing residents adapt to one another.'[50] A 'cohesive community' they described as one with a 'clearly defined and widely shared sense of the contribution of different individuals and different communities to a future vision for a neighbourhood, city, region or country'. There would be a strong sense of trust in institutions to 'act fairly', affording similar life opportunities to all, and a recognition of the contributions made by both the long-standing and newly arrived parts of minority communities.[51] It set out practical proposals for building cohesion according to four key principles. First was the sense of shared futures; second, a new model of rights and responsibilities involving a sense of citizenship and obligation; third, a new emphasis on mutual respect and civility, what they called 'an ethics of hospitality'. Finally came 'a commitment to equality that sits alongside the need to deliver visible social justice'.[52]

Our Shared Future was emphatic in maintaining a local focus, placing the responsibility firmly on local authorities. It contained case studies to illustrate good local practice. Interestingly, the passing of a Localism Act a few years later testifies to a rather generalized concern in this period to devolve activity to local levels. The Act (of 2011) set out a series of measures to achieve 'a substantial and lasting shift in power away from central government and towards local people'. They included 'new freedoms and flexibilities for local government; new rights and powers for communities and individuals; reform to make the planning system more democratic and more effective, and reform to ensure that decisions about housing are taken locally'.[53] What's more, not only local authorities but also the local voluntary sector, especially ethnic minority community organizations, were seen as a necessary part of the action in achieving cohesion and integration. Back in 2003, soon after the riots, a Commission on the Future of Multiethnic Britain had stressed this. What was wanted, they wrote, was not something 'drafted by some benighted local council official who has been locked away in a cupboard for a few months to draw up the latest plan, but an attempt to challenge each local organization to identify what it can do'.[54]

A further concept that features in *Our Shared Future*, in tandem with community cohesion, is 'equality'. Not a few critics noted that the interpretation of equality here is limited to a single dimension, that between ethno-cultural groups. As did the Equality Act of 2010, which drew into a single legislative framework the issue of discrimination by sex/gender, 'race'/ethnicity and ability/disability, *Our Shared Future* entirely ignored that other key dimension of inequality: economic and social class inequalities, the matter of differential wealth and power and its expression in class advantage and disadvantage. Yet, in the case of diverse ethno-cultural communities, *both* ethnic and class inequalities and resentments are clearly significant, and they are visibly intersected. The job you have, the assets you possess, determine what kind of home you can afford, and thus what street or district you live in, and who your neighbours are. In London today 40 to 50 per cent of all renting households are living in poverty, while 40 per cent of owner-occupied homes have two or more bedrooms going spare.[55] This, the critics of *Our Shared Future* pointed out, surely has a bearing on 'how you get along', on cohesion.[56] In coming chapters we shall see some local authorities handling these ongoing responsibilities, as their particular minorities are swollen through war-driven inward migration and settlement. First, to Hackney and its many Kurds.

2

From South-East Turkey to North-East London: Kurds in Hackney

Living in an area that straddles the borders of four nation states – Turkey, Iran, Syria and Iraq – the people identifying as Kurds sometimes term themselves the world's largest stateless people.[1] Around half of an estimated total of between 25 and 30 million live in Turkey's south-eastern region, with sizeable groups in western Iran and northern Iraq, and a smaller cluster in the north-eastern corner of Syria. Their principal languages (Kurmanji in the northern regions, Sorani in the south) are of Indo-European origin, as distinct from Turkic and Arabic, and some claim that the Kurds descend from the very earliest cultivators, the Upper Neolithic people of the sixth and seventh millennia BCE, whose settlements have been excavated in the region.[2] Today there is a substantial Kurdish diaspora. Many have lived for generations in Armenia and other former Soviet Republics, and in the last half century possibly a million have migrated to Europe and beyond.

Throughout their long history the Kurds have herded livestock and harvested grain in their remote steppe-lands and mountain ranges. They were monotheistic Zoroastrians from before the Christian era, and were forcibly converted to Islam in the eighth century CE and later. They became, for the most part, Sunni Muslims, though a substantial minority, including many living in Turkey, are Alevis, practising a relatively undogmatic and mystical mode of Shi'a Islam, akin to Sufism, and owing much to Zoroastrianism. The experience of the First World War, in which elements of the Ottoman Empire fought in alliance with Germany, sparked modern Kurdish identity to life. With it came an aspiration to unity and nationhood. It is the British that many now blame for having betrayed their hopes. An article in the 1920 Treaty of Sèvres, in which Britain, France and Italy carved up the Ottoman Empire, provided for 'local autonomy for the predominantly Kurdish area' with an early prospect of independence. But it was superseded by the Treaty of Lausanne three years later, in which the Western victors expediently recognized the new Republic of Turkey with neither provision nor protection for its Kurdish minority, which comprised 10 per cent of the population.[3] From the accession of the fiercely nationalist, secular and modernizing Mustafa Kemal 'Atatürk' to the Turkish presidency, the state's constitution stressed the unitary nature of the Turkish people, understating or denying the existence of a Kurdish or any other ethnic minority. In 1924, with the aim of extinguishing their identity, a law was enacted enabling the forcible transfer of communities for whom Turkish was not the mother tongue to areas in which they would be less than 5 per cent of the population. In the course of the 1920s the Kurds rose twice in armed rebellion against the Turkish state and met with brutal reprisals. Insurgencies continued in the following decade, and in 1937 a devastating action by state forces against the mainly Alevi population of Dersim, involving three army corps and 40 airplanes, is estimated to have killed 40,000, including many women and children.[4]

MODERN TURKEY: THE STRUGGLE FOR KURDISH RIGHTS

In the 1950s and 1960s, the modernization of agriculture drove more and more Kurdish villagers to leave the land in search of jobs in the towns and cities of the region. Tribal leaders and cultural conservatives lost their influence over this more mobile generation, some of whom migrated westwards to Ankara, Istanbul and other urban labour markets. These were natural recruits to the new (but short-lived) Turkish Workers Party founded in 1961, and some became a more leftist and intellectual Kurdish resistance. On 8 May that year there were huge protests in Mardin, Diyarbakir and other towns in the south-east for recognition of the Kurdish language and place names. Banners proclaimed 'We are not Turks, we are Kurds'. The state's forces were recorded as shooting dead 315 demonstrators and wounding 754. 'Only the most blinkered observer could fail to recognize the growing antiphony between state denial and national expression.'[5]

It would be another 20 years, however, before a specifically Kurdish nationalist party, the PKK (Partiya Karkerên Kurdistan, Kurdistan Workers Party), would mobilize to fight back against the state with a series of attacks and ambushes on Turkish forces in the Kurdish region. Initiated by Abdullah Öcalan in 1978, and inspired by Marxist-Leninist thought, the PKK at first sought secession from Turkey and the creation of a united and independent nation state of Kurdistan. For some years thereafter its activists withdrew into the borderlands, and lay low during the early 1980s when the military were ruling Turkey. But in August 1984 the PKK's armed force, the ARGK (People's Liberation Army), began a major campaign involving attacks on government supporters in the rural areas, including many of the tribal leaders, landlords and (from 1985) the new state-appointed 'village guards'. By now the Turkish military was deploying 200,000 troops to keep control in the region, where street uprisings, or *serhildan*, and military actions by the ARGK were frequent. An estimated 3,500 villages would eventually be sacked, leading to the displacement of between three and four million people. Apart from many deaths in battle on both sides (an estimated 30,000 between the mid-1980s and late 1990s), thousands more combatants and civilian activists were arrested and imprisoned by the security services without trial and for indefinite periods in inhumane conditions. The use of torture and extrajudicial killing was commonplace.[6]

Over the course of the 1990s, Abdullah Öcalan and the PKK leadership moved away from Marxism-Leninism towards an ideology closer to the anarchism of Murray Bookchin. They simultaneously shifted their political demands somewhat radically, abandoning the aim of statehood and arguing instead for a negotiated status of constituent minority with full cultural and political rights within the Turkish state. In his writings on 'democratic confederalism', Öcalan stated his belief that nation states had become serious obstacles for any social development. Instead he articulated a 'contrasting paradigm of the oppressed people', stating that 'all areas of society need to be given to self-administration, all levels of it need to be free to participate'.[7] Democratic confederalism would later be experimentally introduced in some Kurdish localities of south-east Turkey and northern Syria by activists. Each institution would be headed by a male and a female leader.

Attempts to build legal Kurdish political parties – the Kurdish People's Labour Party, followed by the People's Democratic Party (HADEP) – did nothing to temper the state's attitude to the movement. Kurdish elected representatives were denied the immunity from prosecution afforded those of other parties, and some received long prison terms for associating with the PKK. The war continued, with short remissions, and in 1999 Öcalan was captured, tried and condemned to death, a sentence later commuted to life imprisonment in response to pressure from the European Court of Human Rights.[8]

The PKK now called a ceasefire, and subsequently underwent a series of developments to reflect pacification. In 2002, the year Recep Tayyip Erdoğan's Justice and Development Party (AKP) came to power in Ankara, the organization was nominally closed and replaced by, or renamed as, KADEK, the Kurdistan Freedom and Democracy Congress. Soon after, this name too was abandoned, and the 2003-style People's Congress of Kurdistan was named Kongra-Gel. Yet in 2005 the PKK was re-established under its original name, along with its People's Defence Force (HPG). Sporadic fighting against the state continued, and was met with counter-insurgency efforts by the security forces.[9] A reform package initiated by the AKP government in 2009 did little to improve the situation. The years 2011–12 were particularly violent, resulting in several hundred deaths. Late in 2012 the Turkish government began talks with Öcalan. He in turn called a ceasefire in March 2013, and would reiterate this two years later. Yet the United Nations High Commissioner for Human Rights reported that in the year and a half from mid-2015 to the end of December 2016 no less than 2,000 people were killed and entire neighbourhoods of south-eastern Turkey razed in government security operations characterized by massive destruction and serious human rights violations. Up to half a million people, mostly Kurds, had been displaced.[10]

This ongoing war notwithstanding, in recent years the Turkish state has introduced some modest measures of liberalization. Limited airing of Kurmanji, the principal language of Kurds in Turkey, and its teaching in private institutions was permitted at last, though it continued to be forbidden in state education at any level. Many had hoped that Turkey's candidature for membership of the European Union, accepted in 2004, would oblige them to offer a democratic and inclusive settlement to their Kurdish minority. The admission process stalled, however, at first due to Turkey's failure to resolve the Northern Cyprus issue, later on its poor human rights performance. Throughout the negotiations, the European Commission disappointingly evaded the Kurdish issue.[11] Meanwhile, on the one hand the Kurdish population of Turkey continues to grow at twice the rate of the Turkish population, making Kurds ever harder to ignore as a cultural, economic and political presence in the nation's future. And on the other, the Turkish state holds thousands of journalists, trade unionists, lawyers and other human rights defenders in prison, and the PKK remains a 'terrorist organization' proscribed by the EU, NATO, the USA and the UK among other countries. Sporadic violence continues in south-east Turkey.[12]

HACKNEY AS A PLACE OF RE-HOMING

These then are the circumstances from which many Kurds fled, seeking asylum particularly in Germany and other northern and western European countries, including the UK. Home Office asylum statistics do not distinguish Turkish Kurds from other Turks. However, since from the late 1980s to around 2003 more Kurds had reason to flee their situation than other citizens of Turkey, we may assume that a high proportion of 'Turkish' asylum seekers in the statistical record for these years were in fact Kurds. The numbers of individuals giving their country of origin as 'Turkey' applying for asylum in the UK rose to a high of 2,415 in 1989 and stayed well above 1,000 a year till peaking again in the year 2000 at 3,990. In 2001, no less than 7,827 decisions on accumulated Turkish asylum pleas were made, with a massive 7,340 being refused. Numbers of 'Turkish' applicants fell away markedly from 2005 and have remained at only a few hundred since then.[13]

Many of the Kurdish asylum seekers chose London as their place of re-homing. Until the Immigration Act of 1999 they were free to do so, and even thereafter many continued to find their own way to London. Over the years they have created an extensive network of Kurdish organizations. The majority reflect the large presence of Turkish Kurds, but Iraqi, Syrian and Iranian Kurds, each with a distinct history, are represented here too, and presiding over all of them is a UK Kurdish Assembly.[14] There are Kurdish advice and information centres, a housing association and a disability organization. The Kurdistan

Human Rights Project is an important resource, supporting Kurdish human rights defenders, including the pursuit of their cases under national and European law.[15] There is a Kurdish Cultural Centre in South London, which provides Kurdish language classes, and has a music studio and a sizeable library. An energetic British campaigning organization, Peace in Kurdistan, is closely linked to the London branch of the Brussels-based Kurdistan National Congress (KNK) formed by exiled Kurdish politicians, lawyers and activists. They support Kurdish demands for self-determination and cultural rights, and for ending deportations from the diaspora to countries of origin.

In Hackney and neighbouring boroughs are a number of Kurdish community associations, such as a Kurdish Community Association in Manor Gardens (postcode N7), the Day-Mer Community Centre in Howard Road (N16), and the Alevi Community Centre in Ridley Road (E8). Halkevi, in Dalston (also E8), is a particularly active centre with left-wing political orientation, that is unusual in bringing together Turkish Kurds with other progressive Turkish-speakers of North London boroughs. The London Borough of Hackney itself was a particularly popular destination for Turkish Kurds during this period. However, the vagueness of Home Office statistics that prevents us knowing how many Kurds there are in Britain, similarly makes it impossible to know how many are living in Hackney. The only hint comes from an optional 'write-in box' in the census form where an individual may volunteer additional information about him or herself. In 2011 it was used by 2,083 individuals in Hackney to identify themselves as Turkish Kurds. This, then, is the assured minimum of Kurds in the borough. The actual number is certainly many times greater. During the late 1980s, and in the course of the following decade, they became a substantial and recognizable community. As in their place of origin in south-east Turkey, if they espouse a religion at all they tend to be Alevi, an identity that differentiates them from the borough's Turks who, if they are observant Muslims, are mainly Sunni and cluster around the very active Sulemanya Mosque in Kingsland Road.

Hackney is demographically a rather distinctive borough. With a population of nigh-on a quarter of a million, it has been growing fast, seeing a 20 per cent increase between the census of 2001 and that of 2011. It is the third most densely populated borough in London. It is also rather young, with a quarter of its people under the age of 20. Having long been an area that welcomes inward migration, it is today the sixth most 'diverse' borough in London. At just over a third, the 'white British' population remains the single largest ethnic group (by census categories) but is relatively declining. 'Country of birth' data show that just over 39 per cent of the borough's population were born outside the UK. The single largest group of them, about 3.6 per cent of the total population, originated in Turkey. Other sizeable communities include Chinese, Vietnamese and Eastern Europeans. So, very diverse, yes. But also very poor. In 2014 Hackney was judged, by a government index of multiple deprivation, to be (bar one) the most deprived local authority area in Britain. Fifteen per cent of its population were benefit claimants, compared with 11.6 per cent for London as a whole. Unemployment was higher than average at 8.8 per cent. Thirty-seven per cent of the borough's children were living in poverty, significantly more than the London average and almost double the rate for England. The needs of the Kurdish community today, therefore, as experienced by the children of those refugees of 25 years ago, while they are still acute are not the citizenship needs of their parents (asylum, a right to remain, a passport). Rather they are better social and health provision, job opportunities, benefits and housing. But demographic trends are outstripping these 'ethnic minorities', for the dramatically visible newcomers to Hackney today are not a group of asylum seekers from a current war, but rather an influx of wealthy individuals and families, mainly but not only 'white British' – those who alone can afford to buy the freeholds of Hackney dwellings as the property boom impels their price upward year on year. The threat to social cohesion in Hackney, a worry alike to minority community organizations, the voluntary sector and responsible policymakers in the Town Hall, is less a concern over ethnic disunity than this ever-widening division between rich and poor, the wealth gap.

I learned of this concern from encounters with several individuals engaged from different perspectives in community relations and policy work in Hackney. I first attended a reception held in the Town Hall by the Deputy Mayor, Councillor Sophie Linden, and a number of senior officers, at which community representatives were invited to express their needs and aspirations, and to hear about council policy. There I met, and was later able to interview, a Kurdish councillor,

Feryal Demirci. Part of the strong Labour majority in Hackney, Feryal was first elected in 2006, the very first Kurd on the borough council. Since then she had become a member of Hackney's 'cabinet' and thus a senior policymaker, with special responsibility for 'neighbourhoods'. From Feryal, and from a later conversation with Sonia Khan, Head of Policy in the Chief Executive's Directorate, I learned that Hackney's approach to its Kurdish and other minority communities is firmly and explicitly founded on the national 'cohesion and integration' policy as outlined in Chapter 1. That is to say, in the first place, 'cohesion' is firmly twinned with 'equality'. This makes particular sense in Hackney, given, as we've seen, social class dichotomy. Hackney Council can hardly fail to see the challenge as being *both* to ensure that ethnic, cultural and religious differences do not disrupt the sense of local community and belonging *and* to mitigate an increasingly stark divide between the seriously wealthy and the long-term poor. Provision of 'affordable' housing is clearly key to achieving both these aims, and the borough council aims to achieve an increase of 1,000 homes a year, at least half for rent or shared ownership.[16] Interestingly, too, Sonia Khan was explicit that Hackney was well in tune with the national debate on a change of paradigm in community matters. This borough, like many others, was seeking to move beyond both the discredited strategy of 'assimilation' (subsuming diverse cultures into the dominant host culture) and at its opposite extreme, 'multiculturalism' (in which deference is uncritically accorded to community leaders, regardless of their attitude to social matters such as gender equality). Rather, as Sonia puts it, the council's approach should be 'valuing people's heritage while creating spaces that are tolerant of difference'.

Integration and cohesion, as discussed above, are one aspect of a London borough council's concern for its inward migrants viewed as new groups joining established communities. But what of the individual – the asylum seeker or refugee, mum, dad or child, who needs a helping hand to access local services? A close scan of Hackney Council's website generates curiously little mention of asylum seekers and refugees. There appeared to be no unit, department or committee whose sole and specific responsibility is dealing with their needs. Rather, the role seems to be handed down to the borough's voluntary sector. The council is strongly focused towards its 'Local Strategic Partnership' – which it terms 'Team Hackney'. Team Hackney, says the website, 'is dedicated to improving the quality of life for everyone in the borough by bringing together the key people in the public, private, community and voluntary sectors'. One of the very scarce mentions of the word 'refugee' on the council website refers to the 'refugee crisis' of 2015–16. No council service or department is mentioned. Rather, the public is invited to offer help, and interested readers are deflected away from the council itself, and advised rather to contact the Hackney Refugee Forum, described as 'an umbrella network for refugee organizations, hosted by Hackney Council for Voluntary Service'. It is the Forum that keeps a database of the 60-plus refugee organizations in the borough, and works between them and the various local public services (such as health care and education) to improve mutual knowledge and access. A second member organization in the Partnership is the Hackney Migrant Centre, which opened in 2008 in response to a need expressed by the local Primary Care Trust and other local services for an advice centre for refugees.

In so far as Hackney Council contributes to meeting the needs of individual asylum seekers and refugees in the borough, then, it appears it acts mainly indirectly, by affording grant aid to its voluntary sector partners. However, Ali-Riza Aksoy, the Director of the Hackney Refugee Forum, feels this not good enough. 'Many refugees in Hackney are living in terrible, frightening conditions. Hackney is facing its own refugee crisis because the resources are simply not there to help them.' The council 'listens and consults, they have good intentions – but there's not enough action', he says. Nor enough cash. 'Community organizations have to compete for council support, and funding is scarce.' Nobody, inside the council or without, is in doubt that what most impedes the fulfilment of their aspirations is Whitehall's spending cuts in an era of 'austerity'. Hackney is required to 'save' 80 million pounds by the financial year 2017–18, on top of the 100 million they have been obliged to trim from their expenditure over four financial years to 2015. Meanwhile, the migration crisis in the Middle East has presented local authorities with a new challenge. As we shall see in Chapter 6, Hackney Council has been pressured into taking on the care of some refugees entering the country in 2015 and 2016 under the government's 'resettlement' schemes. This emergency response may well oblige the council to feature asylum and refugee operations and policies more visibly in its committee and departmental structure

In Hackney and neighbouring Haringey, in North London, Kurdish restaurants are popular with local residents of many and diverse origins. They have come to be seen as 'characteristic', as part of the boroughs' culture.

in future. Caitlin Burbidge, of Citizens UK, which pressed for the council's engagement, wrote in the local *Hackney Citizen*:

> Our hope in the long run is that we can translate some of that support into support for people who have the same kind of needs but are from different countries – people who are in the borough already, who have challenges with migration or their refugee or asylum status. This might be a bit of a springboard for us to do that.[17]

KURDISH WOMEN: THERE AND HERE

Women are a visible and active presence in and among the Kurdish organizations of Hackney. My first encounter was with Roj Women, an association founded in 2004, with an office in Halkevi, the busy community centre in Dalston. Roj Women describe themselves as 'a Kurdish grassroots women's rights movement', and have a membership of several hundred, from all Kurdish regions. Their activity has broadly two aspects. In relation to women of the Kurdish migrant population in the UK they work in 'community development' mode, providing a place of contact and connection between women living in various localities, running language courses and training women in the know-how that can help them get and hold jobs. They run seminars and offer counselling. Despite the passing years in their new home far from Turkey, oppressive and traditional gender relations persist in some families. So Roj Women need to give psychological and legal support to many women and girls suffering violence, forced marriages and other forms of abuse. They mark International Women's Day. And they organize events in a way that is banned in Turkey – for example the annual Zilan festival in June 'for free women towards a democratic nation'. This links to their second role, of looking outwards and eastwards, to the several regions of Kurdistan, where they lobby and campaign to improve the lives and expand the opportunities available to women, and address the double discrimination they face on the one hand as females, on the other as a Kurdish minority. Roj Women have launched several fact-finding missions, and have reported on the struggle of women human rights defenders in Kurdish regions of Turkey.[18]

It was Roj Women who led me to the three women whose stories I tell later in this chapter. To understand them, and other women now living in the diaspora, it may help to know something of the gender relations that have shaped the experiences and chances of Kurdish women in Turkey. The transition from the ancient Zoroastrian religion to Islam brought a profound patriarchalism, which intersected in Kurdish culture with structures of tribalism and an economic hierarchy built on land ownership. *Namus*, the honour of the community and of the family, became located in the body and demeanour of the woman, who has consequently been subject to rigorous control by men, within and outside the family. Until recently very few Kurdish women (less than 10 per cent) participated in the labour market in Turkey. Their literacy rate has been half that of other Turkish women. They have experienced considerably more violence at the hands of men, particularly behind the closed doors of the family home. Age at marriage has been lower, forced marriage more common and maternal mortality higher than elsewhere in Turkey. Until recently the community has been known for the prevalence of honour killings. These oppressive practices, however, are less marked among the Alevi Kurdish population than among those who are Sunni, and a higher incidence of schooling for girls, the greater mobility of Kurds within and beyond Turkey, and the energetic intervention of women's organizations have gone some way to change gender relations.[19] Nonetheless, while Kurdish men have necessarily learned the Turkish language during their obligatory state military service, many women continue to speak only Kurmanji. As a consequence, Kurdish women have been seen, from the perspective of the western cities of Turkey, as 'eastern', 'rural', 'feudal' and 'backward'.[20] As for Kurdish women's own view of the matter, this had little reach, for their authentic voice was largely drowned by the violent noise of the ongoing war with the Turkish state.[21]

The mobilization of women in the Kurdish movement of recent decades is therefore all the more striking. When armed conflict began between the state and the PKK in the mid-1980s, the upheaval of displacement from villages to the towns and cities put women under stress, but simultaneously opened up new possibilities for them. They began to be visible in meetings and demonstrations. Many organized in support of relatives imprisoned by the state and campaigned for the return of the thousands of 'disappeared'. Some women became PKK militants. Several became suicide bombers and two set themselves alight at Newroz, the Kurdish new year festival, in defence of Kurdish rights. By the early 1990s women were beginning to 'go to the mountains' to join the armed units, so that by 1993 they comprised as many as one-third of PKK troops.[22] In 1991, Leyla Zana became the first self-identified Kurdish woman to win a seat in the Turkish parliament. She provoked the state's fury when, during the swearing-in ceremony, she spoke some words of the oath in the Kurdish language. She was arrested and charged with treason and imprisoned. But, consistently active and vocal on democracy and human rights, she has been a huge inspiration to a generation of Kurdish women.

Abdullah Öcalan, founder of the PKK and leader of the Kurdish movement in Turkey, is a prolific writer. Along with his creative formulations of democratic confederalism,[23] he has written, first from the mountains and later from his prison on Imrali Island, in extraordinarily critical terms of the patriarchalism of Kurdish society.[24] He looked far back to the late Neolithic village culture of the region, which archaeologists suggest was egalitarian, or even woman-centred, in marked contrast to the patriarchal civilizations of the Sumerian city states that developed in the third millennium BCE.[25] The development of private property, cities, exchange, commodification and monotheistic religion was, Öcalan writes, 'essentially the history of the enslavement of women'.[26] This condition has lasted to the present day, for 'no race, class or nation is subjected to such systematic slavery as housewifisation'.[27] Although Öcalan doesn't cite them, his analysis is similar to that of second-wave feminist theorists of patriarchy (see for instance Gerda Lerner[28] and Maria Mies[29]). But often his language is more colourful: 'On top of being an unemployed childbearing and child raising machine that is inexpensive to purchase and can be run cost free', he writes, 'the woman can be used as scapegoat, carrying the guilt for all that is wrong'.[30] He calls for the total transformation of the family. But more than that, his critique of capitalism and the nation state includes their implication in patriarchy. These systems are, he says, 'the monopolism of the tyrannical and exploitative male'.[31] In short, 'Power is synonymous with masculinity'.[32]

The male has become a state and turned this into the dominant culture. Class and sexual oppression develop together; masculinity has generated ruling gender, ruling class and ruling state. When man is analysed in this context, it is clear that masculinity must be killed.[33]

It is remarkable that these avowedly feminist polemics on masculinity have not led to Öcalan's rejection by the male militants of the PKK. His thought has certainly encouraged many Kurdish women and was reflected in the activism of the Democratic and Free Women's Movement, which gained adherents throughout the Kurdish areas of Turkey to become one of the most united and energetic mobilizations of women in the Middle East. In a major study of Kurdish women, researcher Handan Çağlayan conducted a survey of women working in the head office and local branches of HADEP, and went on to interview 40 Kurdish women in the city of Diyarbakir in south-east Turkey.[34] The women she encountered manifested many changes of thinking and lifestyle due to these developments of political theory and practice in the Kurdish movement during the preceding decade. At last women had begun to be honoured in the community for something other than the mothering of sons.

Women's consciousness has been developing concurrently in the communities of the diaspora. In February 2014 a landmark conference on 'jineology', or 'women's studies' (from the Kurdish word for women: *jin*) was organized in Cologne by the Kurdish Women's Peace Office in Germany, widely known as CENI. Its aim was 'to question and deconstruct the ruling sciences and their patriarchal and capitalist structures and to create, share and discuss alternative concepts of women's studies, and alternative ways of thinking and living'.[35]

* * *

Let me tell you now something of three Kurdish women of Turkish origin who shared with me their experience of migration to the UK. They represent three 'generations' of migration, the 1980s, the 1990s and the post-millennium years. I will start with Suna Parlak, the most recent of the three to arrive in London, in 2007.

SUNA'S STORY: PERSECUTION IN TURKEY

I met Suna for the first time in the autumn of 2014, at the Kurdish Community Centre near Green Lanes in Haringey. She was 42 years of age and had by then been living in London for seven years. She was studying for a masters degree in politics in an evening class at Birkbeck College, and earning her living through restaurant and shop work, interpreting and basic accounting. But in 'reality', in another life, the life of 'before', Suna is a skilled and experienced writer and editor. Journalism is a competence she acquired in prison. This is how it came about.

Suna's father, Asaf, was an employee of the Turkish state, working in a publicly owned chain of factories making cheese and other dairy products. He was Kurdish, a leftist, an atheist and a known supporter of a Kurdish political organization, the forerunner of the PKK. The government harassed him for his politics by continually moving him from one branch of the company to another. Thus, Suna, born in 1972 in Kars, up in the far north-east of Turkey where it borders Georgia, experienced a semi-nomadic childhood. By the time she was 18 she had attended 14 different schools. For some years the family lived in the province of Dersim, in the heartlands of Kurdish south-eastern Turkey. In 1980, however, soon after the military coup, Asaf lost his job altogether. Suna says of her father, 'It was his experiences that shaped my ideas. My first political consciousness, gained among his friends, was leftist rather than Kurdish. It was revolutionary songs I learned first!'

Although moving from school to school had deprived her of enduring friendships, Suna had obtained good grades. In 1991, at the age of 19, she made a far-reaching decision: to leave the Kurdish region and follow many other westward migrants to the city of Istanbul. At this time, the violence in the south-east of the country was at its height. The Turkish military were sacking and burning villages to destroy the support base of the PKK. Their motto was 'drain the water to kill the fish'. Many displaced families went first to Diyarbakir and other urban centres of the region, but work was scarce and Istanbul, like other western cities, seemed to offer more chance of a living. Suna took the entrance exam to Istanbul Technical University and, with a leap of imagination and daring that I now know to be characteristic of her, obtained a place on a course in space engineering. Soon she was deeply embedded among the Kurdish student community in the city.

That first year in Istanbul Suna got involved with other students in the highly active local branch of the PKK. They flew the banned Kurdish flag, and celebrated the festival of Newroz, which was illegal. She says, 'It was so nice to have a bunch of close friends at last.' All the same, she felt a little different from them. She explained: as a teenager she'd been a believer in Islam, like her mother. But it gave rise to feminist questions in her mind. Observing that girls got high marks in school, she'd wondered, 'Why should men be privileged? If God had created us all, we should be equal! And why should I wear head cover?' Reasoning this way, she had tended to dress 'girlish', as she put it, in defiance of Islamic gender expectations. Now, among the students in Istanbul, her dresses and make-up set her apart from the average student in jeans and T-shirt. Nonetheless, 'I was accepted', she says.

Suna remained at university until 1993, deeply involved in Kurdish matters. 'We were a kind of youth PKK', she says. They organized events inside and outside the university. They did support work with impoverished rural migrant families in the city, and travelled to make contact with Kurdish migrants in other towns. These activities amounted to little more than social work, and were not, strictly speaking, illegal. But the very fact of this self-organizing among Kurds made the government suspicious of them. In 1994, just before Newroz, the Turkish police made a sweep, arresting more than a hundred activists. One was Suna. She was held initially for 18 days, and for the first five she was herded with others into the basement of a particular police station, Gayrettepe, in Istanbul, well known as a place of torture. And Suna was indeed tortured at this time. Seeking to extract from her the names of other activists, they applied electric shock to her tongue, hands, breasts and genitals. She was hung from her wrists, tied together behind her back. This crippling maltreatment, she tells me, is known as 'Palestinian hanging' or *strappado*. She was also suspended with her arms spread out, crucifix style. Often the prisoners were blindfolded, to prevent them recognizing their individual torturers. They would be forced to stand upright for hours, forbidden to lean against a wall. From time to time the police would return and recommence the questioning, and the torture. On one occasion they broke Suna's arm. The bone was literally broken in two, the limb hanging askew. One of her friends died from such treatment. 'These practices were quite normal for them', Suna says now. 'It was routine. They were doing it everywhere.'

Suna did not give away any information during her torture. After those 18 days of imprisonment, when they took their prisoners to the court hearing, the police threatened those who had refused to speak: 'You will certainly get a long sentence'. This was the first case brought against Suna: of being a key member of the PKK in Istanbul. She got a conviction known as a '125', reserved for people high up in the organization. It can ultimately carry a death sentence. Suna was now imprisoned, along with 40 other defendants, mainly students, in Bayrampaşa Prison where she would remain for seven long years from spring 1994 to winter 2000. Her experience was hardly exceptional: in the decade of the 1990s the Turkish government is estimated to have imprisoned more than 100,000 Kurds.

In Bayrampaşa she found herself among 50 or more women in one big room, stacked with bunks. Such was the overcrowding, extra beds were often crammed between the bunks, and inmates at times slept two or three to a bed. Her court case, with intermittent hearings, would go on throughout the seven years. This is not untypical. The legal process in Turkey, barely recognizable as such by international standards, is extremely long-drawn out and opaque. She and her fellow inmates were not tortured in Bayrampaşa. But pain was inflicted again whenever the police took them out to court hearings. Then for example they would apply handcuffs, Suna said, screwing them on so tightly the metal cut into the women's wrists.

> The police vehicles were very high, and they forced us to jump up into them with our handcuffs on and that could be very painful. I couldn't use my hands for some days afterwards. Often the vehicles were suffocatingly hot. We were thirsty, held for hours without water or food. If we complained, they would beat us.

Of these seven years, Suna says,

> Prison life is what made me who I am, it made me Suna. Before, I was very impatient, I was a perfectionist. Perhaps I was a bit self-absorbed. Because my mother and father were open-minded people

48

I had been free at home, and I could do as I liked. In prison I had to learn patience. You had to be able to be with everyone, anyone, even people you might not particularly like. The big cell was a huge family, you learned to get along with everybody.

Most of the inmates had a university background, and they educated each other. Indeed, they ran a kind of university in the prison. Fortunately they were given access to books. The women shared their resources, and started a library. 'The authorities allowed it to keep us quiet.' In truth, Suna had known little about the history and ideology of the Kurdish movement before. Now she was able to read into it, and about the programmes of Turkish leftist groups too. 'We had all their literature.' The women chose to divide each year into three terms, and for any one year they would choose five or six subjects to study. One, Suna remembers, was the history of religion. She herself was interested, at that moment in her life, in asking questions about the influence of religions on the lives of women. They would focus the first term on research; the second on giving talks and presentations – but interactively; and the third term was cultural – for theatre, writing articles and poems, and drawing.

In Suna's second year in the prison they started to publish a monthly women's magazine. She was the editor, and also did drawings for it. The prisoners managed to get hold of a huge old-fashioned typewriter, arguing that they needed it to prepare their defence for court cases. On this they were able to type a single copy of their magazine and pass it to their lawyers, who would then print and distribute it in the Kurdish areas of Istanbul. They heard later that even PKK women militants in the distant mountains had received copies. Some Kurdish publications noticed their magazine and invited Suna to write for them. So these years in prison brought her a wider knowledge of the women's movement and also developed her journalist's skills.

On 18 December 2000 (Suna has a very precise memory for dates), she heard the court pronounce her release from prison. However, she chose to go back to prison for one more night in order to say goodbye to her friends. To this the prison director agreed. It just so happened that on that very night, in response to a widespread hunger strike, the state launched an aggressive military operation throughout the prison system. (Prisoners had been protesting against the government's threat to remove them from collective accommodation into separate small cells to impede their mutual politicization.) An armed force brutally attacked the inmates in prisons across the country, causing several deaths. At Bayrampaşa, Suna recalls, the violence continued for six hours. 'Then they took us to another prison. I was put in a small cell of the kind that's used to constrain mentally ill people. And there I stayed locked up two days longer, until 20 December, when my family managed to locate me, and I was finally released.'

Suna's family – mother, father, two sisters and a brother – had moved to Istanbul soon after her original imprisonment so they could be nearby. Her mother, Sultan, had visited her every week in prison, and this had led to her own harassment by police. Now at last the family could take Suna home. Injured in the attack, she stayed indoors for two months recovering. Then, instead of returning to her university course, she chose to continue educational work among women in a Kurdish organization, Dicle Kadin Kultur Merkezi (Tigris Cultural Women's Organization). Though the work didn't bring a wage, her parents willingly supported her. Suna says, now, 'They never judged me. They were fantastic!' Soon she was also writing a weekly column in a Kurdish newspaper, and articles for a Kurdish paper published in Germany, and a women's magazine in the Netherlands. Her theme was mainly women's issues, from a Kurdish political point of view, with a feminist critique of both Kurdish and Turkish society. She won a competition for some of her writing. But every few months the police would visit and search the women's office, and before long opened a court case against the organization. Suna says, 'The police knew me, and were watching me'. Then, in 2003, when she had been out of prison for three years, Suna obtained her first paid employment: the Kurdish newspaper for which she wrote a regular column asked her to become the editor of its daily women's page. It was a job she would hold for four years.

In 2004, however, harassment markedly increased against Kurdish civil society such as women's groups and newspapers. The state launched a big operation against the KCK (Koma Civakên Kurdistan, or Group of Communities in Kurdistan), an organization that had been founded by the PKK (called KADEK at that moment) to put into practice Abdullah Öcalan's ideology of democratic confederalism in Kurdish areas. There were more than 5,000 arrests in this sweep. At that time they published a list of high-ranking members of the PKK, and Suna's name was on it. Many activists fled Turkey at that moment. She however stayed put.

> I said, I have nothing to hide. I have my job, my family. So I stayed and went on working. But after the list was published in 2004, on December 5, the police came to our home. My sister was in bed recovering from an operation. Mother had gone back to the village, where my grandmother was dying. Twenty armed police came to our home at six in the morning, with maybe ten vehicles. They said they had a case against me. They searched our house for five or six hours. They ransacked my father's bookshelves, went through the books page by page. They took our computers, all our papers.

Then they took Suna to the police station. They questioned her about KADEK, about her travels to Lebanon, Iraq and Iran where she'd attended conferences and spoken on TV. No physical torture this time, but hours and hours of questioning. Every half-hour they fetched her from the cell for more interrogation. Each time, it was 'different men, same questions'. She told them: 'I write for my rights and my people's rights. I'm doing my job. You have access to my phone calls. You know I'm not doing anything illegal.' This time they held Suna for five days, then took her to court and charged her with being a member of KADEK. This, while true in spirit, was not in fact the case. She denied it, and supplied the evidence they sought about her activities abroad. This time the judge, taking account of her past prison term, released her pending pursuit of the case in court. However, before leaving the building Suna requested the police to return her identity card. She had begun to read the writing on the wall.

> I saw they would hold me if they could. There and then I called my solicitor and asked her to do whatever was needed to recover my ID card. Meantime I requested her husband, also a solicitor, to come urgently to the court and get me out of there. He should call my sister, I said, and ask her to come with a taxi and wait for us outside the building.

The plan worked, and Suna escaped the authorities. But she wisely did not go to the family home – the police went directly there to look for her, she later learned. Instead she took shelter with a distant relative. Thereafter for some years she kept moving, but kept writing. Only in 2007, seeing imprisonment looming again, she reluctantly began to consider leaving the country. She signed up for an English-language course in Cambridge, and applied for and obtained a twelve-month UK student visa. She arrived at London's Heathrow Airport on 31 March 2007, and was admitted through passport control without hindrance.

Suna didn't know a living soul in England. But, taking up her student place in Cambridge, she struck lucky. She was introduced to Turkan Budak, a Kurdish woman who already knew Suna through her writing. Turkan welcomed her into her home, and they became close friends. Suna studied English and worked in a restaurant. Warned by her solicitor back in Turkey that she would certainly be arrested if she returned, when her student visa ran out she set in train the long process of seeking asylum in the UK. A solicitor here, to whom Turkan introduced her, believed she would have a strong case. Her story had been widely aired on the Internet. She had clearly been persecuted in Turkey for her Kurdish identity, yet at the same time she was a women's rights activist and had never been a guerrilla fighter with the proscribed PKK. She submitted her application for asylum in October 2007. Within three months she was given an appointment to attend a Home Office department in Birmingham, at which she was granted asylum, with five years' leave to remain in the UK. In 2013 this was increased to 'indefinite leave to remain' and in 2014 she acquired British citizenship. Now, living in London, although involved in the Kurdish Community Centre in Haringey, and with Roj Women's Association, she is left in peace by the British authorities. As for the Turkish authorities, though they harass her parents back home, they have so far not pursued Suna to London. That both the Turkish state and the host state are capable of making trouble for Kurds in the western European diaspora, however, is evidenced in the story told to me by Suna's friend Turkan, whom we shall meet later in this chapter.

BERCEM: THE EXPERIENCE OF ILLEGAL IMMIGRATION

Meanwhile, meet 'Bercem',[36] who was 27 when we first met in 2014. She is one 'generation' back from Suna in the migration story, having first travelled to the UK as a child in 1998. Her story illustrates the perilous journeys many migrants make to reach the UK. I bumped into Bercem when visiting the Day-Mer Kurdish community centre in Stoke Newington, where she was employed as a youth worker.

Bercem's family don't come from the majority-Kurdish south-eastern region of Turkey, but from Mersin, on the Mediterranean coast. Her grandparents and parents lived in a Kurdish ghetto in the town, and were very poor. She was born, she says, in the basement of her father's uncle's house. She remembers the moment her father was first able to rent a home for his family – the landlord had been a Turkish nationalist with a bitter hatred of Kurds. Her father was, however, fortunate in finding steady employment, albeit very low paid, as a caretaker at a private primary school. Her mother was for a while a cleaner in the same school. What's more, the school administration had a practice of permitting one child of each of its employees to attend the school without paying fees. Bercem, the oldest of three siblings, was the one who got the place and, among these rather privileged children, obtained an excellent early education. Among other things, she had a good start in English as a foreign language, and this, as we'll see, has been a significant factor in her life.

In 1989 Bercem's grandfather decided to take the step of migrating to western Europe in an attempt to lift his family out of the deep poverty of the Kurdish minority in Mersin. Bercem's father was his parents' firstborn, and having obtained secure employment, he had married and started his own family ahead of his siblings. It was decided they would follow, but not until Bercem had finished primary school and obtained a leaving certificate. Then they obtained passports and set off in the wake of the rest of the family, first flying to Germany, a country for which they were able to obtain visas. Their elders were by now in the UK however, and the onward journey across the Channel was going to be a very different matter, for Britain had introduced a visa requirement for Turks and they had no legal right to enter.

Bercem's mother and father, with herself and two little brothers, now travelled overland to the port of Calais, where her father paid for the services of a people smuggler. Bercem remembers at a certain moment arriving at a dark, wild place, near a motorway, somewhere near the ferry terminal. Waiting there was a large, white, windowless van. Her father had been told it would be empty except for themselves. When he opened the door he saw it was already packed with at least

40 people. 'He was furious!' Bercem says. 'He turned on the smuggler as if he'd like to beat him up!' The family squeezed in, for all that. 'The guy instructed us to listen for the sound of a tap on the side of the van by which he would indicate the moment everyone must fall completely silent. After that, not a breath should be heard by anyone outside, while we were driven on to the ferry.' Once on the ferry, the smuggler parked the van in the vehicle hold, and went to the passenger lounges up above, leaving the van unlocked. 'My dad said we must get out. He took my mum and us three, plus a couple of the young men from the van, and a girl who was on her own. But we found that because the ferry had set sail, all the exits from the vehicle hold had now been closed. Dad was shouting and swearing.' However, with her English skills, Bercem was able to understand the signs. She directed the family to one that said 'E-X-I-T'. They found a gate blocking the way up the stairs. Her father pushed and pulled it in vain. Then Bercem saw that it had an instruction saying 'lift'. 'Look, dad, L-I-F-T. You have to pull it up.' And indeed, this was all it needed. He lifted the barrier and they were able to pass up the stairs into the passenger area.

Nobody troubled them on board the ferry, or as they disembarked in Dover. The passengers were met by a fleet of minibuses that transported them to passport control. The police now came and checked them out. Those who, like Bercem's family, had no valid documentation were herded to one side. They were held for several hours. Her dad phoned her grandfather, asking him to come quickly from London with an interpreter. There was nothing to eat in the place they were being held, but Bercem found a dispensing machine and was able to read the instructions to obtain a succession of free hot chocolate drinks. (The memory recalled by the taste of hot chocolate has put her off this beverage for life, she says.) Eventually the police took them into an interview room. They did body searches of them all, including her. But the family were eventually allowed into the country to join their relatives. Apart from that delay on entry, nothing negative happened in the course of their reception in the UK. They were not at any point held in a cell, nor were they put in a detention centre. They were simply released. It would take just a few years to have asylum granted, be given a period of 'leave to remain', and eventually obtain citizenship.

On arrival in London, the family went directly to the grandparents' flat in Stamford Hill and stayed there for some weeks. Then, something that would scarcely be possible today, they were allocated a council house of their own, in Enfield, paid for with Housing Benefit. 'We loved it!', she says. It was difficult for her parents to get work because of their lack of English. Her father was in and out of casual jobs, manual work in shops and depots. Her mother stayed home with the two younger children. Bercem entered Year 7, the first year of secondary education, at Lea Valley High School. Her good English served her well. She recalls, 'There was a Turkish teacher in the school. She gave me a worksheet and said "Write one to ten, in letters". But I told her, "I know English", and proved it by writing from one to a hundred. I felt the joy of it!'

Bercem was quite lonely in those first two years, though. There were incidents of bullying. The native English pupils made no approach of friendship to her, seldom including her in their chat. In her tutor group there were only three other Turks, all boys. In the year as a whole, however, there were 10–15 Turkish-speaking pupils, and by her third year in school she had started to have a more social time, hanging out and speaking Turkish with them. 'It was being a teenager by now. We clustered together, in the playground, in the canteen.' 'A kind of Turkish-speaking ghetto?' I asked? 'Yes', she said. 'There was a bunch of black kids, mainly boys, who used to take the micky. But by Year 10 we were a strong group, and weren't bothered any more.'

Settling into migrant life in London, despite her young age, Bercem played quite an adult role in the family. She was effectively doctor, accountant and interpreter for the household. 'It was Bercem, do this, do that! Every oldest child in that situation would probably tell the same story, because we were the ones to pick up English first. We were more adaptable than the adults.' I asked Bercem about the family's relationship to Kurdish politics, both before and since their migration. Among the family members, all Kurdish, the men had been more concerned with Kurdish politics than the women. Though none of Bercem's relatives had been fighters in the PKK guerrilla forces, some of the cousins and uncles had been politically engaged, and tortured as a result. Her father, less political, was nonetheless at one moment arrested, roughed up, and then released without charge. He is deaf in one ear from the beating, and he has a burn on his inner leg. So Bercem's family would more correctly be said to be economic migrants rather than asylum seekers. As we shall see in other chapters, however, it is difficult to separate the two causes of displacement. It is Turkey's political oppression of Kurds that has brought about their economic disadvantage. Kurds have not only been deprived of political and cultural rights in the Turkish state, they have also been limited to second-rate education and a poor job market.

Once in London, although her father and mother didn't become actively involved in London's Kurdish community organizations they didn't discourage Bercem from doing so, and gradually a greater awareness of Kurdish-Turkish politics awoke in her. As a child in Mersin, she told me, though she perceived there were two languages, she knew little of the cultural and political differences between Turks and Kurds. Her parents had sheltered her from 'all that trouble'. Thus, she had little understanding of Kurds' political reasons for migration. To illustrate her ignorance she told the story that while in primary school in Turkey they had been shown a typical Turkish video about Ataturk, extolling the great man. Far from being critical of it, she had found it very moving. Indeed, she loved it so much she asked if she could borrow it to take home! She took it for granted that all the pupils, every day, would pronounce the national oath, standing to attention. 'I was proud to do so', she says. But once in the UK, she became more conscious of her Kurdishness. The teachers asked her to help a Kurdish girl who spoke primarily Kurmanji and was having trouble not only with English but also with Turkish. They became friends, and it was from her that Bercem began to learn, for the first time, things she had never known about Turkey's oppression of the Kurds. The learning continued when she started attending the community centre, Halkevi. Meanwhile, Bercem was progressing from school to a BTech in sport at a further education college, and thence to a degree course in sport science at London Metropolitan University. Leaving university, now in her early twenties, she started getting more involved in Turkish and Kurdish events in London. She started visiting the Day-Mer Kurdish neighbourhood centre in Hackney, and found it friendly. After a while she was offered a job there, working with young people, and this is where I met her.

I asked Bercem about her own identity today, does she feel herself to be Turkish, Kurdish or British? She says:

I don't feel I belong to Turkey, as if I'm a Turkish citizen, because I've not lived there for the last 17 years. But on the other hand I don't really feel attached to the UK, as a British citizen, because I don't originate here. I feel I'm lost in my identity. I prefer to live here because of the better standard of living, and we have more freedom of speech. I'd love to go back to Turkey if only I could live there freely and equally as a Kurd. But that won't happen.

Bercem seems to exemplify the young migrants studied by Ayar Ata, hesitating on a cusp between being merely 'Kurds living in London' and what he calls 'Kurdish Londoners', more integrated into the multicultural city.[37]

TURKAN: HARASSMENT IN THE UK

Turkan, the third and last woman to tell something of her story in this chapter, is of a yet earlier 'generation' of migrants than either Suna or Bercem. Fifty years old now, she entered the UK back in 1984 when she was only 20. Her story is especially interesting for me as it illustrates the anomalous situation of someone simultaneously subject to risk from the Turkish state and the British authorities, due to the proscription of the PKK under the Terrorism Act of 2000.

Turkan comes of a Kurdish family, many of whom were activists contesting Turkish repression. Her mother, of whom she's immensely proud, reared nine children, born over a span of 20 years. Much of that time, after Turkan's father died of cancer, she brought them up single-handedly. Many of Turkan's brothers and cousins had already sought refuge in Sweden, Switzerland and the UK, after episodes of imprisonment and torture, by the time Turkan herself came to join her partner in London. It was November 1985, before the imposition of a visa requirement. She was 21, and pregnant. The couple found lodging in Walthamstow, and Turkan was at first busy caring for her newborn son, and a second born soon after. Meanwhile, she learned English of which she scarcely had a word on arrival. Many Kurdish women in London at that time were in similar circumstances, mostly married, raising children and confined to the home. Turkan is struck, looking back, how things changed just a few years later, with the influx of 'plane-loads' of Kurds fleeing the escalating conflict. 'Thousands came in 1988 and 1989', she recalled. 'Turkey wanted rid of them, and England at that time had an open door.' Many were women, active in the Kurdish movement. Few spoke English, and today's raft of Kurdish community resources did not yet exist. Turkan remembers herself with a baby in a buggy and a toddler in tow, leading 40 Kurdish women to the Department of Health and Social Security to get the assistance they needed. In the 30 years she has been in the UK, Turkan has made a living running cafés, and has done so in several different towns, while maintaining links with the Kurdish activism that thrives in Hackney and neighbouring boroughs of North London where she's been a consistent and valued member of the 'Peace Committee', a customary mediation initiative found throughout Kurdistan. She is also active in the Roj Women's Association, in which latterly she has served on the Administration Committee.

On 9 January 2013, an act of extreme violence shook the Kurdish diaspora. In Paris that day, three women were shot dead in the Kurdish Information Centre, where their bodies lay till discovered next morning. They had all been killed at close range by bullets from a single gun. Sakine Cansız, aged 55, was a founding member of the PKK, for which she was a leading organizer in Europe, and had at one time been involved in the armed struggle. The other two victims, however, were less politically prominent. Fidan Doğan was a member of the Kurdish National Congress, and Leyla Söylemez was a youth worker. The Turkish government condemned the assassination, which they averred was the outcome of conflict within the PKK. However, it was widely believed in the Kurdish communities in Europe to have been the work either of the Turkish security services or of clandestine extremists of what Kurds know and fear as 'the deep state', aiming to derail the peace talks between the Turkish authorities and Abdullah Öcalan. The deaths were certainly intended as a warning to Kurdish activists in Europe.

A year later, the anniversary of their murder was to be marked by a demonstration in Paris, protesting at lack of progress in investigating the case and identifying the killers. Women prepared to travel to the event from all over Europe. Coaches were hired to carry a contingent from Britain. Two of them set off from London on a January evening to catch a night-time train through the Channel Tunnel. Turkan was one of the Roj Women organizing the trip, and had taken responsibility for making a list of those travelling on her coach, gathering their travel documents so as to pass speedily through passport control. When they were stopped by the UK Border Agency at Dover, around midnight, Turkan's coach was leading the way. Their passports were collected. But then all passengers were asked to alight and the two vehicles were subjected to a thorough search. One bus was cleared, reloaded and allowed to pass through border control, while Turkan's coach was held back. All 56 passengers were taken indoors by plain-clothes Metropolitan Police officers. After a long wait in a bitterly cold room, Turkan asked, 'What's going on?' The Border Agency staff replied, 'It's not up to us, it's the police.' The police said, 'This is normal.' Turkan answered, 'It's not!' But she'd noticed that the police officers seemed to be observing her keenly and particularly. She'd experienced this before when playing an organizing role. She believes it's deliberate harassment, to discourage Kurdish activism. She told the coach passengers, 'I think this is all to do with me.' They said, 'We don't care. We stand with you!'

Eventually the police began taking the passengers, one at a time, into a separate room, and when they were done with them, sent them off into a different area so that they had no contact with those waiting to be screened. Turkan, seeing them at a distance through a glass wall, noticed that some seemed distressed as they emerged from questioning. After some hours, one of the women, using the excuse of needing a toilet, managed to make her way back into the waiting room. She told Turkan, 'They found some money on one woman. Now they are taking all our money.' As it happened, Turkan was carrying £2,000 in cash. Her younger son had asked her to convey this sum to his brother, living in France.

The authorities left Turkan till nearly the last. When her turn came, she stepped in and simply stated, 'It's me you're looking for! Why waste everyone else's time?' First the Border Agency staff spoke to her. A female officer greeted her by name. 'Turkan', she said. 'We've met before.' Turkan had indeed come to know quite a few such officers by name in the course of her trips abroad. The officer said, 'This operation is not to do with us in the Border Agency. It's the Met. Police. They think you're carrying money for the PKK.' Then she was questioned by a plain-clothes police officer who introduced himself by name. Turkan addressed him very directly and personally. 'Jeremy,'

Opposite: Suna Parlak (left) and Turkan Budak on a demonstration in North London, calling on the Turkish Government to free Kurdish leader Abdullah Öcalan. Their banner commemorates Sakine Cansız, a PKK founder, and two other PKK women activists assassinated in Paris in 2014, see p. 58.

Above: London Kurdish women from several countries of origin came together in 2014 with other women's organizations in London, forming an alliance to support Yazidi and other women captured by ISIS.

she said. 'I have a political role here. You represent the state. But be careful of your actions.' He replied, 'Are you warning me?' Turkan said, 'I'm telling you the truth. We're humans. I'm Kurdish by nationality, but I'm a human being. We should behave well as human beings.' She went on, 'I do have something to do with the PKK, I'm a supporter. But I'm not taking money to them. I am taking it to my son.' She gave him evidence of how she'd obtained the money. He said, 'I believe you, but I have to take it from you.' She told him, 'Keep it, but you will pay it back. You should be embarrassed by what you're doing. You're wasting tax payers' money here tonight.' She placed her money in an envelope, without allowing him to touch the notes, and took his signed receipt. She warned him that she had a list of journalists' phone numbers and was ready to alert the press to what was going on this night in Dover.

By the time Turkan was released, ten hours had passed. They all got back on the coach – but of course the train on which they'd been scheduled to cross to France had long-since gone. They were told they must pay for the crossing again. But now they had no money! At that point Turkan said, 'Enough!' and called a BBC reporter and told the story. She told the police she had done so, and also threatened to mobilize a thousand Kurdish people living in Kent to come and blockade the Tunnel route. At that point the authorities agreed to load their coach on to the next train without additional cost. The group arrived in Paris at 4.00 pm, by which time the commemorative event to which they were travelling was long-since over.

Along the way, Turkan learned from the women travellers that the UK police had been unpleasant and intimidating in dealing with them. Women wearing head cover had been obliged to remove them, regardless of the presence of men. Women officers conducted intrusive and intimate body searches, while male officers looked on. Everyone's money had been confiscated, to a total of £17,700. It was held by the court for three months, 'pending investigation'. Turkan was named personally in the case, the only passenger who was, and her name appeared in all subsequent correspondence. The incident, she says, is characteristic of the surveillance to which the UK authorities subject politically active Kurds. Their homes are visited and questions asked, their cars are stopped and searched. This harassment is directly due to UK government asylum and terror legislation. In a report drafted by the London-based Kurdish Human Rights Project the impact on the Kurdish community was described this way:

> While facing substantial problems as a minority immigrant community, they are, in particular, subject to restrictive asylum policies and poor asylum decision-making, impediments to cultural expression, intolerance, discrimination and criminalization generated by police activity and the association of immigrant communities with terrorist threats, deprivation and social exclusion, including problems in employment, skill levels, language ability, political participation and concentration into areas of multiple deprivation.[38]

* * *

In Chapter 6 we shall be looking at the major political disturbances that have shaken the Middle East and North African region since 2011, and at the 'migration crisis' that has ensued. The Kurdish women with whom I was in touch in Hackney were closely following these developments, which were deeply affecting Kurds in Turkey, Iraq and Syria. They were establishing contact with a community of Kurds living in the north-eastern corner of Syria, just across Turkey's southern border. It's an area in which Kurds of both Alevi and Sunni belief live side by side with Arabs and Turkmen, mainly of Muslim belief; with Christian Assyrians and Armenians; and Yazidis, who have their own brand of monotheism. Here, in November 2013, two years into the civil war, the Kurdish leadership had declared self-rule, first forming what they called a 'transitional interim administration' and then, in early 2014, holding elections to generate the government of an autonomous region: Rojava (which signifies 'western Kurdistan'). Its leading political party is the mainly Kurdish PYD, the Democratic Union Party. Inspired by the ideology of Abdullah Öcalan, it is in the process of creating a polity wholeheartedly embodying his principles of democratic confederalism. Women comprise 40 per cent of all assemblies in Rojava, and all bodies of governance have a woman co-chair. The Assad regime of Syria of course strongly denies the legitimacy of Rojava, but it has become an inspiration for many Kurds worldwide, and especially for Kurdish women.

Kurdish women in London were watching these developments with the closest attention. Roj Women organized a small group to travel to Rojava to gather news and give support. They visited camps to find out the condition and needs of refugees. They learned at first hand about the progressive democratic and feminist processes being established by the PYD. They also travelled to Diyarbakir, north of the border in Turkey, and met Kurdish women there working hard to apply the principles of democratic confederalism and feminism in 'North Kurdistan'.[39] On returning home, Roj Women, together with the Peace in Kurdistan Campaign, an energetic, ethnically mixed group of activist supporters based in London, started an initiative to draw concerned groups together in a 'Women's Alliance for the Defence of Women in Kurdistan, Iraq and Syria'. In this way, developments in a distant world have spurred women of the Kurdish community in Hackney and elsewhere in London to greater awareness and activism, and have, at the same time, drawn them closer to local feminist organizations with whom, on International Women's Day, they now march to Trafalgar Square.[40]

3

From the Horn of Africa to the Isle of Dogs: Somalis in Tower Hamlets

It must have been some time after the millennium that we began to notice growing numbers of Somali women, men and children among us on the streets of Camden and Kentish Town. I discovered they were just our little local cluster of thousands of migrants from Somalia now swelling a worldwide diaspora. It is hardly surprising that those with the wherewithal to migrate from Somalia have been doing so, for the country is among the most distressed in the world. As I write these words, in April 2017, it is one of four (the others are Nigeria, South Sudan and Yemen) in which famine is impending. United Nations agencies are warning that more than six million people are facing severe food insecurity, including a third of a million acutely malnourished children in need of urgent treatment and nutrition support.[1] Hunger and thirst, however, are nothing new for Somalia. Only six years ago, in 2011, failure of the seasonal rains caused an episode of hunger, thirst and cholera that cost the lives of an estimated 260,000 people, half of them children. The most recent United Nations Development Programme (UNDP) report on Somalia, that of 2012, states that Somalia's meagre national income per head of population, at $284 a year, places it among the four poorest countries in the world.[2] More than half the individuals of working age are without employment, and the figure is two-thirds for those under 30, one of the highest rates in the world. The effect is that 73 per cent of Somalis are living in poverty, less than a third have access to safe drinking water, and less than a quarter have adequate sanitation. Life expectancy is no more than 50 years. Only 42 per cent of school-age children are being educated.[3] Such circumstances are the reason that perhaps one million Somalis, one in seven of the population, are living outside the country, making them one of the world's largest diaspora groups. The life chances of many back home are dependent on these individuals now struggling to make a living abroad. Their remittances to Somalia, amounting to more than a billion dollars a year, account for a third of the country's gross domestic product.[4]

CLAN AND HUNGER: THE DISASTER THAT IS SOMALIA

It is not lack of resources that is holding Somalia back from development, for 95 per cent of land deemed arable is as yet uncultivated, and there are massive untapped oil and mineral reserves. Nor is the hot, dry climate that afflicts the country entirely to blame. The main factor turning drought into famine has been political chaos and war. As the UNDP's *Human Development Report 2012* recalled:

> Between 450,000 and 1.5 million people have died in Somalia's conflict or directly due to hunger since 1991. Millions have been affected by disability, rape and sexual violence, and the spread of disease and famine. Conflict has disrupted and destroyed family structures and the social fabric of societies through human rights abuses, forced recruitment of children and youth into rebel groups, massive displacements, and losses of life and property.[5]

Many of today's problems derive from the past, when various parcels of the country we know as Somalia today were colonized by competing European powers during the West's 'scramble for Africa' from the late nineteenth century. The north-western area, Somaliland, together with the adjoining eastern peninsular of Puntland, came under the control of Britain; Italy held the south; and France occupied the adjacent northern enclave of Djibouti. Ethiopia, which itself avoided colonization, took control of the Ogaden, a large area in the west. Somalis, from the linguistic and cultural point of view, are a rather homogeneous population, and historically they were spread much further afield than this, with sizeable communities across the northern border in Ethiopia and in the region to the south that would become Kenya. But when the colonists withdrew in 1960, the independent Republic of Somalia comprised only the British and Italian territories, while hundreds of thousands of people identifying as Somali remained apart in neighbouring states.[6]

Somalia is one of the oldest Muslim communities in the world. From soon after the death of the Prophet Mohammed in the seventh century CE, the religion spread south to this coast, bypassing Ethiopia, which had been Christian since the fourth century CE. The Somali population is largely Muslim today, adhering to a Sunni variant that some Somalis term 'African Islam', to emphasize its differences from that of the Arab world.[7] Though relatively united by religion, the population is nonetheless fragmented on lines of clan. There are six major clans: the Darod, Dir, Digil/Mirifle, Rahenwein, Hawiye and Isaaq, groups that are again differentiated by sub-clan and family. Clan belonging is a kind of insurance policy, affording individuals support and protection in a conflictual world marked by scarcity and hardship, and Somalis often cite and recite ancestral family names to clarify and affirm relationships. After the withdrawal of the colonial powers in 1960, this clan and family identification gave rise to no less than 60 political parties competing for power in the new state. The chaos was interrupted in 1969 by a military coup, led by General Mohamed Siad Barre.[8]

Barre banned clan identification and discouraged religion too. His intention was to introduce a regime of Marxian 'scientific socialism'. He built roads and schools and promoted literacy, introducing a written form of the Somali language for the first time. He would eventually install a new constitution involving equal rights and duties for men and women. But the Horn of Africa hit the world's headlines several times in the 1970s and 1980s due to drought and famine, which uprooted and displaced many thousands of people. To add to this chaos, the repressive and dictatorial nature of the military regime spurred clan-related opposition groups into guerrilla warfare. One was the Somali National Movement, an insurgency of mainly Isaaq people in Somaliland, in the north-west of the country, to which, in 1988, Barre's forces responded with a massively destructive bombardment of its capital, Hargeisa. Another was the Somali Patriotic Movement, based in the south-west. A third was the United Somali Congress (USC), drawing its support from the Hawiye clan in south-eastern Somalia. They would eventually form a united front and, on 26 January 1991, force Barre to flee from Mogadishu. In the power vacuum that followed there was vicious inter-clan conflict, marked by rape, looting and massacres of unarmed communities by rival clan militias.[9]

The ousting of Siad Barre occurred at the very moment that, following the collapse of the Soviet Union, the United States was aspiring to establish itself as the uncontested world superpower. Washington therefore saw Somalia's descent into chaos as a test of that intention – for by its very location the country has strategic importance on the world stage, with 70 per cent of the world's petroleum-related products passing through the Indian Ocean. The USA therefore sent 20,000 military personnel in support of a UN mission and relief effort, Operation Restore Hope, only to pull them out two years later after ignominious defeat at the hands of General Mohamed Farrah Aydeed , leader of the USC, and other warlords.[10] Though the UN mission, UNISOM, was replaced by African peacekeepers, these international efforts at nation-building continued to be frustrated by clan-minded war-makers. Author Lidwien Kapteijns sees this period as marking what she calls a 'key shift' towards 'clan cleansing' in Somalia, prefiguring the 'ethnic cleansing' that would soon follow in Bosnia and, within a couple of years, in Rwanda.[11]

Another actor also stepped into the Somalian power vacuum of the 1990s: Al-Itihaad Al-Islamiya, a Salafi fundamentalist Islamist movement. After the attack on the Twin Towers in New York on 11 September 2001, the US administration began to perceive Somalia as a potential source of international terrorism. It proscribed Al-Itihaad as a terror group. But the Islamist movement continued to grow, and in late 2005 a relatively new faction, Al-Shabaab, with connections to Al-Qaeda, the supposed authors of the 9/11 attack, joined with two other Somali Islamist groups in opposing the warlords. They were instrumental in establishing administrations in many local areas under the name of the Union of Islamic Courts (UIC). By 2006 the UIC had stabilized Mogadishu and southern Somalia, and, while by no means all Somalis welcomed the rule of *sharia* law and the prospect of an eventual Islamist state, many could not help but appreciate both the UIC's determined opposition to clannism and its efficient administration, which permitted the establishment of much needed social services, health provision and schools. However, Meles Zenawi, Ethiopia's President, saw this manifestation of political Islam as extremely undesirable. Backed by the USA and Kenya, he attacked

Somalia and toppled the UIC. The fighting cost an estimated 10,000 lives, mainly in Mogadishu and south-central Somalia, and displaced a million people from their homes. Ethiopian troops would remain in the country for a further three years.[12]

Many Somalis resented the overthrow of the UIC, and were all the more inclined to value Al-Shabaab as a resistance movement. Joined by Hizbul Islam, another anti-Western, anti-government and anti-clan alliance of fundamentalists, Al-Shabaab launched suicide attacks on government figures and representatives of the African Union Mission to Somalia (AMISOM). Also active across the border in Kenya, in 2011 they kidnapped a group of tourists there, leading the Kenyan military to retaliate with incursions of air and ground forces into Somali territory, where it joined AMISOM in fighting Al-Shabaab and eventually driving them, for a while, out of Mogadishu.

There have been a score of conferences to try and resolve Somalia's problems, sponsored by and held in a range of countries, in the two and a half decades since the fall of the Barre regime. Somaliland, being relatively stable, has long-since unilaterally declared itself to be separate and independent. Puntland also aspires to autonomy. Meanwhile, following an international summit in London in 2012, a National Constituent Assembly was set up that introduced yet one more in a succession of transitional governments of the Somali state. Despite this, in 2013 Somalia was listed as having the highest level of 'conflict events' in Africa.[13] Many were down to the continuing use of IEDs (improvised explosive devices), grenades and suicide devices by Al-Shabaab. In September 2013 the group mounted a devastating attack on a shopping mall in Kenya, killing 67 and wounding 200.[14] Eighteen months later, they would massacre 150 carefully selected Christian teenage girls in the dormitories of a college in the town of Garissa.[15] Notwithstanding an internationally brokered 'New Deal Compact' and a fresh initiative for a 'Somalia of federated states', the violence continued. The USA added to the mayhem through drone strikes against Al-Shabaab that caused significant collateral civilian deaths. It has become 'normal' that hundreds of thousands of Somalis, the majority of them women and children, live in refugee camps, within Somalia and outside its borders, in conditions of extreme poverty, malnutrition and disease. We must add to this, according to a recent Human Rights Watch report, the continuing presence of AMISOM, known more for its soldiers' exploitation of local women and girls than for its success in peacekeeping;[16] harassment of the media and other critics by the authorities, particularly the National Intelligence and Security Agency; and arbitrary justice, including summary executions, by military courts.[17]

Some term Somalia a 'failed state'. Indeed, one widely cited index ranks it among the four highest of 'high alert' countries and second only to South Sudan among the world's 'most failed' states.[18] Others, however, believe that Somalis should be judged more generously. David Hayes and Harun Hassan point out that 'Somalis recreate and sustain their homeland even in the absence of a functioning state – through local institutions and networks, through mobile and virtual connections, through conferences and gatherings, through clan solidarities.'[19] As Mary Harper writes, 'It is as if the Somali community somehow floats above the world, having reached a postmodern stage of development, beyond the nation state.'[20]

WOMEN IN SOMALI SOCIETY

Historically, as well as in recent years, the conditions of life in Somalia have brought many hardships for women. The greater part of the country is grassland, home to pastoral nomads rearing camels and cattle. In this culture women have tended the smaller livestock, and made and traded milk products. They have been the ones to raise children and care for the old while seasonally on the move, with responsibility for making and unmaking the *aqal*, the nomadic home. In the south, where fertile river valleys allow a settled life, women have been hardworking horticulturalists as well as home-makers, growing and trading maize, sorghum and vegetables.[21]

Traditional culture has inflicted particular hardship on women. Somalia is in the bottom four countries worldwide for gender equality, by United Nations development criteria.[22] The clan system, patriarchal and patrilineal, controls women's lives and chances, both in the family and in the wider social and political context, formally subordinating them to men. Boys are favoured in all respects, so that, of children who make it to school, only a third are girls. Women are customarily married exogamously, to men they do not choose, as a way of forging social connections across clan lines. The effect is to place a woman in a clan that differs not only from that of her husband but also of her sons, so that inter-clan warfare often severs women from close family members. Rape used to be relatively rare, deterred by cross-clan punishment. That changed during the clan wars that followed Barre's downfall, when hundreds of thousands of women were raped, and frequently gang-raped, in a pandemic that has continued in the refugee camps both within Somalia and across the border in Kenya and Ethiopia. Female circumcision (termed *qodob*, or 'sewing up') is normal practice in Somalia, and the mutilation has been performed on an estimated 98 per cent of girls. During rape, therefore, razor blades, daggers and bayonets are commonly used to penetrate the infibulation, inflicting severe injuries.[23] Men often reject and abandon their wives when learning they have been raped. Meanwhile, women continue to have six children each on average, and childbirth is itself hazardous: maternal mortality is the highest of any country in the world, excepting only Chad. One out of every 18 Somali women dies from pregnancy-related causes.[24]

More Somali men than women have been killed in the fighting of recent decades, and yet more have been obliged by famine and scarcity to leave their families in order to seek work in towns or abroad. Women have picked up the roles and responsibilities men left behind and are thus even more economically active today than they were in earlier historical periods. Amina Mohamoud Warsame describes how many have become merchants, travelling not only within the country but as far afield as Italy, India and Pakistan, selling Somali products and returning with medicines, clothes and pasta. She points out, however, that this new-found economic activity has 'not translated into political power, nor any meaningful economic power beyond the family ... Somali women continue to be absent from decision-making at the wider societal level'.[25]

A 2005 report on *Gender Justice* by UNIFEM, the United Nations Development Fund for Women, states baldly that women's equality is unattainable under any of the three legal systems coexisting in Somalia. Under customary law, *xeer*, women are essentially commodities, items of exchange between families and clans. They can't inherit, and the only punishment for rape is monetary compensation to husband or father, or an obligation on the rapist to marry his victim. In the Somali interpretation of Islamic *sharia*, a woman's worth is measured at half that of a man, such that two women witnesses are considered equivalent to one male witness. To prosecute a rapist, a woman must present the court with evidence from four Muslim male eyewitnesses to the actual penetration. Secular law, favoured and pressed on Somalia by the international system, while more supportive of women's rights, is costly, intimidating and all but inaccessible to those without influence, connections or resources. The UNIFEM report concludes, besides, that 'there is a lack of awareness of what constitutes women's human rights among the judiciary, law enforcement agencies, men and women in general ... [and] law enforcement agencies, particularly the police, are not gender sensitive'.[26]

The only remedy for such inequality in Somali society is for women to organize, and to obtain a presence in civil society organizations, peace negotiations and political power structures. The first women's organization in Somalia dates back to 1959, when the Somali Women's Association was founded to promote women's welfare. The following year there emerged the Somali Women's Movement, which was more political, seeking political and cultural rights. Siad Barre, taking power in 1969, banned such independent organizations and substituted for them a Women's Section of the Political Office of the Supreme Revolutionary Council. In the two decades since Barre's fall many women's organizations have come and gone, but women have gradually managed to obtain a presence in peace negotiations. Some intervened to try and stop the intra-clan fighting among the Isaaq in Somaliland in the 1990s.[27] Others attempted to stop the inter-clan wars that broke out at that time in Wajir, across the border in north-east Kenya.[28] Despite death threats to women activists such as these, from both clan and religious male traditionalists, a significant breakthrough occurred at a peace conference in March 2000 held in Arta, Djibouti. On this occasion – the thirteenth formal attempt at reconciling differences – women were for the first time officially recognized as participants. Their presence was fostered there by an orientation towards civil society and away from warlords. Among the 3,000 delegates were not only individual women leaders but representatives of women's NGOs (non-governmental organizations).[29] As to the political system, the parliamentary elections of 2012 were something of a test case, being governed for the first time by a legally ratified 30 per cent 'quota' for women – 82 seats out of 275. The voters returned less than half that number. Nonetheless, history was made by the appointment of one woman as Deputy Prime Minister and another as Minister of Social Development.[30]

RESETTLEMENT IN LONDON: TOWER HAMLETS

There has been a community of a few hundred Somalis living in Britain since the late nineteenth century. Somalia's coastal geography drew many Somalis to seafaring, and those early arrivals were mainly crew from merchant vessels who stayed to work in the docks of Cardiff, Liverpool and London. Later came sailors on Royal Navy ships. Additionally, during the colonial period, British Somalilanders came to the UK to study. The number of these world travellers, however – almost entirely male– was negligible compared with the mass migrations that began in the late 1980s, impelled by the mayhem of Siad Barre's final years, and continued into the warfare and famine of the 1990s.[31] The rate of arrival peaked in 1999, a year in which they comprised 11 per cent of the refugees arriving in Britain. From the 6,465 individual Somali asylum applications received that year, the figure stayed above 5,000 until 2004, after which it gradually fell away to a mere 373 by 2015. But likewise the reception accorded to Somalis by the British state changed over time. Asylum was ever-more grudgingly granted, with a turning point in 2003 when 1,664 applications were granted, against 3,833 refused. By 2012 Somalia was only tenth in the list of countries of origin of those granted leave to remain.[32] Many of the later arrivals reached the UK after periods living in or transiting through other west European and Scandinavian countries, and today we have by far the largest Somali migrant population in the EU.

London's Somalis, at first economic migrants, increasingly refugees, gradually spread from the docklands to other areas of the metropolis, predominantly north-western and north-eastern boroughs. Stepping as I did from a case study of the Turkish Kurdish community in London to one of the Somali community, I was immediately struck by the contrast. While refugees of both groups began to arrive in Britain in significant numbers in the late 1980s, and during the middle years of the following decade were both among the top-ten nationalities applying for asylum here, the reality is that they came from very different kinds of conflict. The Kurds had been fighting the

Turkish state, united in their quest for either a state of their own, or recognition of their identity and rights within Turkey. The Somalis by contrast were rent apart by clan warfare and thrown to the winds by a collapsing state. In a study comparing and contrasting the two communities in London, David Griffiths found this difference had profound implications for their sense of belonging to a united group of exiles here in the London context. Due to their lack of a 'coherent political project', Somalis' community organization was 'negligible and fragmentary', he wrote, in comparison with that of Kurds, who, as we've seen for ourselves, had been able to establish many solid and enduring associations in their new home.[33]

The various boroughs of London, and their elected councils, furnished different kinds of terrain for the incoming Somalis. Aware of the long history of Somali settlement in East London, I chose the London Borough of Tower Hamlets for my first walks in search of Somali life. Tower Hamlets is the borough that lies immediately east of the City of London, and is thus prototypically what is known as the 'East End'. It is bordered to the north by the London Borough of Hackney, where we saw Turkish Kurds settling (Chapter 2). And its southerly boundary is the winding River Thames, including the meander that encloses the marshy promontory known as the Isle of Dogs, with the West and East India docks, now long past their colonial heyday, and the relatively new high-rise business district of Canary Wharf. Many East End districts with evocative names and interesting histories lie within the relatively new borough boundaries of 'Tower Hamlets': to the north is Bow; eastwards lie Bromley, Poplar and Lansbury; and down on the south-western river bank are Wapping and St Katherine's Docks. The western wards, closer to the City boundary, include Bethnal Green, Spitalfields, Whitechapel, Stepney Green and Shadwell.

Walking the streets of Tower Hamlets, at first I found the Somali community hard to descry. Inescapable, on the contrary, was the lively presence of Bangladeshi people and their market stalls, shops and organizations. The 2011 census showed the demography of Tower Hamlets to be highly unusual, even in the London context. The overall population of the borough (just over a quarter of a million) is growing extraordinarily fast. Its already high density has been augmented by an increase in overall population of 30 per cent since the previous census

(2001), the largest rise of any local authority in England and, astonishingly, four times the rate of increase in London as a whole.[34] Tower Hamlets is also notable for the fact that 'white British' residents are a clear minority (down from 43 per cent to 31 per cent in the decade). This places the borough fifth from bottom in the ranking of English local authority areas by the proportion of white British among their residents. Even when 'white British' are summed with the 'other white' census category, and with 'Irish' and 'Gypsies', they remain less than half of the population of Tower Hamlets. The second most notable demographic feature is the presence of one very large ethno-cultural element. Those defining themselves as 'Asian' or 'Asian British' were 41 per cent of the total population. The great majority of these in fact have their origins in Bangladesh. Almost a third of the population of the borough is Bangladeshi, making it by number and percentage the largest such community anywhere in England.[35] Other non-white ethnic groups are many but relatively small, the most notable being Chinese, Indian, 'other Asian' and Black Caribbean.

Of special interest to us is the group the census calls 'Black African', accounting for 3.7 per cent of the borough's population, because herein are hidden our Somalis – a category the census totally fails to 'see'. While 'country of birth' data are available, they generate only 2,925 Somalis in Tower Hamlets, seriously underestimating the actual number, which of course swells with every child born here to Somali parents, and every Somali arriving here who was born, let's say, in a refugee camp in Kenya, or who has moved here from some earlier foothold in the diaspora such as Norway or Canada. Various estimates derived from statistics of housing and education suggest we have to double that figure of Somalis in Tower Hamlets to between 5,000 and 6,000. Indeed, academic research and voluntary sector estimates put it higher still – at between 8,000 and 12,000, or between 3.3 and 5 per cent of the borough's population. This wild variation in estimates is not limited to Tower Hamlets – the touted Somali population of England and Wales is a guesstimate suggesting anything from 108,000 to more than 200,000.[36]

As I set about discovering the condition of Somalis in Tower Hamlets, I came across a substantial document, *Understanding East London's Somali Communities*, published in 2010 by five borough councils, including Tower Hamlets, who got together for this purpose, calling themselves the East London Alliance.[37] It reported qualitative research commissioned from Options UK. In the following account I draw on this and other studies issuing from Tower Hamlets Council,[38] from the London Centre for Social Impact[39] and other bodies. One thing I learned is that the Tower Hamlets Somali community is surprisingly young: two-thirds are under 20 years old, and only 4 per cent are older than 50. Young – and poor. Almost as poor as Hackney. In 2012 it was the second most 'deprived' borough in London (and third nationally). It had the highest child poverty rate, at 42 per cent, of any local authority area in the country, and it is certain that Somali children were contributing to that figure. According to a Joseph Rowntree study, Somali poverty in Tower Hamlets, severe as it is, is almost matched by that of Somalis in the UK as a whole.[40] Among the largest 25 migrant groups, Somalis have by far the highest level of working-age adults who are economically inactive (71 per cent), and the estimated average gross annual income of those who are working is the lowest, at £13,700, because such employment as Somalis find is notably unskilled and low paid.[41] This is due to job scarcity, lack of recognized qualifications, language difficulties and (no doubt) discrimination. A contributing factor is the lack of qualification with which Somali children leave school – though this is gradually improving. Underachievement in the past has been due partly to parents' lack of English. Boys have been faring worse, apparently because of peer pressure in a culture involving 'a version of masculinity which is not compatible with success at school'.[42] From low and unreliable family incomes must be subtracted the considerable sums many households must send, month after month, as remittances to sustain relatives, family businesses and charitable work in Somalia – for ties with home are strongly maintained. East London Somalis, besides, feel they lack access to social and public services, and they live in substandard housing. A report by the Karin Housing Association describes long waiting lists for accommodation and high levels of overcrowding in dwellings, many of which, especially in the private rented sector, are unsuitable for their tenants and in a poor state of repair. As a result, not a few Somalis are reduced to finding shelter in night hostels or on the streets.[43]

THE BOROUGH COUNCIL: SCENE OF ETHNO-DRAMA

In recent years, the Bangladeshi community has been dominant in Tower Hamlets Council affairs. In the local elections of May 2014 the Conservative party won four seats, Labour 22, and Tower Hamlets First 18. Since many Labour Party representatives were Asian, and the Tower Hamlets First party was founded by Lutfur Rahman, a prominent Bangladeshi, people of this ethno-cultural category predominated among councillors. Lutfur Rahman himself became the elected mayor. Only one councillor, a woman, Amina Ali, was a Somali – although there had been another, Ahmed Omer, who, for a while from 2009, was (unelected) mayor. The sheer weight of the Bangladeshi presence in the local scene has been discouraging to many Somalis, who have felt that their community tends to be neglected both by local politicians and officers of the council.

In November 2014, however, a few months before I first set out in search of Somalis in Tower Hamlets, central government had made a dramatic intervention in local affairs. The findings of an inquiry commissioned by the Department for Communities and Local Government from accountants PricewaterhouseCoopers had prompted the Communities Secretary, Eric Pickles, to announce that his department would despatch commissioners to Tower Hamlets Council to restore good governance and public confidence. Pickles, hardly mincing his words, told the House of Commons that Mayor Lutfur Rahman had been dispensing public money like 'a mediaeval monarch', and the administration for which he was responsible was 'at best dysfunctional, at worst riddled with cronyism and corruption'.[44] The press release announced that the commissioners were to 'take control of grant making within the council and ... approve any sale or disposal of property'.[45] Rahman was to be dismissed as mayor and banned from standing for office for five years. (At the next mayoral election he was succeeded by a white, British, Labour activist: John Biggs.) A local failed state? Home from home for the local Somalis! While some Somali comment on this extreme measure was favourable, community leaders I spoke with were circumspect in their evaluation of the events and the personalities involved. Some analyses in subsequent weeks robustly defended Tower Hamlets First, believing (as Rabina Khan put it in *Red Pepper*) that 'a dodgy Labour-Tory alliance [was] trying to undermine an independent left-wing administration' and, what's more, showing unapologetic racism as they went about it.[46] Those who hoped stability might be restored at the elections of May 2015 were disappointed. Right up to the vote Scotland Yard were asserting that 'sixteen allegations of electoral malpractice are being assessed by the Met'.[47]

Curious to know how community integration and cohesion policies might look in such circumstances, I sought an interview with responsible officers in Tower Hamlets Council (see Acknowledgements). They directed me first and foremost to the borough's successive Strategic Plans, wherein one objective is 'to promote community cohesion, bringing different parts of the community together, tackling divisions and encouraging positive relationships, thus fostering the principles of One Tower Hamlets'.[48] This was to be achieved in part through a Community Engagement Strategy and Delivery Plan. I learned from the council officers I spoke with that Tower Hamlets, like Hackney, had obediently espoused the 'equality' framework advocated by the government in approaching 'cohesion'. As we know, in the Equalities Act of 2010, 'race', religion and belief are among the 'relevant protected characteristics' (along with age, disability, gender reassignment, pregnancy and maternity, sex and sexual orientation), and the Public Sector Equality Duty requires a body such as a local council to 'advance equality of opportunity … between persons who share one of these characteristics and those who do not share it'.[49] However, given the electrifying ethno-drama being enacted in this borough, Tower Hamlets Council were at pains to steer well clear of any focus, even a corrective one, on a particular ethno-cultural group. Too explicit a concern with Somali needs might be counterproductive for cohesion.

My informants mentioned two policy areas that might illustrate their ethnically alert 'equality' approach. Take housing. There are 20,000 names on the housing waiting list in Tower Hamlets. Six hundred of these 'households in need' are known to be Somali families. In particular, as already mentioned, overcrowding (size of unit relative to number of occupants) is a serious problem for Somali families in the borough. But wait – overcrowding is a problem for more than Somalis alone. It is a problem for Bangladeshis. It is a problem for 'white British'. The council's approach is to research housing need *generally*, and set about improving supply *generally*, in so far as it has the capacity to do so. 'If the problem of overcrowding is solved for the population of Tower Hamlets generally, we will inevitably be helping Somalis.' This is not to say that there will be no directed efforts, although grant-giving is increasingly curtailed by government spending cuts, as well as (now) carefully monitored for probity. I was given an example of circumstances where a small grant can quietly make a difference. The council has a Housing Options Department that works with registered landlords. One of its 'arms-length management organizations' is a very substantial housing association called Tower Hamlets Homes. In partnership with them, the council has undertaken some 'engagement work', providing Somali-speaking staff for the association's office, so as to improve both the accuracy of their data and Somali families' understanding of their options.

Employment is the second example I was given. Tower Hamlets Council is itself a big employer and a valuable source of work for local people. Somalis are known to suffer high levels of unemployment and underemployment, and thus to be 'unequal' by this measure. This being so, it's a matter of 'equality' that the number of Somalis benefitting from council employment should reflect their presence in the community fairly. They have been under-represented till now. In fact, available figures suggest that they have not yet achieved half their 'due' presence on the council's workforce. Under the watchful eye of Mr Pickles' commissioners, however, the recruitment process has to be scrupulously 'fair'. 'We can't favour a particular group,' my council informants explained, 'but we can advertise the jobs widely to attract applicants.' However, placing adverts in the Somali-language pages of the council's newspaper has not generated enough job applicants to produce equality of outcome for Somalis – yet.

However, notwithstanding this cautious avoidance of 'favouritism', Tower Hamlets Council had, I learned, recently established a Cabinet Commission with the title Somali Task Force. In identifying 'being Somali' as a potential source of inequality in this way, it seems the council may in future be prepared to apply its Equality Framework a little more boldly to the dimension of 'race' and 'religion or belief'. The Task Force is to work with a consultative group of Somali citizens so as to achieve 'co-production' of programmes of action. It had started by examining Somali needs within the remit of each of the council services – including housing, education, mental health and social care, to which the 'Somali citizens' themselves have proposed the addition of 'youth, safety and the justice system'.

SOMALI COMMUNITY SELF-ORGANIZATION

Over and above the council's Strategic Plan is something they term the Community Plan, more inclusively conceived, in which, in pursuit of its 'vision', the council engages others it terms its 'partners'. These partners are the various public services (such as education, health and policing) delivered in the borough, and local businesses. But they also, and importantly, include all the voluntary organizations and structures in the local community. So, with a marked lack of elected representatives in senior or elected office in the council, let's see what Somali community organizations exist out there in Tower Hamlets on whom the council may draw for this kind of advice. And ask, besides, do the Somali clans speak with one voice? After all, while the importance to Somalis of clan belonging fades in the diaspora, it doesn't vanish. Somali families maintain links with their clan community at home, and clan rivalry has been known in the past to cause serious tension and division among them here. David Griffiths, in his study of Kurdish and Somali community organization, cited above, noted that 'clan divisions and factionalism inherited from the home country [had] … contributed to the invisibility and marginalisation of Somalis in London'. As a result, the most notable feature of their life here was 'lack of community in the sense of an inclusive network of support mechanisms and forms of identification'.[50] Likewise, the researchers who carried out the East London Alliance study were frustrated by the fact that many more Somali community associations exist in name than in material reality, and all too often reports and references cited are nowhere to be found on the web or the bookshelf.[51] In 2009, alerted by the terror attack in London in which a Somali national was involved, the Trust for London funded research into issues facing the Somali community.[52] The researchers found, as had many before them, a scatter of fragmented and transitory community organizations without central coordination or infrastructural support, resulting in a lack of 'meaningful engagement' with central and local government agencies. The outcome was the creation in 2011 of the Council of

Somali Organisation, a nationwide umbrella organization, in an attempt to fill the gap.

Tower Hamlets Somalis, I quickly discovered, are less likely than those of other boroughs to suffer residual clan conflict. This is because they are predominantly Somalilanders, and of the Isaaq clan. As we've seen, this northern region of the country, formerly a British colony, has long considered itself autonomous, or even entirely separate from the Somali state. Thus, in the Tower Hamlets context clan identity tends to be a unifying notion and signifies cohesion and support. This is certainly the reason that Somali community organization is better sustained in Tower Hamlets than other boroughs. There is a Tower Hamlets Somali Organizations Network, fostering the management of the various Somali associations, encouraging networking and speaking for them to the larger world. Kayd Arts, which runs the Somali Week Festival each year, is based in the borough, as is the group that produces *Somali Eye* magazine. The Somali-led Al Huda Mosque is located here. And there are two substantial community associations, Wadajir, in East India Dock Road, and the highly reputed Ocean Somali Community Association (OSCA) in Burdett Road.

One day I set out from home in Kentish Town helped by the speedy above-ground North London line, to look for OSCA. The weather was bleak and windy, with squalls of sleet. I'd forgotten to bring my street guide. Mile End Road? What Mile, for goodness' sake, was this the End of? OSCA gives its address as 'The Railway Arches' – but beneath which of the many railway tracks round here was I to search? I was lost, cold, tired. Then a thought crossed my mind: imagine I'm a Somali woman, newly arrived in England. I speak no English. I have no warm clothes. I'm hungry, have nowhere to sleep tonight. And I'm looking for the Ocean Somali Community Centre. Now how do I feel? When I eventually located OSCA, next to the screaming tyres of a go-kart track, beneath a rumbling railway line, and was greeted by its friendly team of community workers, I felt almost as happy as she. First, Aydarus Sarman and Mohamed Adan sat me down for an impromptu chat. Later I had an informative interview with the director, Abdi Hassan. He expressed a positive opinion of Tower Hamlets Council that I later heard confirmed by other community figures, an appreciation that would certainly have been welcome to my council officer informants: it is an active, hands-on borough

Opposite: Top, Behind the go-karts and 'under the arches', Ocean Somali Community Association, Bow, London Borough of Tower Hamlets. Bottom left, Women's Officer, Khadra Sarman. Bottom right, Director, Abdi Hassan.

Above: Dahabo Ahmed, prize-winning hair and henna artist and founder of Voices of Somali Women.

when it comes to community cohesion, Abdi told me. This makes it, he says, 'very different from other local authorities. You feel welcome here.' Statistically under-represented though they may be in council offices, what Abdi sees is many Somalis glad to have public sector employment as care providers. Where the council is failing to support community organizations it is due not to council policy, he feels, but to government spending cuts. The consequent loss of grant funding had recently obliged OSCA drastically to reduce its staff – from 15 to five.

On a third visit to OSCA I met Khadra Sarman. Besides contributing to management, fundraising and youth work at OSCA, Khadra runs a number of activities for women. Listening to her, I learned what's different about Somali women's lives, 4,000 miles from their birthplace, re-homed here in London's East End. 'It's hard for them!' she says.

> Women are more housebound than men because most of them have responsibility for children. They miss out a lot on opportunities while they are at home raising kids. They don't learn English sufficiently. They carry a lot of trauma with them from their experiences in a war zone. Of course as migrants they encounter social barriers. And they lack employment.

If Somalis have one of the lowest levels of employment of all ethnic groups in the UK, the situation is even more extreme for women – one study shows only 18 per cent of working-age females to be in employment, compared with 23 per cent of males.[53] OSCA's brochure describes Somali women in much the same terms as does Khadra: isolated in their homes, with limited English-language skills, living in poverty, many experiencing depression and other mental health problems. They are, it says, 'some of the most socially excluded people currently living in the UK'. Responding to this perception, Khadra and other community workers at OSCA try to draw women out of isolation and involve them in community activities. They run basic training in cooking, sewing, gardening, health, numeracy and language; they offer workshops on citizenship and leadership to build confidence and self-esteem; and they address sensitive issues such as female genital mutilation and the relation of mothers to their daughters.

There is something of a contradiction in the portrayal of the Somali experience in London. We see them, not infrequently, described as above – characteristically sunk in poverty and joblessness. We know besides that they are objects of suspicion to the British state, called on to scrutinize their children for signs of 'radicalization' and *jihad*, subject to the vigilance of the Prevent programme and harassment by the security services. Yet many Somali migrants are success stories, justly celebrated. Some are lively entrepreneurs, travel widely, contribute to peace and development back home, and are especially competent with communications technology.[54] Not a few achieve academic and professional success,[55] and many of these are women. I was very struck in October 2015 by the presence of women among the well-known academics, dramatists, poets and singers who featured in the performances of the annual festival of Somali art and culture they call 'Somali Week'. On the opening night, not only the organizer, but the first panel of three speakers and their chair, were all female. The speakers were an archaeologist, Dr Sada Mire; a professor of sociology, Dr Cawo Abdi; and author Ladan Osman, winner of a prize for African poets. We shall see below, the experience of war, displacement and migration may, by lifting women out of traditional family relations, be increasing their independence from men and propelling some into activism.

WOMEN'S TALES OF FLIGHT FROM WAR

It was at this event, in a packed-out hall in Bethnal Green, that I got talking with two women sitting beside me in the audience. Hinda Ali and Ubah Ibrahim were both, as it turned out, residents of Tower Hamlets, and later I had a chance to visit these friends in their neighbouring homes in Stepney Green and learn something of their stories of displacement and their perceptions of Tower Hamlets as a place of resettlement.

Four years separate Hinda and Ubah. Hinda was born in 1973, Ubah in 1977. So, mature women now at 42 and 38 respectively, they were both teenagers-going-on-twenties when they experienced war in Somalia. Ubah's family lived up in the north, in Hargeisa, capital of Somaliland. Her mother and father had a small business in the city, a store selling clothes and food. And she looks back on her childhood, as a primary school child, the oldest in a family of seven children, as 'a good life'. A good life that was about to change forever. For it was in Somaliland, as we've seen, that one of the first major insurgencies against Siad Barre occurred, with the formation of the Somali National Movement and a reawakening of Isaaq identity in response to the oppression of Barre's regime. This is Mary Harper's description of that moment in May 1988:

> The authorities' response to the rebellion was extraordinarily vicious; Siad Barre's ground and air forces carried out such heavy bombardment of the regional capital, Hargeisa, that it was known as the 'Dresden of Africa'. Barely a wall was left standing and almost every roof of every building was blown off or looted. The city was smashed and stripped; its population eventually left, walking all the way to Ethiopia in a biblical-style exodus.[56]

An estimated half million civilians trekked out of the country in this way. At the time it was one of the fastest and largest forced movements of people ever recorded in Africa.[57] Ubah's family were lucky. Her parents and siblings survived the bombing, though other family members perished. But the fighting continued, on the ground, in the streets. Ubah remembers, 'They would come into our houses, take things, kill people'. Their shop was destroyed and looted. So the family abandoned their home in Hargeisa to live with grandparents in a relatively safe rural area. And as war continued to rage in the south of Somalia, Ubah, her mother and one brother were enabled to travel, first to Ethiopia, and eventually to England, their entry facilitated by an uncle who had previously migrated to London, and was living in the West London Borough of Harrow. By now Ubah was 14.

Hinda's experience, no less traumatic, had been different because her childhood was lived far away to the south of Somalia, in the capital city of Mogadishu. She remembers it as having been 'a good city – the sea was nearby, it was beautiful. The weather was fine, the food was good. It was a simple life, but we experienced happiness as children, playing outside, going to school, being with our mum and dad'. Her mother and father, like Ubah's, were shopkeepers, owning a small sweet store on a busy street. It was her father who mainly ran the shop, since her mother had twelve children to care for. Hinda was positioned, age-wise, in the middle of this large band of siblings, and was a teenager as the war between the Barre regime and its enemies gathered momentum. Hinda says now:

> Of course, there was always war in Somalia. My father, my grandparents, my ancestors, they always lived in war. In the old days, one clan would fight another over camels. And water. People would wait and hope for rain, and when it came the clan would have to defend their water source against others who would come to try and take control of it. But it was a new and different kind of war that broke out in 1989 and 1990.

And it didn't end until 1998, so Hinda was there to experience the worst of it. She remembers, 'Our neighbourhood was crowded, like Tower Hamlets, people living close together. There was fighting in the streets all around us. We heard the guns very often, men running around shooting.' She remembers how, at a particularly bad moment, their parents locked the family into the house for a week in order to keep them safe. 'We couldn't go out to the shops. We had only water to drink, no food in all that time.' From the window they saw dead bodies lying in the street. 'There were hundreds – too many to bury. They were piled up, swollen, rotting, threatening disease.' When Barre was finally ousted, in 1991, by the forces of the USC and its allies, the fighting continued all around Hinda and her family, but now it pitted the USC's General Aydeed and other clan-identified factions against each other. Hawiye fought Darod, Hawiye fought other Hawiye. Thousands continued to be killed, a bloodletting scarcely interrupted by the ill-fated United States' mission, Operation Restore Hope, in 1992–3.

It was in 1993, when Hinda was 20, that her father was killed. He was a religious man, she explained, 'a well-known person' thereabouts. He was doing his ablutions before praying, when he noticed a fight threatening to develop between two groups of men in his vicinity. He stepped between them, trying to make peace. And was shot in the head. The family were terribly shocked by this loss. Her mother and father had loved one another dearly, and Hinda herself had been very attached to her dad. They continued their life in Mogadishu as best they could, each family member helping the others. But eventually Hinda's mother reluctantly decided that her daughter should leave

Somalia, with two of her brothers, to live with an aunt in the relative safety of Kenya. Hinda has very clear memories of the seven perilous days the three young people spent together on the road to the Kenyan border, travelling by bus and by foot:

> We had very little money, barely enough to eat. We were scared of the Kenyan soldiers. It was especially dangerous for a woman, a young woman like me. They can so easily rape or kill you. Rape is a big issue for us. You are punished for being raped. In Somalia, when you think of rape, you think it would be better to die.

In Nairobi, Hinda attended English classes and was also able to earn enough to contribute towards the family's income. But she didn't feel safe there, among the impoverished Somali minority, swollen by new waves of refugees. 'If you aren't Kenyan, the soldiers can take you from the street at any time.' So when another aunt, living in London, offered to send money to enable Hinda to join the many thousands of Somalis fleeing to Europe, she set about finding a trafficker who could supply a travel document with a fake visa. 'He could fix it!' Hinda says. 'It was easier to do such things then. Lots of people were doing just what I did, to be honest.' The fixer in question purchased an airline ticket with her aunt's remittance, and Hinda took off, nervously, into the international skies. She landed at Heathrow, to be met by her aunt and taken to the family home in Leyton, in the North London Borough of Walthamstow.

Ubah and Hinda, though they arrived in the UK several years apart – Ubah in 1991, Hinda not until 1998 – had equally easy transits through the UK Border and Home Office immigration procedures. The famine, oppression and war scenario of Somalia was receiving attention on the international stage at that moment. So, Hinda says, 'They understood very well what we were running away from'. Both were granted asylum and five years later, albeit after much paperwork and many interviews, acquired British citizenship. In those days, unlike the present, legal aid was free. 'I feel grateful to the UK government from the bottom of my heart', Hinda says now. 'After all the dead people I saw back home, I feel so lucky. You can feel nothing but respect for the ones that welcome you. The people I hate are the ones who destroyed my country.'

So Ubah and Hinda began their new lives in Britain, respectively in West and North London. How did they end up neighbours in Stepney Green, in the Borough of Tower Hamlets? In both cases it was the accident of marriage. Hinda met her partner Ali in 2000, when she was 27, and they married the following year. His needs were dictated by his studies. While Ali was a student at South Bank University, the couple lived in Elephant and Castle. Later, when he began working, as he still does now, as an assistant in a secondary school resource department for children with special needs, Tower Hamlets became more convenient for him. Ubah, for her part, met and married her husband Hussein in 2008, at the age of 30. He had obtained steady employment as a bus driver, and they moved to Tower Hamlets as it was more convenient for his daily journey to work. Ubah's job, at that period before marriage and motherhood, had been less 'localized' and more casual – caring, cleaning. She lost nothing by moving to Tower Hamlets with Hussein. And here the two households have established themselves. They have become East Enders. Ubah and Hussein have two sons, boys of six and one, and the family is relatively secure with a bus driver's salary assured. Hinda and Ali have six children, including a new babe in arms. Ali struggles to get the work for which he is qualified by his higher education – accountancy studies at London Guildhall University (as it then was) and a masters course in development studies at South Bank University. He is trapped in the familiar vicious cycle: how do you get the work that will give you the 'work experience' without which you cannot obtain work? Meanwhile, the family depends entirely on his three-day-a-week job in education. Somehow, by extraordinary frugality, the couple manage to pay for their food, £100-a-week rent, and extra tuition for the older children. They even send remittances to family members at home in Somalia. 'How on earth?' I exclaimed. 'Yes,' Hinda insisted, 'even yesterday I did it. People say we're crazy. But how can we not? Whatever I have I must divide between my kids here and my family there. We have to help each other. If we don't, they may die. That will continue to be the case until life there becomes normal.'

I got some sense from Ubah and Hinda and their partners of what it means to live in Tower Hamlets. As we've seen, it has a strange demography – with its huge and dominant Bangladeshi community, and a much smaller, but nonetheless characterful, Somali minority. Hinda said, promptly and emphatically, 'I love living in Tower Hamlets.

I do! The reason is … [she hesitated for a moment] … I feel like I'm safe here.' 'Safe from what?' I asked.

> Safe on the streets. Most of these Bangladeshis who surround us in Tower Hamlets are very respectful people. They are Muslims, they believe in God. So for instance, you might go out in the evening, there maybe is a wedding, the street is full of people, smoking, talking. As a woman you might feel insecure. But if an Asian man sees you looking afraid, he will say, 'Sister, don't be scared!' It's different in North and West London, where there are teenage gangs, stabbings.

I asked, 'But do you not feel overwhelmed by their sheer numbers, their presence in local businesses, their control of the local council, their dominance in the mosque?' And she answered, thoughtfully,

> It's true – the Bangladeshis 'own' Tower Hamlets, and we Somalis are the outsiders. We are less educated than them. We can't achieve as much as they do. We don't have their long history here, and the connections they have. They support each other, whereas we Somalis still think in terms of our different clans.

We've seen, earlier, that most of Tower Hamlets' Somalis come from Somaliland and are mostly of the Isaaq clan, whereas Hinda and Ali were located in southern Somalia. So Ali added here, 'Yes, we're a minority here among the Bangladeshis. And as southerners we're a minority among the Somalis. We're not very integrated. But there is no conflict between us.' Hinda was reluctant even to name, let alone talk about their own clan identity. 'I believe we've left that ignorance behind', she said. 'We're here now, looking to the future. If we hold on to clan rivalry we won't succeed.' But she did admit to feeling excluded, at times, by the Somalilander majority in the community. In projects like OSCA or Kayd, you could feel that Somalilanders were more welcome than other Somalis. She said, 'You sometimes hear people saying "This is a Somali project", when actually, correctly speaking, it is a *Somaliland* project.' Nevertheless, these hesitations about majority/minority relations were not overemphasized by either Ubah or Hinda. They represented them as mere facts of life to be pragmatically negotiated.

DISPLACEMENT AS A PROMPT TO ACTIVISM

Searching for a specifically *women's* organization among the Somali community in London, in which I might find the experience of women in the Somali conflict translated into diaspora life, I located a website called Voices of Somali Women. Following this lead took me out of the Little Somaliland of the East End, back to the western reaches of London from which Hinda had 'migrated' eastwards, specifically to the London Borough of Brent.[58] Here I discovered Dahabo Ahmed, founder of Voices, who describes herself as 'a feminist advocate for women's rights'. To my delight I found she was a familiar face, for we are both members of the Women's International League for Peace and Freedom (WILPF), and had recently met at conference in The Hague. It is significant, and says a lot about the degree of Dahabo's present integration and engagement in London life, that she has found the time and enthusiasm to join this century-old and (it has to be said) rather white and elderly peace movement. She has done so because her concern with war in Somalia by now, 16 years after her flight from that country, has translated into a concern for ending militarism and war not just in her home country but on a world scale. WILPF, however, is only one facet of Dahabo's present activism. One among several projects deriving from Voices of Somali Women is Mudnaan, with which she is currently most concerned. The first three letters of this name stand for Mothers United Development. The organization's main aim is to inspire Somalian mothers and young girls in London by the provision of activities and facilities. The logo shows a woman with a small child in her lap. 'I feel this could be me!' Dahabo said. And this was the prompt that led us to embark on the story of Dahabo's migration. It took us back in time to the events in Somalia in the late 1990s that caused Dahabo to set off for Britain, a lone woman with a baby in her arms, and before that to her own childhood.

Dahabo was born in 1969 in Makar, her mother's family home, in the central region of Somalia that stretches along the coast northwards from Mogadishu, and is home to people mainly of the Hawiye clan. Her father was a well-off businessman operating in the capital, not engaged in politics but nonetheless a prominent figure among the Hawiye. Due to his prosperity, he married and maintained four wives. Dahabo's mother was the first and, refusing to countenance a second, had moved away from her husband while Dahabo was still little. Though she continued to receive his financial support, it was effectively she who raised and educated Dahabo, in her home town of Makar. To continue into high school Dahabo had to go to Mogadishu, and here, in her late teens, she progressed to college to study nursing. Then, at the age of 20, she married. 'Why so young?' I asked her. 'Well', she said, 'that was the age you did get married. Nobody thought of going on to university. There were no models for that.' Besides, this was a young man she herself had met, liked and singled out for marriage. She asked her parents to fix up the marriage. She says, 'I was very happy. And they were happy that I was happy. So they agreed to it.' Bride price was arranged between Dahabo's absent father and that of the groom. All was well. Dahabo now took up hairdressing, which has remained her principal occupation and source of income ever since.

Dahabo's marriage took place in 1989, a moment when the situation in Somalia was unravelling fast. Two years later, as we've seen, Siad Barre would be driven from power amid horrendous violence across Somalia, not least in the capital. In 1991, Dahabo's father and one of his sons, brother to Dahabo, were shot dead by Barre's forces – not because they were militant with the opposition, but simply as two among the many thousands of civilians caught up in the killing. At this point, just before the United Nations and US forces launched their violently militarized relief operation, Dahabo left the capital and retreated to Makar to live near her mother. There, in the following years, two children were born to her. They would have been five and six years old when she made up her mind to leave the country. 'It was the situation', Dahabo explains. 'I didn't want to go. But it was terrible. Everywhere was burning, everywhere bombs. I don't like even to remember it. The militias were attacking civilians. Taking people from their homes in the night, killing them.' But here was the problem. She had responsibility not only for her own two children, but for a third. Dahabo had a sister, a profoundly deaf woman with many problems, who had recently abandoned a newborn daughter, now in Dahabo's care. What was she to do? She made the hard decision to take the baby out of the country with her, leaving her own children in their grandmother's care, to follow as and when Dahabo could arrange it.

To achieve her migration, Dahabo contacted an organization of people smugglers. They told her they could fly her to 'South Africa, or perhaps Canada', with the possibility of transferring thence to the UK. Dahabo paid up front without question. 'Anywhere', she told them, 'where there's peace!' The first step of the journey involved a 15-day bus journey to Addis Ababa, capital of Ethiopia. The bus was overloaded. 'You had to fight your way on', Dahabo remembers. 'If you were weak, it would have been impossible to do it.' During the day, she dozed in the bus, the six-month-old baby in her arms. At night they would curl up on the ground, under a tree. Security was a worry. Dahabo was carrying a considerable sum of money with her. In all, this migration was going to cost her no less than $12,000. 'If we saw men with guns, we had to hide.' On arrival in Addis, the smugglers lodged Dahabo in a hotel. The following day they took her to the airport, for a flight to an unknown destination. By now, Dahabo didn't care where she might be taken. 'There was no time to consider. I thought: just go!'

A man from the smuggling organization boarded the plane with her. When they landed, after many hours, he led her through passport control (a remarkably uneventful transit) and into a lounge area where he told her 'Just sit here', and abruptly walked away. She never saw him again. Hours passed, night fell, and Dahabo slept right there on the benches, the child in her arms. 'I was just so tired', she says, simply. Next morning she happened to see a man who looked Somalian. She approached him and asked, 'Help me please!' It was he who broke the news to Dahabo that she was actually in London. This was Heathrow Airport. 'I was so pleased!' she recalls. The man was helpful. He bought milk for the baby. He approached another Somali, a woman seeing off a friend in departures. He enlisted her help, and she agreed to take Dahabo home with her, 'just for one night'. Crucially, this woman called a solicitor, who came to see Dahabo and explained the UK border process, accompanied her to the Home Office, and obtained a letter of identification which would afford her temporary reprieve from deportation and the right to receive benefit. Then Dahabo was taken to the local council, which happened to be the London Borough of Brent, whence she was transferred, with bag and baby, into a bed and breakfast used by the council as emergency lodging. 'And that', she told me, 'is how I started life here. That's how I came to Brent, and I've stayed here ever since.'

That bed and breakfast would be the first of 14 that Dahabo and child would eventually inhabit. But, first things first. There and then, Dahabo remembers, on that February day in 1999,

> It was so cold! I was shaking. It was so difficult. I only spoke 'African English', and nobody could understand my strange accent. I didn't understand the system. In the hotel, I didn't know how to use the equipment in the kitchen – the microwave, the toaster. I had never seen a room heater, I thought it was some kind of decoration. And there was nobody to explain to me. The hotel receptionist didn't help – she just shouted at me, 'At eight o'clock the kitchen will shut!' And all the time the baby was crying.

So Dahabo made her way back to the offices of Brent Council and said to them, 'I don't understand how to use the kitchen'. A man went back with her to the hotel. But his visit was uninstructive, and indeed discouraged her yet further. Seeing a knife lying on the table (Dahabo had been cutting up oranges), he shouted, as Dahabo recalls the moment,

> Why have you left a knife lying on the table? It's very dangerous! Do you want to kill the baby? Listen, you came from the jungle, right, and here you have a bed and a clean place to live. The receptionist complains about you. She says you're a difficult person. Just follow the rules, OK?

It is the 'unkindness' of some of these early encounters that Dahabo remembers most painfully. For the most part, she stayed in her room. 'It was room 105', she remembers. 'I worried, if I went out would I ever find this room again? And what if I should lose the key?' She lay awake at night listening to her neighbours' loud music, and dogs barking in the neighbourhood. Gradually, over the weeks, she reached out. She made friends with another resident in the bed and breakfast, a Moroccan woman, with whom she managed to get along, finding a few words to span Arabic and Somali. Eventually she was able to contact some relatives, an uncle and a cousin living in London. Thereafter she would visit them from time to time, and when she started college, her aunt took on a few hours a week of childcare. The council moved her into a shared rental flat in a terrace house. Dahabo improved her English rapidly, and gained a formal qualification in hairdressing. She set up a salon, offering both African and European styles, and even won third prize in a Europe-wide hairdressing contest.

In 2002 Dahabo, now divorced from her distant husband in Somalia, married again – a brief partnership in which she had another child. But on her mind all the time was the question of reuniting with her two children and mother, back in Makar. They were not linked in the way that is so customary among Somalis today, by e-mail and mobile phone. Her first news from them was in a letter transmitted by hand by means of a contact in Dubai. Then she approached the Red Cross in London to ask for their help in establishing phone contact. It was several years before the overwhelming moment when she first heard their voices on the line. Twice Dahabo applied to the authorities for permission to bring her family to join her in London, and was twice refused due to her own insecure status. It was only when, in 2005, she obtained 'indefinite leave to remain' in the UK, that a third attempt was successful. It was 19 October, she recalls, when she was at last reunited with her own children, who flew to London with her deaf sister and husband. Her mother remained, and still remains, in Somalia.

It was soon after her children had arrived and settled in with her in Brent that Dahabo applied for her British passport. She had already gained a certificate of proficiency in English. Now she set about the 'citizenship test', in which the candidate must answer questions about British geography, history and culture, an exam that would dismay many native-born-and-educated citizens. Undefeated, Dahabo achieved British nationality in 2007. The process had taken eight years and cost her more than £1,000. She still, however, lives in 'temporary accommodation'. Sixteen years after arriving in the UK she has lost hope of being allocated a permanent tenancy, let alone accommodation suited to her increasing disability from arthritic pain in back and legs.

Nonetheless, her home, impermanent though it may feel, furnishes a room in which Dahabo can continue her hairdressing profession and other endeavours – her daughter insisted that I must understand Dahabo as 'an artist', who works creatively not only with hair but with henna and textiles. Most importantly, however, this little terrace house is a base from which she has been able to pursue the social contact and frequent meetings that occupy her as a Somali feminist activist.

It was from 'get-togethers' of her hairdressing clients, gathering to chat about their own and their families' circumstances, both here in Brent and at home in Somalia, that the Mudnaan project developed. When the umbrella organization Voice of Somali Women was formed, other Somali initiatives clustered alongside Mudnaan, among them the Gargar Foundation for Development and the Midaye Somali Development Network.

Dahabo's story is interesting for contradicting the picture of the characteristically home-bound Somali woman, constrained by motherhood and domestic responsibilities, that Khadra, community worker at OSCA in Tower Hamlets, had earlier painted for me, and which indeed is the prevailing image. Here was a woman whose life in London, 16 years after settlement here, was outgoing and connected, socially and politically creative. In trying to disentangle the reality, I was helped by a conversation I had with Hinda's husband, Ali Jimale.

Ali's study of development issues at London South Bank University had awoken in Ali an interest in the effect on women's gender status of resettlement after flight from violence and war. He set up a small project of empirical research which resulted in an essay, titled 'Does Displacement Reinforce or Weaken Pre-existing Gender Inequality?' His paper began by describing the abuse of women in patriarchal systems, not least that of Somalia. He reviewed other authors' work on gender and displacement. And finally, using a questionnaire devised for the purpose, he interviewed, by telephone or face to face, a small sample of Somali refugees. He chose them as being located in two contrasted situations. Some were inhabitants of Dadaab refugee camp in Kenya, just across the border from the home from which they had been driven in Somalia. Others were resident in London. He found that living in Dadaab camp was not in any way lessening women's pre-existing subordination to men. Several factors were sustaining their dependence. One was the heavy demand of physical labour – obtaining food, gathering firewood and building dwellings. Another was that men, having lost so much in the wars, now felt disempowered, and vented their frustration by oppressing their wives even more than before. And women were even more vulnerable in such a camp to other men, gangs and militias liable to rape, rob or kill.

By contrast, the women in Ali's study who had reached and settled in London were less economically dependent on men by virtue of access to state benefits and, in some cases, a wage. An income gave them more bargaining power with their husbands, and enabled them to participate more effectively in family decision-making. Besides, both social expectations and British law served to protect women (better, if not wholly) from violence and sexual abuse. Ali concluded that in comparison with either war-torn Somalia or a Kenyan refugee camp, for Somali women in the UK 'gender inequality had been weakened dramatically in the course of displacement'. His findings are borne out by other, published, research. David Griffiths notes of his study among Somalis in London that 'a state of flux or tension in gender relations is a notable feature of my sample and is a central dynamic of refugee adaptation'.[59] Another study, made ten years previously, had already shown that the transformed situation of women was resulting in community activism. A distinctive feature of Somali organization in London, already at that time, was the independent role of women, working in key positions alongside men, and the existence of women-only organizations, founded by women, promoting health and education.[60]

What Dahabo's activism and achievements show us is that displacement to a 'developed' country, where there is a degree of support for women's autonomy and at least an appeal to human rights, modifies patriarchal power relations to the extent that a woman can indeed step out more independently in her own life, and, what is more, find scope for empowering other women around her. Undeterred by lack of grant funding, the small organizations she has founded or supported work for the improvement of Somali women's lives both in London and Somalia. Raising the funds entirely from their own economic activities, these activist women of north-west London now travel frequently to Somalia. And thanks to this, I am happy to be able to tell you, Dahabo is now back in touch with her mother. Makar is no longer on another planet.[61]

4

Home for Whom?
Tamils in Hounslow and
Home Office Detention

Sri Lanka experienced bitter armed conflict between 1983 and 2009, yet, for some reason, the country was not imagined by the wider world during that period primarily as a war zone, in the way that Bosnia, Afghanistan and Rwanda were during their years of conflict. One reason for this may be that the economy continued to prosper. With an income per head almost twice that of India, Sri Lanka had an undiminished reputation as (in the words of the *Economist*) 'a bright star of South Asian development'. Another could be that the island is renowned for its natural beauty, 'well-watered hills, rolling green tea estates and miles of palm-fringed white sands', and managed to remain, for much of that time, a tourist destination, particularly popular with western Europeans. The devastating Indian Ocean tsunami of 2004, in which 35,000 people died, dented the tourist statistics more than the fighting did. Even in 2006, while war persisted, no less than half a million tourists visited the country.[1] And with the government's victory in 2009, the tourist arrivals kept on climbing – to one and a half million in 2014.[2] Yet war – for war it was – between the government controlled by the Sinhala Buddhist majority and the mainly Hindu Tamil population of Sri Lanka, cost possibly 100,000 lives in those decades, displaced up to half a million people, and devastated large areas of the north and east of the country.

Myth has it that Buddhism reached the island of Sri Lanka from India in the very year that Buddha himself is said to have died, 483 BCE. Over the next two and a half millennia, Buddhists (of North Indian, and thus Aryan identity) became dominant in Sri Lanka. The largest minority on the island were Tamils, darker-skinned Dravidians historically associated with South India, and of Hindu belief. They too are at pains to date their arrival in Sri Lanka back at least 2,000 years. A smaller community of Muslims, including some Arabs and Malaysians, had also long been present on the island by the time the European colonists arrived in their tall-masted ships – the Portuguese in 1505, the Dutch in 1656 and eventually the British in 1796 – and set about converting as many as possible to Christianity.[3] Today, the ethnic breakdown of this densely populated island is: Sinhalese, 75 per cent; Tamil, 15 per cent (of whom about a quarter are of recent Indian origin); and Moors (the name by which Muslims are known here) 9 per cent. Vedda aboriginals, the 'first people' of the island, have been reduced to a fraction of 1 per cent.[4] In terms of religion the distribution is (to the nearest round number): Buddhist, 70 per cent; Hindu, 13 per cent; Muslim, 10 per cent; and Christian, 7 per cent.[5]

It was during the period of British colonial rule in Sri Lanka, effectively from 1815 to 1948, that the seeds of the late twentieth-century war between Sinhala Buddhists and Tamil Hindus were sown. The British favoured the Tamil minority, recruiting them as their preferred civil servants. As Gordon Weiss puts it, 'With their English and academic skills, the Tamils started as errand boys, clerks and managers, before they evolved to become doctors, lawyers, engineers and senior civil servants, who oversaw much of the administration of the country.'[6] Unsurprisingly, at independence in 1948, the Sinhalese majority that assumed control of the country vented its resentment on the Tamils. In laying the foundations for a constitution, the outgoing British imperialists had attempted to build in democratic rights for minorities. But an elite club of Sinhalese families had influenced the path to self-rule, and the Sinhalese, numerically dominant, were bound to prevail in post-independence elections in which votes were mainly cast on ethnic lines. Weiss continues: 'As the modern state took form, excessive Sinhalese Buddhist nationalism would dismiss the complementary claims of other of the islands communities.'[7]

THE CREATION OF ENMITY

The first significant action against Tamils was the denial of rights to a million 'Plantation Tamils', imported by the British as labour for the tea-growing regions of central Sri Lanka. Half a million of them were now expelled to the mainland. Though, to their discredit, some Sri Lankan Tamils of the north and east were complicit in this purging, Sinhala Buddhist nationalism soon turned against them too. In 1956 an act was passed through parliament making Sinhala the only official language, in which all state business would be conducted. The intended effect was to cost Tamils, fluent mainly in Tamil and English, their secure civil service jobs and any remaining political influence they possessed. In 1956, Tamils, who accounted for about one-fifth of the population, held about 30 per cent of the administrative positions. Within 20 years, that figure would have fallen to just 5 per cent.[8] The result was a succession of Tamil riots in which hundreds were killed. In 1961, Tamils in the north-east launched a campaign of *satyagraha*, or non-violent protest, and were brutally attacked by government forces, who thereafter maintained a military occupation of the region. In 1973 the government introduced a second discriminatory measure, a requirement that Tamils must achieve higher grades than others to enter university, thus greatly reducing their presence on science, medicine and engineering courses, subjects in which they had till then excelled. Tamils were also deprived of their land through the state-aided and aggressive colonization of Tamil areas by Sinhalese settlers, with the support of security services. Many Hindu places of worship were destroyed in the process.

It was in the early 1970s that Tamil representatives in the parliament in Colombo first introduced a demand for a separate state for Tamils. For years already, Tamil activists had been organizing against their growing oppression and exclusion. Their resistance groups and political parties divided and reformed many times, but in 1976 a young man named Velupillai Prabhakaran created an entity that was destined thenceforth to dominate the movement: he called it the Liberation Tigers of Tamil Eelam (LTTE, or the Tamil Tigers). In a referendum in 1977 among Tamil-speaking people, the overwhelming vote was for secession, in short for the creation of Tamil Eelam, a new nation state. Prabhakaran was a fearsome leader, eliminating without hesitation not only disloyal informers but many moderate and guiltless Tamils. In 1975, when he was only 21, he launched his career of violence by assassinating the (Tamil) mayor of Jaffna. Youngsters flocked to join him, and the ultra-violent elite of the movement began to be known as the 'Black Tigers'. Within a few years the LTTE would dominate the political and armed resistance in the north and north-east of the country.

In 1983, Tamils were deprived of the effective use of their vote by an amendment to the constitution which rendered vacant the parliamentary seats of elected representatives of the Tamil people. The same amendment introduced an oath, to be sworn by members of parliament and holders of official posts, undertaking not to support the establishment of any separate state in Sri Lanka.[9] The Tamil movement for secession, unsurprisingly, gathered momentum from this moment. In July 1983 (it would later be called 'Black July'), an incident occurred that has since been taken to mark the beginning of outright war. Tamil forces in Jaffna killed 13 government soldiers. The response was a pogrom, fired by a violently nationalistic coterie of Buddhist monks but orchestrated by the authorities. Sinhalese mobs rioted in Colombo, attacking Tamil shops and properties, killing between 1,000 and 3,000 Tamils.

If the Sinhalese Buddhist nationalists and the state's armed forces were violent in the extreme, the Tamil Tigers developed a matching ferocity. This is how, in his book *This Divided Island*, they are described by Indian Tamil author Samanth Subramanian:

> The history of the Tigers' struggle for Eelam is less a succession of political manoeuvres than a parade of slaughter, and they had no reservations about slaying their own. Tamil families in Tiger-controlled areas were forced to contribute one of their offspring to the movement; the Tigers promised they would extract just the single sacrifice per household, but when the war went awry, they came back for more. They recruited boys and girls, turned them into ill-prepared combatants, and hurried them to their deaths.[10]

In this way, long before they were defeated in the armed struggle, the Tigers forfeited the hearts and minds of their own people. They lost 'the war for the unconditional affections of the island's Tamils and for the uncontested right to fight on their behalf'.[11]

In 1987 the Indian government signed an agreement with India's Prime Minister Rajiv Gandhi for an Indian intervention force to invade the north, notionally to restore peace but in reality to subdue the Tamils. For three years, while the Sri Lankan Army (SLA) and police were busy suppressing a left-wing insurgency in the south, the Indians battled the Tigers in the villages and forests of the north. They eventually withdrew, defeated, and the LTTE exacted revenge, sending a woman suicide operative to India to assassinate Rajiv Gandhi. By the early 1990s the government had turned its attention northwards and was achieving an economic and humanitarian blockade of the entire Tamil region. Within it, the Tigers were consolidating control of their prefigured Eelam 'homeland', ruthlessly raiding, evicting and frequently killing not only residual Sinhalese but also Muslims and other non-Tamils.

At various moments in the late 1990s negotiations between the Tigers and the government were attempted, but were confounded by the latter's refusal to consider third-party mediation. Only in January 2000 did it relent and accept the involvement of the Norwegian government in shuttle diplomacy. At the end of that year the LTTE declared a unilateral ceasefire, but the government failed to reciprocate and intensified its attacks in the north. The Norwegians nonetheless persisted in their mediation, through three rounds of peace talks. These, followed by a conference in Tokyo of 51 nations and 22 international agencies, resulted in principles for a negotiated settlement with internal self-determination for Tamils in a federal state.[12] However, in an election in 2005 Mahindra Rajapaksa displaced Chandrika Kumaratunga as President of Sri Lanka. The political pact on which he achieved power involved rupture with the Norwegian mediators and reaffirmation of a unitary state. Indeed, his arrival promised 'revenge, glory and the possibility of a new political dynasty built on a military victory that had eluded the Sri Lankan government for almost three decades'.[13] A man with much invested in definitive triumph over the LTTE, Mahindra Rajapaksa appointed his belligerent brother Gotabhaya as Defence Secretary and granted him virtual rule over the north-east, where the devastation intensified.

It was in 2008 that the endgame began. The 57th Division of the SLA began combing north and east through the Vanni region, capturing towns as they went, herding the LTTE into a smaller and smaller area. On 1 January 2009, the 50,000 front-line SLA troops seized the key town of Kilinochchi from the Tigers. It then closed in on a triangle of land in the north-east corner of the Vanni region, where one-third of a million displaced people, predominantly Tamils, were huddled, under the control of Prabhakaran and his several thousand Tamil fighters, waiting for the final assault. As the SLA advanced, this Tamil horde were driven on to a tiny sliver of coastal land about 14 kilometres long, separated from the mainland by the five-kilometre-wide Nandikadal Lagoon. Curiously termed by the government a 'no fire zone', this landspit has become known to history as the 'Cage'. In the Cage, the violence came from within and without. The desperate LTTE ruled violently inside the enclave. This is how Samanth Subramanian describes the moment:

> Almost until the very end, the Tigers reached into their people and plucked out the able-bodied to press into service. Many of them were in their early teens. They would first be instructed to dig trenches and bunkers, or to erect tents; after a few days of such labour, they would be armed and sent to the front lines, where it was a near-certainty that they would be killed.[14]

Meanwhile violence rained down from the air. Regardless of the cost in civilian casualties, between February and May 2009 the Sri Lankan Army bombarded the Cage with heavy artillery fire from across the lagoon and from ships at sea. A small number of international humanitarian workers remaining among the captive population insistently informed the United Nations agencies of what was happening. But, impeded by the veto-power of the Russians and Chinese in the Security Council, the UN shamefully stood by and took no action. In May, Barack Obama urged the regime to show restraint and offered the services of the US Navy to evacuate the Tamil civilians. But the Sri Lankan government denied it was shedding civilian blood and refused all entreaties for intervention. Eventually, the mass of Tamil survivors were impelled to the least-worst option: evacuation of the landspit towards the mainland, and thus towards the Army. As they went, wading neck-deep across the waters of the lagoon, the Tigers fired on them punitively from the rear. On 18 May 2009, Velupillai Prabhakaran and the LTTE leadership were cornered by the Army and executed on the spot. The Tigers as a force were finally spent. The 16-week siege and its closing moments led to the deaths of at least 40,000 people. In the measured assessment of Gordon Weiss soon after these events, ruthless though the Tigers had been, it was 'the Sri Lankan Army that had brought the bulk of deaths upon the captive population'.[15] His assessment was supported by the graphic documentary films made by Britain's Channel 4 News, which shocked the world with full-on footage of summary executions of Tamils on the battlefield, carried out by government troops.[16]

Mahindra Rajapaksa remained in power. Indeed, in the presidential election the following year his victory was decisive. His brother, Defence Minister Gotabhaya, effectively remained governor of the north-east, where ill health and food insecurity plagued the Tamils. As the internment camps were slowly emptied and hordes of internally displaced people (IDPs) returned home, they found themselves lacking not only employment but even, in many cases, shelter, water and sanitation facilities. Buddhist nationalist extremism and its influence in and on the government intensified, its brutal persecution now extending from Hindus to the Muslim and Christian minorities throughout the island. In 2010, though still asserting that his hands were clean of civilian blood, Rajapaksa appointed a Lessons Learned and Reconciliation Commission. Designed to appease international criticism rather than to uncover the truth, it was neither independent nor impartial and predictably whitewashed the government. The UN Human Rights Council stepped in, and after several inconclusive exercises, in 2015 carried out a thorough international investigation that produced conclusive evidence of war crimes by the Sri Lankan government.[17] In response, the government pledged to address the legacy of the war through a wide-ranging set of measures. Its promises were contained in Human Rights Council Resolution 30/1, agreed in October 2015. Meanwhile a presidential election earlier that year had resulted in the ousting of the Rajapaksa brothers. The incoming moderate, Maithripala Sirisena, elected on a platform of democratization, the rule of law and reduction of presidential powers, gave many inside and outside Sri Lanka a new optimism.[18]

LEAVING THE ISLAND

Sri Lanka is positioned in the UNDP's *Human Development Report* for 2014 among countries with 'high human development'.[19] For all that, many Sri Lankans emigrate. They leave for two reasons, economic and political, although of course these overlap – political emigrants also seek employment. In 2009 the estimated figure for all Sri Lankans living abroad was 1.7 million, annually increased by a further 200,000 departures.[20] The principal destination of the Sri Lankans of majority Sinhalese ethnicity has been Middle Eastern countries, where employment opportunities are abundant. The trajectories of Tamils have been different. Many left the country in the wake of the discriminatory Sinhala Only Act of 1958 and the legislation of 1973 that reduced their access to universities. These tended to go to the West, looking for the opportunities now closed to them at home. It was only with the government's genocidal response to the riots of 1983 that the large-scale flight of Tamils seeking safety in Western countries began, notably in Canada, Australia and the UK.[21] Even these emigrants, however, were not the poorest of the poor. It is estimated that the cost of political migration would have been at a minimum $10,000 per person, and thus feasible only for those with significant assets.[22] Since, for the most part, statistics of migration record country of origin rather than ethnic group, it is impossible to know exactly how many of the 'Sri Lankan' diaspora are 'Sri Lankan Tamils'. An array of post-war estimates from various sources, however, suggest that by now not much more than half of Tamils born in Sri Lanka (that is to say, excluding Indian Tamils living in Sri Lanka) are resident in their homeland. Many have gone to nearby India. The rest are scattered far and wide.

Of the Tamils who fled Sri Lanka in the war years, some were evading maltreatment by the LTTE, but more were Tiger supporters fleeing persecution by the Sri Lankan government. The latter were of great significance to the Tigers, since many remained active in homeland politics wherever they settled. Indeed, as Sarah Wayland wrote, 'In the diaspora, it became possible to explore and express Tamil cultural, linguistic and religious identity as never before.' She points out, 'Persons who migrate from a closed society to an open society are able to capitalize on newfound freedoms to publish, organize, and accumulate financial resources to an extent that was impossible in the homeland.'[23] Tamils widely dispersed around the world were actively connected through the swiftly developing Internet.[24] They had offices in numerous countries that raised significant funding in support of the war. Shortly before the end, the LTTE's businesses abroad, licit and illicit, were believed to be generating up to $300 million a year.[25] That the Tigers had eventually acquired up to ten ocean-going ships and as many light aircraft, capable of bombing Colombo, was largely due to revenue reaching them from the diaspora. In turn, feeling still part of the struggle 'back home' served to unite many Tamils overseas, helping them overcome the trauma of migration, loneliness and marginalization in the receiving country. 'Associations were formed, both with an eye toward facilitating integration in the host country as well as toward maintaining ties with the homeland, namely through supporting the quest for Tamil independence.'[26] By contrast, when the war was lost, Tamils in the diaspora felt powerless and demoralized.

Many Tamil refugees have terrible stories to tell of the journey to 'freedom'. First, it was hard enough to reach Colombo, and once there they had to locate and pay an agent to get them out of the country. 'Without passports, with only the stamp of illegality, they left,' writes Selvy Thiruchandran, 'paying huge sums of money to unscrupulous agents. The agents took them to unknown places, kept them locked in dingy rooms, made them travel by road, by boats, by planes, and finally left them at some airport to face the immigration authorities.'[27]

For many, that airport was London Heathrow. The UK was always a destination favoured by conflict-driven Tamil asylum seekers, both because of the former colonial connection and because even in the 1980s many Tamils continued to be English-speakers. As we've seen, Tamils are not distinguished as a census category from the cultural majority of Sri Lankans, so we can't know with any certainty the number actually present in Britain at any one time. However, it is reasonable to assume that while 'normal' immigrants from Sri Lanka tend to be Sinhalese, the great majority of 'asylum seekers' are in fact Tamil. Thus, the fluctuations of Tamil arrivals in the UK over recent decades can be inferred from Home Office statistics of Sri Lankan asylum applications, and some instances when Tamil refugees hit newspaper headlines. Looking at the four-year period 1994–7, the early war years in Sri Lanka, Home Office statistics suggest that almost 7,590 applications for asylum were submitted by Sri Lankans, of whom a mere 90 individuals were granted secure refugee status, while 6,005 were actually refused entry.[28] The Asylum and Immigration Act of 1996 would further restrict refugees' chances of settlement in the UK, and more and more would be forced down illegal entry routes. Figures of Sri Lankan applications for asylum in the UK for the period 2001 to

2014 are striking both for the extreme variation in applications made, year on year, and the much greater number refused than are given 'leave to remain'.[29]

It is relatively straightforward to turn back an asylum seeker at the port of entry. It is less so to deal with the one who is already, illegally, living in the country. Deportation is the ultimate tool – but it's costly, highly visible, and evokes adverse publicity the authorities would rather avoid. As early as 1987 the Home Office, deaf to the protests of the UN High Commissioner for Refugees, had arbitrarily deported 64 Tamils, including 25 women, ignoring legal safeguards and the right of appeal.[30] Until 2009, however, deportations to Sri Lanka were in comparatively small groups on scheduled commercial flights. From that year (and just as the assault of the Sri Lankan state on the northern Tamils was culminating in great bloodshed and displacement), the UK Border Agency switched to the use of chartered flights to get its unwanted refugees out of Britain and deliver them back to the mayhem. In mid-2011 the programme was further stepped up. In the following 18 months, a succession of charter flights would carry away a total of 297 Sri Lankan Tamils – of whom at least 24 were women. The departures were attended by fierce protests by groups such as No Borders. In one case a protestor chained himself by his neck to the axle of a coach being loaded with deportees on their way to the airport.[31] Such delaying tactics bought time for barristers to win injunctions from the High Court cancelling the deportation orders of some already seated on coach or plane.[32] The protests were fired by detailed studies of Sri Lankan security practices which showed beyond doubt that deportees were being arrested as they landed in Colombo, imprisoned indefinitely and subjected to torture.[33] The methods of torture uncovered included anal and vaginal penetration, burning, cutting, beating, binding, 'Palestinian hanging', cramped confinement, drawing of nails, electrocution, gouging of eyes and forced consumption of faeces or flesh.[34] Yolanda Foster, Amnesty International's Sri Lanka researcher, reported on a deportee's attempt to hang himself in an airport holding facility the night before his flight, following threats he had received by phone to kill him once he returned to Sri Lanka. He had been recruited as a Tamil Tiger child soldier at the age of 13.[35]

It was undeniable that the UK government was fully aware of the danger into which it was returning Tamils. Sri Lanka was one of 20 countries for which the UK government held updated Country of Origin Information.[36] Yet they had put in place no precautions to ensure justice for returnees, other than thoughtfully furnishing the phone number of the British High Commission in Colombo – more an insult than a favour.[37] While the number of Tamils shipped out slackened off a little after 2012, deportations did not cease. Nor did the torture and maltreatment to which they returned. The Medical Foundation for the Care of Victims of Torture reported that it had had more victims from Sri Lanka referred to it for treatment in 2013–14 than from any other country.[38] The UK government appeared immune to an avalanche of criticism of its deportation policies from bodies ranging from the House of Commons Foreign Affairs Committee to the United Nations Committee against Torture.[39] What UK practice amounted to, these human rights defenders argued, was 'refoulement', that is to say the forcible return to a country of origin where the returnee has a well-founded fear of persecution. Refoulement is banned under the Refugee Convention of 1951. The UK Border Agency's bulletins, however, continually rubbished reports of continuing torture, and reiterated their mantra: there is no risk for those we deport to Sri Lanka.

RE-HOMING IN LONDON

A substantial proportion of the Sri Lankan Tamil population of the UK live in London. The most recent generations of arrivals, those since 1983, joined relatively small existing communities with a very different history from their own. The Tamils who had come to live in London in the 1950s, 1960s and 1970s may have chosen to leave Sri Lanka due to increasing discrimination and resulting acts of violence,[40] but they were, compared with later incomers, relatively well-off, educated professionals, including many doctors, engineers and lawyers. Though not quite so socially 'elite', they were not all that different, in fact, from the many Sinhalese living in London at the time – economically secure professionals and business people. In sharp contrast, the refugees of the late 1980s and following decades were mainly young, single Tamil men (and a smaller number of single women), often of lower caste, Karaiyars and Nalavars. Some of the long-settled migrant communities here referred to the newcomers as 'people like that', and resented them for throwing 'an unpleasant and wrong light' on the Sri Lankan community in London.[41] Unsurprisingly, many of these Tamil youths felt despised and inferiorized by both the London Sinhalese and the British host community. With their radical politics, low-status jobs and Tamil 'street culture', they boosted their confidence with the one resource left to them: machismo. But the key to macho self-respect, money, was lacking. They might have liked to follow the Tamil tradition of higher education, but the first priority was to earn enough to pay off the debts their families had incurred to get them out of the country. And the two routes to cash were long hard hours of underpaid work in the 'black economy', or crime. Ahalya Balasunderam wrote of gang-related credit card fraud and money laundering, turf wars, and even kidnapping and murder, among the younger immigrants of this new wave. This Tamil criminality was first registered by the authorities in 2000, and following ten homicides between 2001 and 2003 the police launched Operation Enver against Tamil criminality.[42]

In London, many Tamil asylum seekers went first to Newham and other easterly boroughs, subsequently moving north and west to relocate in Harrow, Ealing and Hounslow. The Tamil population of these boroughs then continued to grow with the arrival of family members seeking reunion. In 2015, when embarking on research for this chapter, I chose Hounslow for my study of a local authority and its Tamil residents for the simple – perhaps simplistic – reason that the only significant Tamil community initiative I could identify in London, the Tamil Community Centre, was based therein. The council calculates, projecting from the 2001 and 2011 census figures, that Hounslow's population in 2015 was likely to be 273,000, of whom 48.4 per cent would be white British, with 'black, Asian and minority ethnic' having crept up to just over half: 51.6 per cent. Around three-quarters of these 'BAME' would in fact be Asian.[43]

Hounslow is one of 13 local authority areas classified by the census-takers as a 'super-diverse cluster' with very high rates of migration from a range of places of origin. It's also one of the boroughs in which the population is fast-growing: the census of 2011 showed a 17.6 per cent increase since 2001 – the fifth highest rate of increase in the country. It has a rather young population, more than 50 per cent are under 35 years of age. There is a high degree of 'churn', with almost one in five residents 'on the move': an annual turnover of 182 individuals per 1,000. There are indicators suggesting considerable deprivation: average household size is growing; 42 per cent of households are renting their accommodation, either in the council, social or private sector; and 28 per cent of children in Hounslow live in poverty – compared with a national figure of 21 per cent.[44] Sketchy data from the census are taken to suggest a presence of 3,196 Sri Lankans in Hounslow in 2011, and an associated guesstimate of Tamil-speakers was 1,776.[45] While suggesting this is one of the largest clusters of Tamils in any local authority in Britain, these putative numbers are small compared with the presence in Hounslow of Indians of many cultures and religions. The territory of Hounslow is long and thin, stretching from Feltham in the west to Chiswick in the east. Between these districts lies Hounslow Town, and it is in its western wards that Sri Lankans, including those of Tamil identity, notably cluster. In his thesis on the Tamil diaspora in London, Nirad Pragasam describes these 'enclaves of habitation that in various ways have begun to emplace a sense of Tamil-ness in London'. He notes 'the grocery shops with a wealth of foodstuffs catering to the Tamil palate, the boutique shops selling the latest in South Indian fashions … outlets selling a variety of Tamil magazines and newspapers' and describes the 'almost compulsory sounds of Kollywood music, which seems to follow you from shop to shop, ushering you out of one and beckoning you into another'.[46]

Hounslow Council was, at the time I interviewed there in mid-2015, Labour-controlled. Of the list of 60 councillors, a quick scan of names suggests that 25 might be of ethnic minority identification, apparently from South Asian communities including Indians, Sikhs, Pakistanis and Bangladeshis. I learned that none of the elected members were Sri Lankan Tamils, and that this identity group were also absent from the ranks of senior officers. In this sense the Tamil community lacked direct representation in Hounslow Council. The elected leader was Steve Curran, a white British councillor, who headed a cabinet system. Of his ten-person cabinet, only two, judging superficially by name, appeared to be non-white British. The cabinet member for communities, Sue Sampson, was white British. The principal structure in the civic centre to which this cabinet member relates in her 'communities role' was the

Community Partnership Unit (CPU), which I found to be an energetic team of ten officers, headed by Uttam Gujral, a Sikh woman.

Laura James, a member of the CPU, afforded me time for a briefing on the council's approach to its 'cohesion and integration' policy. The unit's job includes absorbing government policy on community cohesion and relaying it throughout the council. Its principal brief is a document titled *Thriving Communities and VCSE Sector Strategy: 2015–2019*.[47] This reflects a strong council focus on the 'voluntary community and social enterprise' (VCSE) sector (no less than 600 organizations) with whom it aspires to forge a working partnership for the delivery of many essential services to local residents and communities. The coalition government that came into power in May 2010 made 'the biggest cuts in living memory' to local authority funding, with the effect of removing £60 million from Hounslow's budget prior to 2015, with even fiercer cuts in prospect to 2019. The aim of council policy towards its community in this 'financially constrained environment' is necessarily to reduce its reliance upon public services. It is hardly surprising then if the Hounslow Voluntary Sector Compact, a code of practice for the council and VCSE working together, is a core document for the unit. The CPU must use its limited resources to give modest grants to voluntary and community associations (up to £20,000 to any one organization) in the hope that *they* will provide services for which residents might otherwise look to the council. The unit is closely involved in the functioning of various structures linking the council to other actors. One is the Stronger United Communities Group, a multi-agency partnership with representatives of various council departments, in collaboration with police and other public agencies. Its aim is 'to provide strategic coordination and support to Prevent and Cohesion Activities' in the borough, 'taking account of national legislation and guidance and local policy and intelligence'. Then there is the Local Strategic Partnership, governed by the Hounslow Together Board, with representatives of the council alongside other public providers, the voluntary sphere and local businesses. This has developed a Future Borough Strategy with a forward vision to 2030. There is also a Hounslow Community Network (bringing together the voluntary organizations) and a Hounslow Voluntary Sector Support System.

The CPU strategy is 'objective driven', and its three objectives all, with clear intention, put the emphasis on what the community will become, rather than what the council will do.[48] The first speaks of 'empowered residents actively shaping their local areas and enhancing civic pride'; the second aims for 'independence and resilience by building the skills, resources and capacity of residents, neighbourhoods and communities'; and the third seeks 'a vibrant, self-sustaining and ambitious VCSE sector'. 'Cohesion' is formulated by Hounslow Council as 'the extent to which residents of Hounslow bond around common interests and goals, mutual knowledge, a sense of collective identity and belonging, shared understanding and trust'. They see it as 'positively related to the number, variety and/or intensity of shared interests and interactions that provide a basis for solidarity, mobilisation and joint action'.[49] The council carry out a resident survey every two years to ascertain what people are feeling. The most recent showed 73 per cent of residents 'agreeing that people of different backgrounds got on well together' – three percentage points lower than the London and national averages. But a sizeable majority of 83 per cent felt that Hounslow people 'treated each other with respect'. Two recent projects prompted by the council in the name of 'cohesion' were commissioning art-based community events organized by local people, and supporting families in given streets to exclude traffic now and then in order to organize children's 'play days'.

On publication of the 2011 census, the council noticed for the first time that a surprising number of Afghans had settled in the borough in the last ten years, a presence they had previously paid little attention to. They wondered then, were there perhaps other communities like the Afghans, somehow invisible to the council? This prompted the CPU to commission researchers at Middlesex University to take a close look at six neglected Hounslow communities: Afghans, Algerians, Burmese, Sri Lankans, Romanians and Bulgarians. 'We felt we didn't have the same degree of relationship with these that we did with the older and bigger communities, like Sikhs and Somalis', Laura James told me. The research report, *Mapping and Needs Assessment*,[50] featured the Sri Lankan community in quite negative terms, particularly the numerically dominant Tamil-speaking segment of it. They found that compared with the Sinhalese-speaking and mainly Buddhist Sri Lankans, the Tamils had a less secure immigration status, a lower level of English-language ability, and despite frequent recourse to council front-line services, they were more likely to have 'no trust in authority'. The authors surmised that Tamils' neediness was related to extensive trauma due to the civil war, resulting in poor mental health, alcoholism and a high level of domestic violence. The researchers found that until then the authorities' response to this neediness had been poor, with little public health engagement, a lack of services targeted at the community, 'a huge unmet need' regarding English-language classes and inadequate support for survivors of domestic violence. Tamil women, the principal victims, the researchers reported, felt that council personnel failed to provide language interpretation, and treated them poorly, made them feel inferior 'because they have dark skin' and looked down upon them because they are refugees. Among the young, particularly teenage males, there was a gang culture linked to drug dealing and use. Unsurprisingly, the report concluded that the predominant attitude among Tamil refugees, affecting their motivation and quality of life, was 'fatalism'.

One might have expected that such a stark portrayal of a suffering minority group would prompt its host council to compensate for past neglect by spending more money on them and providing more services. However, what came into play in response to the Middlesex University research findings was the well-established council approach: encouraging people to help themselves. And here the word 'resilience' came to the fore. The policy would be *not* to increase communities' dependence on the council but rather to encourage them to 'do things for themselves', thus 'building their own resilience'. The term has been energetically promoted by the Local Government Information Unit, an 'award-winning think-tank'.[51] The idea is to identify individual and community shortcomings on the one hand, and impending risks on the other, with the policy aim of developing peoples' strengths to prepare ahead of time and 'cope' with challenges likely to occur in the future. Thus, the *Thriving Communities* document states, 'Closely linked to the concept of cohesion in Hounslow, is the concept of community resilience.' Our work is to enable residents 'to withstand, respond to and recover from a wide range of harmful and adverse local, regional and international events'. It's all about 'unlocking local capacity'. We must, they say, help people to help themselves 'before they need lots of services or more expensive services'.[52] For this the council have established a new team of Community Engagement Officers to support resident-led activities that increase 'local resilience'. It is not easy, however, to detect in the council documents precisely what risks and challenges to local residents they fear lie ahead. In other areas and regions, risk has sometimes been taken to refer to the effects of climate change, such as catastrophic flooding, but it is not clear that Hounslow is particularly flood-prone. Perhaps the crash of an aircraft on its flight path to or from nearby Heathrow Airport?

Like Tower Hamlets Council, Hounslow Council is cautious about fingering particular minority communities as recipients of council attention and grant aid for fear of resentment on the part of other communities or the 'white' half of the population. Thus, while the *Thriving Communities* document states that 'We take the view that tackling inequalities remains a key component of community cohesion', it also commits to policies 'that reach the majority of residents, not just specific groups (such as ethnic minorities or white working class families)'.[53] In light of this it has chosen the conceptual device of directing policy instead towards *place* – a street, a neighbourhood, a housing estate, an electoral ward – and to assume that such an area will be home to a mixture of residents from diverse identity groups.

To return to the Hounslow Sri Lankan community and its Tamils, the Middlesex University researchers described the Tamil Community Centre that I mentioned above, as 'providing the specialist services that the community needs', but as being 'oversubscribed and underfunded with a question mark around sustainability'.[54] In the course of my own interview with Thavarani Nagulendram, the founder and coordinator of the Centre, reported more fully below, I learned that she has never applied to the council for a grant, preferring to maintain the Centre's independence. During my interview with Laura James of the CPU the latter stressed that, had they sought it, the Centre would certainly have had a good chance of obtaining council funding. The council had helped it in a non-funding capacity over negotiation of access to the building in which they are based. They had also invited them to put on a dance performance at the council's event for International Women's Day. Laura stresses, 'we want to support them like that in ways that *they* want'. Nonetheless, Thavarani's preference for independence clearly suits Hounslow Council's budget-restricted strategy.

A TAMIL WOMAN SETTLES IN HOUNSLOW

Let's turn now to Thavarani Nagulendram herself, or Rani for short, who plays such a significant role among the Tamils of Hounslow and other West London boroughs. She tells me she was born in 1970, on the island of Karainagar in the northern Tamil region of Sri Lanka, the firstborn of six children. Her father owned a shop a little way from their home, in the upcountry town of Hapaltele, selling clothes and other commodities. They also owned a few acres of land, including paddy fields, near their home. As a young child Rani experienced no conflict, no danger, she says. It was not until she was nine or ten that the war between the Sinhalese majority and the Tamil minority began, and it was not until the climactic year of 1983 that war became a reality for her. That was the year her uncle (her mother's brother) was arrested by the Sri Lankan Army. She remembers her mother crying about his seizure. He would be held prisoner for five years, maltreated and tortured. But even at this stage her parents told the children little about what was going on – they didn't want them to worry. Rani's parents were not involved with the Tamil Tigers. This, however, did not secure them from trouble. In July that same year, her father's shop was burned down by the SLA. That little property had been their principal asset and their sole source of income. Now they had to turn to their small landholding and work it intensively for a livelihood. Her mother laboured in the paddy field, helped by the children. But it wasn't easy to keep the family fed. Looking back, now, on these early teenage years, Rani says, 'Funnily enough, there was something happy about that time, despite the deprivation and the hard work. It was a simple life. We could just manage. We were independent. We had our own house and fields and water.'

Then, in 1988, the Indian Army invaded the north of Sri Lanka. Called a 'peacekeeping mission', it was experienced as a bald attack on the Tamil region and its rebels. Rani was at that moment studying for her A-levels in a boarding school some distance away from home. The school was bombed and blasted. She and the other students ran from their devastated hostel, and hid in a church school. Her father came from home to look for her, seeking high and low, under Indian bombing and occupation. He was 'asking everyone, asking, asking', Rani says, 'amid the turmoil, everyone running'. He found her eventually, and took her home. But that was the end of schooling for Rani. She never went back to do her A-levels, and feels this now as a huge loss. 'In Tamil society education is an absolute priority – it's felt that children *must* study.' Instead, Rani pursued dancing, informally at first, then, from 1989, she attended a dancing course in Chennai, across the water in India's Tamil Nadu province. In this way dance became her main achievement and, eventually, the source of a slender income.

While living in Tamil Nadu, Rani chanced to meet a visiting Sri Lankan man, and this encounter changed the course of her life. He had been imprisoned in Sri Lanka, had fled the country and achieved asylum in the UK. They decided to marry, and when he returned to London from his visit to India, she followed him, arriving in 1991, admitted without problem as the wife of a citizen. The process of achieving her own citizenship was long, costly and tortuous, but, once achieved, it enabled her to bring others of her family to join them – sister and brothers first, eventually her parents. By 2001 all her close relatives were resident in the UK.

In 1991, when Rani first arrived, she joined her husband in the north-east London Borough of Walthamstow, a relatively prosperous area. They moved to Hounslow in 1995 – and Rani found that very hard. 'I cried', she says. 'It meant leaving my friends. But my husband worked at the airport, and he persuaded me. And some of our friends followed us to West London later.' Rani herself has never been in full-time employment in Britain. She quickly had two children, both daughters, one in 1992 and another four years later, and was a full-time mother and homemaker. It was Rani's father who was the prompt to setting up the Tamil Community Centre. Back in Sri Lanka, he had always been an active and social person. Resettled in London, he felt lost, isolated, confined to home. So Rani decided to start a 'drop-in' facility – first and foremost for him. 'And then,' she says, 'I found people began to talk to me, to confide in me. Why me? I felt they needed something.' So she consulted those more experienced in the voluntary sector in Hounslow, asking for their advice on how to organize a centre. She managed to get some training. Then she created the Tamil Community Centre, still to this day Hounslow's only Tamil NGO. She hired (and still does) a community hall for two days a week, a peaceful quiet space. Her dad enjoyed the Centre. Gradually their activities expanded. An article in *London24* online newspaper describes the Centre this way:

> a vital help service for Tamils living in London which does not get a penny of state help. Thavarani Nagulendram leads the Tamil Community Centre ... More than five thousand came for help last year with problems as diverse as poor health, money worries and domestic violence. The latter is a serious concern for Hounslow resident Mrs. Nagulendram, because cultural norms make it very hard for victims to speak out. ... Mrs. Nagulendram is a well-deserved winner of a London Star award from the Mayor of London.[55]

The many hours Rani devotes to the Centre are voluntary and unpaid. She earns a small income from teaching classical dance. As we've seen, she has never sought funding for the Centre, either from the council or the voluntary sector. She finds application forms, letter writing and evaluations tedious and time-consuming. Besides, 'funding makes you dependent', she believes. 'You lose the initiative.' She has only ever accepted one small grant of £5,000, from an NGO that guaranteed it would not make any bureaucratic demands.

I asked for Rani's evaluation of Hounslow Council's community relations, and its policies and provisions for minority communities such as the Sri Lankan Tamils. She pulled a sour face at the very mention of the council, of which she has a low opinion. 'There are many, many communities of asylum seekers living in Hounslow borough', she says. 'There are Somalis, Iranians, Afghans, Gujaratis. There are 149 languages spoken here. ... I like that!' But as to the council, Rani's view is that they talk all too readily about their provision for communities, while mainly being concerned with cutting the cost of benefits and services, and 'expecting everyone to adapt to their bureaucratic rules and expectations'. So for her it's best for voluntary organizations to stand well back from the council. 'Labour, Conservative, I don't want it', she says.

In 2006, Selvy Thiruchandran published a volume of Tamil women's writing from the diaspora. She found that many felt they had gained by leaving Sri Lanka. 'Judging by their writings, these women seem not to be attracted to the idea of returning "home", despite the many dilemmas and multiple identities and ambiguities they must thrash

Above: Decorated arch celebrating Tamil Heroes' Day, at
Queen Elizabeth Olympic Park, East London, 2016.

Opposite: Top, Rani's Tamil dance class. Bottom,
Rani Nagulendram, classical dance teacher and
founder of the Tamil Community Centre in the
London Borough of Hounslow.

out ... they do not want to lose the gains they have earned in the host country: the independence, socio-economic mobility, the rights and choices available to them politically.'[56] Reading this prompted me to ask Rani whether she might perhaps want to go back to live in Sri Lanka, now the war has ended. No, she said emphatically. 'I only lived there for 18 years of my life, after all. I've been in London 27 years now. It's become home.' The effect is surely the greater for the fact that through her efforts in the Tamil Community Centre she's made West London feel like 'home' for hundreds of other Tamil migrants.

HARDLY HOME: TAMIL WOMEN IN DETENTION

If several thousand Tamil women, like Rani, managed to obtain UK citizenship during the last 20 years, and thus to have a choice as to whether to stay forever in their new homeland, there were many others (and even more Tamil men) who were denied that possibility. And, as we saw above, some were rejected and ejected from the UK in a manner so brutal it seemed to mimic the inhumanity of the Sri Lankan state. The programme of deportation of Tamil asylum seekers was closely associated with increased use of 'detention'. Let's call it by its name: imprisonment. The power to detain immigrants to Britain was first introduced as long ago as the Immigration Act of 1971. There was, and still is, no statutory limit to how long a person may be held. The practice began to gain more public attention in March 2007, when the Home Office introduced an innovatory procedure it called the New Asylum Model (NAM). A key part of NAM is Detained Fast-Track (DFT), an accelerated process for assessing asylum claims, intended for use in cases that appear to be uncomplicated, ripe for speedy acceptance or refusal. The Home Office's five-year strategy for the period 2005–10 stipulated that DFT would be increasingly used, including for women.[57] The corollary was the opening of more detention centres. The Yarl's Wood facility in Bedfordshire, first operational in 2001, became the place of choice for detaining fast-tracked women. Now termed an Immigration Removal Centre, it is designed to accommodate 405 detainees. Some children were also held there with their mothers until, in 2014, this practice was discontinued due to concerns for the children's well-being. There are also a few family units in Yarl's Wood wherein a handful of men are incarcerated with their partners.

During this last decade, while some Tamil women have been addressing the day-to-day problems of re-homing out there in Hounslow and other London boroughs, Yarl's Wood has been an unchosen 'home' to other less lucky ones. An indication that Tamil women have been present in Yarl's Wood from the start is that Tamil is one of two foreign languages used for a welcome sign at the entrance.[58] But they have been tucked away there, out of sight, in limbo – and uncounted. In 2015 the Refugee Council reported that Sri Lanka was one of the six commonest nationalities among detainees in Yarl's Wood (they listed Pakistan, India, Bangladesh, Nigeria, Afghanistan, ending with Sri Lanka).[59] We may suppose they have been, for the most part, Tamils.

From the moment Yarl's Wood came into use in 2001, detainees voiced acute distress at their treatment there. Indeed, only three months after it was opened there was a major fire, apparently started by angry and despairing inmates.[60] Women's organizations rallied to the support of the female detainees. A group of 'Yarl's Wood Befrienders' was set up. Two activist groups associated with the Crossroads Women's Centre in North London, Women Against Rape and the Black Women's Rape Action Project, have worked in and among Yarl's Wood detainees over a ten-year period. In June 2015 they published a dossier based on hundreds of complaints by women inmates recounting the harassment they had experienced there. Stories include being strip searched with men present, and of male guards commonly entering bedrooms when women are in a state of undress. Suicide watch, involving guards spying on you while you are sleeping, taking a shower or sitting on the toilet, women say they experience as deeply humiliating. Male guards are said frequently to proposition women for sex, leading them to believe that compliance will speed their release.[61] The two groups concluded their study with a strong demand for the immediate closure of Yarl's Wood, and went with it to demonstrate outside parliament.

A second feminist campaigning and support NGO, Women for Refugee Women, also carried out research in Yarl's Wood, involving interviews with 38 women detainees held there between June 2012 and October 2014. Thirty-four of the sample disclosed gender-related experiences of persecution in Sri Lanka, 19 reporting rape, while

28 had suffered forced marriage, forced prostitution, female genital mutilation or sexualized torture. Give such a history, detention in Yarl's Wood was understandably having 'an extremely negative impact on their mental health', such that 40 per cent of them had self-harmed, and one in five had tried to kill themselves while there. Women for Refugee Women argued that in future no woman who presented with experience of sexual or gender-based abuse should be held in Yarl's Wood, that an upper time limit for detention of 28 days should be established, and that no male staff should be employed in roles in which they would be in contact with women detainees.[62]

Undercover journalists picked up on such information emerging from support groups, publishing highly critical articles.[63] Cameras have never been allowed inside Yarl's Wood, but Channel 4 News contrived to carry out an undercover investigation that aired in March 2015. The programme cited figures obtained through the Freedom of Information Act recording no less than 74 separate incidents of self-harm requiring medical treatment in the year 2013 alone. The disrespect shown by staff to inmates was indisputable. Unaware of being filmed, staff are recorded referring to the inmates as 'animals', 'beasties' and 'bitches', and officers are heard to say, 'Let them slash their wrists', 'It's attention seeking'.[64] Even official reports have been critical of the Yarl's Wood regime. For instance, the Chief Inspector of Prisons, Nick Hardwick, who was sent unannounced to examine Yarl's Wood, concluded that the centre was indeed failing vulnerable women, and that women should be detained only as a last resort.[65] A study by Medical Justice found serious healthcare failings.[66] Most tellingly, in January 2015 the UN Special Rapporteur on Violence against Women, Rashida Manjoo, on a fact-finding mission to the UK, was refused permission to visit Yarl's Wood. 'Does the government have something to hide?' she asked.[67] Under pressure, SERCO, the private security firm the government contracts to run Yarl's Wood, itself commissioned an investigative study by barrister Kate Lampard CBE and Ed Marsden of the NGO Verita. These notables predictably found 'there is not an endemic culture of abuse, nor a hidden problem of inappropriate behaviour by staff at the centre'. SERCO's main response to criticisms was a better level of staffing by female officers.[68] The Home Office, for its part, responds to all this criticism with bland statements to the effect that 'we are committed to treating all detainees with dignity and respect', while standing by SERCO, extending its contract to run Yarl's Wood to 2022.[69]

The government was bound to defend the existence of Yarl's Wood so long as it had a need to hold women pending a judgment on their case for asylum. The DFT process that deposits males at centres such as Campsfield House in Oxfordshire or Colnbrook in Middlesex, and women at Yarl's Wood, is never 'faster' than two weeks, and on average takes more like three months. There is much to criticize in DFT, in and of itself. However, in addition cogent criticism is levelled at the procedure from a gender viewpoint. Article 1 of the Refugee Convention of 1951 states that to obtain protection and recognition as a refugee a person must establish that they have a well-founded fear of being persecuted in the country of origin 'for reasons of race, religion, nationality, political opinion, or membership of a particular social group'. Note that 'gender' is not one of the reasons for persecution listed here. However, it is widely argued that women may be, and should be, considered 'a particular social group' under Article 1. A foundational document, *Guidelines on International Protection: Gender-Related Persecution*, issued by the UN High Commissioner for Refugees (UNHCR), makes it clear that the assessment of 'grounds' for protection should include 'the gender dimension of persecution'.[70] Even the UK Border Agency in 2004 published an Asylum Policy Instruction on *Gender Identity Issues in the Asylum Claim*, which set out some of the forms of gender-based persecution and violence on which women might base their claim, and sought to improve the gender sensitivity of the UK asylum process.[71] The argument being made here is that women's asylum claims regularly present issues that are different from those presented by men, and can be highly complex and challenging. Many women arrive in the UK in flight from persecution that has included being forcibly held and subjected to sexual violence by individuals, criminal groups or agents of the state. We have already seen plentiful evidence that torture by state agents persists in Sri Lanka, and that sexualized torture is widely used on Tamil women. Recently, Freedom from Torture reported on 148 cases they had examined, writing: 'Both men and women reported the same forms of torture, including beating, burning with different types of implements, sexual torture including rape, suspension and other forced positioning, asphyxiation and sharp force trauma with various implements.'[72] Many, perhaps most, women find it impossible to recount such things in a brief interview with immigration authorities, especially when, as is often the case, the interviewer is a man or a man is present in the room. Even when the process is handled by female officers, reticence is understandable. Yet in the first five years of the DFT procedure (2005 to 2010) no less than 2,055 women were routed into it.[73]

The NGO Asylum Aid made the first in-depth study of women's asylum claims after NAM was introduced in 2007, focusing on the quality and sustainability of the initial decisions made by the UK Border Agency on the basis of the screening interview. They found that the Agency had initially refused 87 per cent of cases for lack of credibility, but that 42 per cent of these negative decisions had later been overturned by immigration judges on appeal – far above the average for all asylum claims, which is 28 per cent. Asylum Aid concluded that the UK Border Agency was badly failing to meet the challenge of the complexity of women's claims, and was consequently achieving an 'extremely poor standard of decision-making'.[74] All in all, its critics have argued, DFT for women not only constitutes a continuation of the inhumane treatment from which they have fled, it is a waste of time and money. Women for Refugee Women reckon that in the year 2013 only 633, or 31 per cent, of women asylum seekers detained at Yarl's Wood were subsequently deported. The rest re-entered British society. One-third deported, two-thirds released, this was the finding too of the Inspector of Prisons. For the most part, detention had served no purpose.[75] Radhika Sanghani, writing in the *Telegraph*, pointed out that if most detainees are eventually allowed to return to their lives in Britain, we have good reason to question the price paid for Yarl's Wood by the taxpayer (£130 per woman per day).[76] Meantime, a sizeable public is less concerned by the price being paid by the taxpayer than the price being paid by women. They monitor detention centres with a critical eye. On 6 June 2015, No Borders and other migrant support groups drew several hundred protestors to a demonstration outside Yarl's Wood, in solidarity with inmates and clamouring for its closure.[77] I was there. My photos overpage show women breaking through the barbed wire fence and communicating with detainees watching from their windows.

CAUGHT IN THE SYSTEM: WOMEN DETAINEES' STORIES

I was fortunate to be able to meet two Tamil women with experience of detention in Yarl's Wood who were willing to speak to me. One, Veena, had been imprisoned there in early 2013; the second, Srisivakumar, 18 months later, towards the end of 2015. Let me tell you how they remember it. For Veena those three weeks in Yarl's Wood were a time of serious stress and deep depression. It was not that she was physically hurt, but the close monitoring by the staff, the intrusive questioning, being checked up on every hour – she found it horrible. 'How can you sleep if you are being watched? The men were unpleasant. They followed me even to the toilet and stood outside the open door.' Veena made no friends during her detention. She tried to kill herself, using anti-depression tablets she had brought in with her and which the staff, strangely at odds with their obsession with surveillance, had omitted to remove from her bag.

For Srisivakumar, too, Yarl's Wood is a memory that haunts her. While there she couldn't sleep. She suffered flashbacks to violence experienced in Sri Lanka. Her physical health deteriorated and mentally she was deeply depressed and disturbed. She found it hard to get the medication she needed, or to see a doctor. She had no visitors while there, no support. 'The place felt airless, suffocating', she says. 'Some prisoners were really rude and difficult.' She says she tried to keep away from the male officers, but every night they would peer into her cell to check on her, which she found 'scary'. The personnel at Yarl's Wood, she says, 'just don't understand your feelings'. Worse, at times they reminded her of the Sri Lankan Army personnel who had tortured her.

To fully understand just how inappropriate, in the circumstances, is this punitive detention regime, let me go on to tell you something of Veena's and Srisivakumar's lives, the history of misadventure that had, over the years – first in Sri Lanka, then in the UK – led them towards Yarl's Wood's barbed wire gates. Veena was born in 1983, into a Tamil and Hindu family living in a small community called Alaveddy, about half an hour's drive from Jaffna in the Tamil north of Sri Lanka. Her father was a farmer and her mother was occupied at home looking after a family of five children. The three boys were all older than she, and there was also a younger sister. A great deal of trouble was inflicted

Veena.

Above and opposite: Demonstration
calling for the closure of Yarl's Wood
Immigration Removal Centre, 2016.

by the state on many members of Veena's family, due to her uncle (her mother's brother) being a leading personality in the Tamil Tigers. First they suffered from the Indian Army invasion of the late 1980s. But it was a few years later, in the early 1990s, when the Sri Lankan Army turned its attention to the Tamils and moved to take control of the north, that the family members began to feel state repression. Her father was imprisoned for a while; her grandfather was likewise in prison, and died from the torture to which he was subjected. Veena was nine years old when the family were first displaced from their home, attacked by the army. After that they were shifted from one place to the next according to the fighting and did not return to her birthplace until 1999. Of course, as a result her schooling suffered badly, but she was nonetheless eventually accepted on to an engineering course at a university near Colombo. University attendance is free in Sri Lanka, and her family helped with her living expenses. Having no relatives in the city, she stayed in lodgings and seldom went out. She didn't finish the course, however.

Veena was 24 years old the first time she was arrested. She says, 'As a student, they were always checking your identity.' Her ID card showed she was from Jaffna. Tamils were a minority down south, and most of them were harassed by the police and army, who assumed them to be Tigers supporters. 'They just looked at us that way', Veena says. On one occasion they took her for another young woman, whom she happened to resemble. This first time she was arrested she was taken to the police station, subjected to questioning, constrained, beaten up and generally treated roughly. Four months later, in the same year, 2007, when the war was at its height, she was arrested a second time. They came for her when she was on the way to the offices of a company to be interviewed for a training position. This time she was held for longer, and the torture was worse. When she was released, her father decided to send her to London where one of her brothers was now living, to stay with him, and to study. She obtained a passport and visa legally, and so experienced a trouble-free arrival in the UK, went to her brother's place in Norwich and studied accounting.

I asked Veena, 'In those days when you first came to Britain were you feeling sad, or were you glad to be away from the dangers of Sri Lanka?' She paused as she considered this – and answered 'Both! Of course!' On the one hand, yes, she avoided the terrible experiences of the culminating years of the war in 2008 and 2009, but she continually missed and worried about her parents and siblings, as indeed she still does. In 2011, accompanied by her brother, Veena went back for a three-week visit to see them. And she was again arrested when in Colombo. She was held for about a week. Her treatment during this detention and interrogation was physically very violent, including extreme sexual abuse, beatings and 'Palestinian hanging'. Eventually they took her to court, and she was granted bail pending a hearing. Released for the moment, she set about returning to the UK. Her father bribed a policeman to give her back her passport, in which she still had a valid UK visa. They used an agent this time to get an air ticket illegally, because she would be breaking bail in leaving the country. In this way she succeeded in getting back to the UK.

The following year, in 2012, Veena had news that her father and brother had been arrested. It was around now that she was due to apply for asylum in the UK. She received an initial rejection, and then missed the date by which she could have lodged an appeal against this. In the intervening time she was under orders to report monthly to the local police station, and on one occasion when she went to do so she was arrested. It was February 2013. They held her in a prison cell for five or six hours – it was, she says, a tiny cell, very confining and scary. It was then that they took her to Yarl's Wood, where she was detained for 23 days. An immigration lawyer helped with her case but, nonetheless, the UK Border Agency ruled that she must be deported. They gave her an airline ticket to Colombo for the last day of February, for a given flight and time. On that day she presented herself at the office in Yarl's Wood with her ticket and papers, prepared to go. Several other Sri Lankan women detainees were gathered there, all due to be deported that day. But her lawyer had appealed against deportation, and at the very last moment it was cancelled. She was not bussed to the airport with the rest. Instead, that evening she was released, and slept at 'home' in her brother's house.

Veena made another suicide attempt in May 2013. She is seriously depressed, mentally damaged by all that she's been subject to, not only previously by the Sri Lankan regime but now by the British state. She receives counselling but, she says, the counsellors change every few months. She is living now with a (female) cousin, supported financially by her brother, and still waiting for her immigration status to be resolved. One step in the hearing has been carried out, the other is still to come. The barrister has failed to turn up in court three or four times. She's been told the next hearing will be in three months' time. Still nothing is decided. So much delay. She's in a bad state. She says, 'I'm really fed up with life. I have no future, it's spoiled. And my parents are still in trouble because of me.' Veena is not politically active. She does a little charitable work, such as collecting support for tsunami victims. When I said to her, puzzled, 'I don't understand why the Sri Lankan state follows you for so long and treats you so badly when you have never actually been, on your own account, a Tiger activist'. She says, 'I don't understand it myself'. The Sri Lankan state, it seems, needs no evidence of wrong-doing to justify arrest and torture of Tamils.

Unlike Veena, Srisivakumar maintains her Tamil political identity openly here in England and has, besides, a prior history of activism in Sri Lanka. She was born in 1988, not far from Veena's birthplace, in the town of Kokuvil, near Jaffna. During her childhood her father worked as a mid-level government employee and her mother raised the children at home. The oldest of three children, all of them girls, she was educated in the Kokuvil school for five years, and then passed the exam to attend high school in Jaffna, to which she travelled daily. The Tamil struggle became a reality for Srisivakumar in 1995, when she was seven. That was when the region was bombed by the Sri Lankan Army and the family was displaced for the first, but not the last, time. When she was a young teenager, in 2002, there were peace talks and a remission in the fighting. This was when she began to be actively involved with the LTTE. She was in a Tamil Youth programme, Pongu Tamil. She says now, 'I supported the aims of the Tigers. We had to do something for Tamils!' When the fighting renewed in 2005, and the Tigers were being driven northwards into the Vanni region, Srisivakumar was still in high school working for her A-level exams. There was a union of students in the school that often joined the Students Union of Jaffna University in demonstrating for the Tigers. Srisivakumar was a leader among them. The government cracked down on them with a heavy hand. 'They assumed automatically that all Tamil students were Tigers', Srisivakumar says.

It was in 2007, the year of her A-levels, that Srisivakumar was arrested for the first time, and detained for one month. She was beaten up (and sexually molested, abused with touch and language – but not raped). She was held in isolation, although she could hear the voices of other women in the prison. When they released her it was all of a sudden, without explanation. They just took her in a van and dropped her in the street near her family home. She was in pain from her maltreatment, and needed a doctor. Her mother and father felt strongly she should get away from the country now, to avoid further attention from the authorities. They pressed her to go and stay with an aunt living in Tamil Nadu, just across the water in India. Reluctantly, Srisivakumar went, and she tried to study, but found it hard. She continued to put her energies into support for the Tiger's struggle. She was active in shipping medical supplies to Tamil groups across the sea in Sri Lanka. She helped find accommodation for two Tiger activist families who arrived by boat as refugees. Only three years on, when the war had finally ended, did her father permit her to come back.

The Sri Lankan government's defeat of the Tigers as a military force was not the end of trouble for Tamils, however. Srisivakumar flew into Colombo airport. At immigration control they took her passport and questioned her intensively, noting the address of her family in Jaffna. Her father had a friend in Colombo, who now took her to his home while her father came down from Jaffna to collect her. While they were all three in the friend's home, Srisivakumar recounts, 'Suddenly, some security people broke in on us, four or five men. They were not wearing military uniforms, but they were speaking Sinhalese, and they had guns. My dad was arguing with them. But they grabbed me, and put a blindfold on me, and shoved me into a van.'

She was detained for ten days and questioned about her activities in India. While they extracted this information and much more, she was beaten badly, until she was bleeding. She was raped. Sometimes she lost consciousness. She says, 'I was helpless. Ten days. It was so long!' The torture ended only when her father's bribe was accepted. Reunited, they travelled back to the family home up north, where Srisivakumar was ordered to report monthly to the local police station. Now her father was determined to get her out to seek asylum in the UK. He engaged an agent who obtained a passport and visa, and booked a flight to London. The cost, Srisivakumar reckons, must have been at least £5,000. She never met the agent, and made the flight to Heathrow unaccompanied.

A relative (her father's sister) was living in Newbury Park, near Ilford in north-east London. This aunt came to meet her at the airport, and took her home to live with her. She helped Srisivakumar to recover from the terrible experiences in Sri Lanka, pressed her to study, to get out and about, and encouraged her to sign up at a college in Oxford Street to start a course in management studies. But Srisivakumar was an unenthusiastic student. She was so badly missing her family and friends, the place she thought of as 'home'. She tried, for a year or more, to make new friends, imagine herself into a new life. But she says, 'I felt at that time my life had ended'. And then came the moment, in 2012, when her visa was about to run out and she had to reapply. At that point she did indeed succeed in getting a three-year extension. However, after some trouble with an expired college enrolment, she now found herself in a curious double bind. The Home Office rules required her to sit a biennial English proficiency test, but they would not accept her candidacy for the test without presentation of her passport. And her passport was being held by – the Home Office! 'They seemed to be playing with me!' she says. With the help of an adviser she wrote to the authorities asking them to give back her passport. They refused, in writing. Instead, Srisivakumar says:

> On 22 September 2015, they came to my home at 6.30 am, and arrested me, on grounds that I had overstayed my visa. They took me to Hounslow Police Station and held me in a cell for 24 hours. Then they took me to Colnbrook, the men's Detention Centre, and kept me there for a week. Then they transferred me to Yarl's Wood.

Once in the detention centre, her visa extension application refused, Srisivakumar became an undocumented illegal immigrant and had no recourse but to seek asylum. She made her case, arguing that if deported she would certainly, as a known Tamil activist, be arrested on arrival in Sri Lanka and subjected to imprisonment and abuse. Her father had been questioned about her by the Sri Lankan authorities and warned, 'We'll get her when she comes back.' Behind this warning lay not only Srisivakumar's past as a student activist in Sri Lanka, but her continuing support for the Tamil movement in the diaspora. Though the LTTE no longer exist in Sri Lanka, an international organization, the Transitional Government of Tamil Eelam (TGTE), was founded in 2010 with representation in many countries, including the UK.

Its constitution commits to a democratic system of government, 'to establish an independent state of Tamil Eelam based on the principles of peace, non-violence, tolerance, pluralism, transparency and accountability'.[78] Srisivakumar had been pursuing her political interests and aims in this framework. She is an interesting illustration of a feature in refugee 'emplacement' stressed by Maja Korac. In her study of Bosnian war refugees, this researcher found that, as they 'nested' in their country of asylum they often simultaneously renewed and extended a transnational 'belonging', within the troubled country from which they had fled, and among their compatriots now settled in other countries world-wide.[79]

The TGTE is just such a diasporic community. The UK authorities certainly knew of Srisivakumar's engagement in the movement of Tamil nationalism, and no doubt for that reason her first application for asylum was quickly refused. Her aunt then found a lawyer, the same professional, as it happened, who had advised Veena. His first action was to apply for bail, in order to get her released from Yarl's Wood. He succeeded after a month. Today, she is greatly relieved to be back at 'home' with her aunt, but she feels depressed and angry. Fed up with waiting, always waiting. She had another asylum interview in January 2016, and was refused again in March. Her lawyer appealed, and there has been a new court hearing. Three months ago, at the time of writing, she received a letter from the judge approving her case. But she is still waiting for affirmation from the Home Office. If she gets it, she supposes this will involve five years' 'leave to remain' before she might ultimately hope to get British citizenship.

Meanwhile, Srisivakumar says of her continuing support for the TGTE, 'In Sri Lanka we can't raise a voice. You get 20 years in jail. Two Tamil university students were shot by the army not long ago, with no justification at all. There are protests, but no justice. Only more arrests.' She's trying meanwhile to live according to her principles. So she goes with the TGTE when they take petitions to the UK parliament, and when they demonstrate outside the Sri Lankan Embassy. But she says, 'We have to do more, we are not being strong enough.' I enjoyed going at her invitation to join in the annual November celebration of Tamil Heroes' Day, which gathered an impressive crowd of several thousand Tamil Londoners at the Olympic Park in Stratford, East London, and where I glimpsed Srisivakumar active behind the scenes.[80]

5

The Sudans' Divided People
Come to Camden

At the beginning of the millennium, when Sudan and South Sudan were as yet a single nation state, its land area, at two and a half million square miles, made it the largest country in Africa. Almost landlocked, but for a short stretch of Red Sea coastline, the territory was bordered by no less than nine countries: Egypt, Libya, Chad, the Central African Republic, the Democratic Republic of the Congo, Uganda, Kenya, Ethiopia and Eritrea. The River Nile is the Sudans' lifeline, flowing down as the White Nile from the Central African lakes and the Blue Nile from the highlands of Ethiopia. The capital city of Khartoum/Omdurman is situated at the confluence of the two great streams, which then flow north as one, linking Sudan to the Mediterranean by way of Egypt. With an extreme climate, and liable to periodic drought and famine, the territory's fertile agricultural land is greatly exceeded in area by grass, scrub and rocky slopes from which nomadic people wrest a pastoral living. In this chapter we shall be concerned both with the Republic of Sudan, as it now is, in the northern three-quarters of the land area, and the Republic of South Sudan, which in 2011 broke away to become an independent state in the southern, more equatorial, region. The Sudanese we shall meet in London are refugees from wars that were fought both before and after the separation, and within and across the states' common border.

The land area known as 'the Sudan' and colonized in 1898 as the 'Anglo-Egyptian Condominium', was home to many tribes, each with its cultural history and religious adherence.[1] Among them is a wide range of phenotype or 'race'. These dimensions of difference have been used, as Jok Madut Jok puts it in his book *Sudan: Race, Religion and Violence*, 'as a mechanism for allocation of rights, resources and social standing' and as such a source of unending strife.[2] Physically, the peoples of the northern regions, especially along the River Nile, have tended to be relatively pale-skinned, with a hint of the Middle East in their looks, and generally thought of and referred to as 'Arabs'. The peoples of the southern regions, and peripheral areas of the north, have tended to have more negroid features, and to be referred to as 'black' or 'African'. It's impossible to categorize Sudanese individuals unambiguously, however, and many 'Arabs' would be seen by an uninformed observer as 'black'. Equally, 'race' is not a sure indicator of religious adherence. Many 'black' Sudanese are Muslims, and not every 'Arab' is one. Before the advent of the monotheisms, the area had many religious beliefs, mainly animistic. Christianity reached the region in the sixth century, via Ethiopia, and there was a Christian Nubian kingdom until the twelfth century. From the seventh century, Islam spread south and west into Africa from its birthplace on the Arabian peninsular. The people identified as Muslim – pale-featured, 'riverain' Arab types – were the dominant class for the duration of the Ottoman Empire, when the south was treated as a gold mine and a field for harvesting slaves. Later, in colonial times, the British imperialists favoured the 'Arabs' and employed them in the bureaucracy. They too drew a hard line between north and south, putting the latter out of bounds to Arabs and introducing Christian missions to civilize the 'blacks'. As a result, it was the northern, Arab elite who alone negotiated independence in 1956, and heavily dominated the first elected government of Sudan.

The 60 years that have passed since then have seen little but military dictatorship and violent strife. Just two years after independence, the democratically elected government was overthrown by Islamist and militarist Ibrahim Abboud, who was himself forced to resign six years later during the protests by students and other democracy activists they termed the 1964 'October Revolution'. But the civilian administrations that briefly followed him were replaced, in 1969, in a second military coup, by Colonel Jaafar Muhammad Nimeiri. War between the regime and the south of Sudan had broken out even as the British departed, for many southerners viewed the moment not as liberation but as the substitution of northern Arab colonialism for the European variety. Nimeiri now pursued with increased ferocity this war against the southern rebels, the Anyanya, led by General Joseph Lagu. Week after week villages, homes, churches and schools were wrecked and burned, crops destroyed and livestock stolen or killed. The rape of women and girls was routine (more on this below), and many were carried off to the north as slaves. Between 1972 and 1982 there was a ten-year remission in the fighting. But Nimeiri espoused Islamist extremism, imposing strict *sharia* law throughout the country. The Christian and native religious affiliations of the south made a reprise of war inevitable. This time the southern dissidents called themselves the Sudan People's Liberation Movement (SPLM) and Army (SPLA). They were led by the inspirational John Garang, a Dinka, in partnership with Riek Machar, a leader of the second-largest southern tribe, the Nuer. Today's President, General Omar Hassan al-Bashir, came to power in 1989. Backed by the fundamentalists of the National Islamic Front (NIF), he banned opposition parties and exiled their leaders, while pursuing the war in the south into the new millennium. It is estimated that half a million people died in the first phase of the north–south war, and over two million in the second. At least four and a half million southern Sudanese were displaced inside and outside the country.

The year 2005 stands out in the tortured history of the Sudans as a moment of hope. A Comprehensive Peace Agreement (CPA) was signed, putting an end to the fighting between north and south. Brought about through the efforts of the Inter-Governmental Agency for Development (a group of nations comprising Sudan and some of its neighbours), supported by the so-called 'Troika' of Western states (Norway, the USA and the UK), it was finally signed in Nairobi on 9 January 2005. The signatories were the government of Khartoum, dominated by the renamed NIF, now the National Congress Party (NCP), and, for the south, the SPLM led by Garang. The CPA established a six-year period during which Sudan would be run by two parallel governments, pending a referendum in which the southerners would choose whether to remain part of the Republic of Sudan or become an independent nation state.[3] The CPA enabled the return to the south from refugee camps and urban destitution in the north of an estimated two million impoverished and alienated southerners. It is hardly surprising that when the big moment of the referendum came, the popular vote down there was overwhelmingly for independence.

AFRICA'S 54th STATE

Many who joyfully celebrated 9 July 2011, hoped and believed that any fighting henceforth would be contained within the north, where the 'Arab' regime of the Republic of Sudan would no doubt continue to harass its despised 'black' minorities. But things were not auspicious for the new state. South Sudan is home to more than 60 ethnic groups, many of whom have a long history of enmity. It was, besides, extremely poor. Something of its underdeveloped condition can be imagined from the fact that at independence there were only 40 kilometres of paved road in the entire country. The now fully autonomous government quickly proved autocratic and divisive. The SPLA began carrying out civilian 'disarmament' campaigns involving shocking human rights violations.[4] As James Copnall put it, 'its tendency to centralise power, and the widespread human rights abuses, reminded some within the country of the successive Sudanese governments they had fought so hard to escape'.[5]

The SPLM/SPLA was deeply riven by rivalry between on the one hand President Salva Kiir and the Dinka tribal units, and on the other Vice President Riek Machar and his Nuer interests. In December 2013, political tension turned to rupture. Fighting broke out in the capital between soldiers of the two factions serving in the Presidential Guard. The armed forces now split into what remained of the SPLA, mainly Dinka loyal to President Kiir, and the Sudan People's Liberation Army in Opposition, mainly Nuer and supporting Machar. It was the start of tank and artillery battles between the two armies, both of which attacked and killed civilians in total disregard of international humanitarian law. There was also widespread violence among and between communities. Within a year, one million had been put to flight within, and a further 400,000 beyond, South Sudan's borders. Several of the largest towns were deserted. One-third of South Sudanese were in need of direct food aid.[6] Soon after independence, the United Nations had deployed a mission to South Sudan (UNMISS), but it proved powerless to stop the slaughter. Now its bases were sheltering 80,000 people, and basic supplies for them were running short. Amnesty International, noting that in a single month China had delivered more than 1,000 tonnes of rocket systems, grenade launchers, automatic rifles and ammunition to the SPLA, called for a comprehensive international arms embargo on South Sudan.[7]

Ceasefires were brokered in January and May 2014, and again in August 2015, but were ignored by forces on the ground. In its report for 2015–16, Amnesty describes how both sides were deliberately attacking unarmed civilians, based on their ethnicity or assumed political affiliations, and destroying hospitals, schools and places of worship. No prisoners were taken: captured fighters were executed. Public and private property as well as food stores and humanitarian aid supplies were looted. Aid workers and UN staff were attacked, detained, harassed and threatened. Of the population forced to flee only the lucky ones found shelter in IDP camps – many were driven into swamps and forests.[8] One of the cruellest aspects of war in South Sudan is the recruitment of young boys aged 13 to 17. The youngest of these child soldiers are used as cooks, bearers and bodyguards, the older ones are fully fledged combatants.[9]

UNENDING CONFLICT IN RUMP SUDAN

And was there peace now in the north, in the new, truncated, Republic of Sudan? Far from it. For one thing, petroleum had become a new source of strife. Exploration for oil had begun back in the 1970s and 1980s, revealing large reserves. At first its extraction by the US oil company Chevron had been interrupted and delayed by the violent response of rebel militias to the displacement and distress the oil operations caused to many local communities. Before long, however, bolder international oil giants weighed in. After the millennium production boomed and, despite much of the revenue accruing to South Sudan, the northern state emerged with plenty to spend on its military, enabling the continuation of violent repression within its own borders.[10] It should be noted that China, Malaysia, Sweden, Britain, France and Canada all had oil companies directly or indirectly involved in Sudan, giving them a vested interest in the regime. Their failure to speak out against its atrocities, as Jok observes, has made them 'partners with the state in human destruction'.[11]

Among the victims of that destruction are the people of the Nuba Mountains in South Kordofan, just north of the new international border. The Nuba are a 'black' African people, long oppressed by the Arab-supremacist regime. They deeply resented being separated from kin in the south by the new state border. The region housed a considerable presence of oppositional forces of the Sudan People's Liberation Movement-North, capable of putting up a fierce resistance to the forces of Khartoum. Open warfare broke out in 2011. Human Rights Watch has estimated that, three years into this conflict, more than a million people had been displaced.[12] The Sudan Air Force drop cluster bombs on civilian areas in South Kordofan. They are reported to have bombed 26 health facilities, leaving only two hospitals to serve a population of over a million people.[13] In May 2016, the Troika were moved to issue a statement of deep concern about continued aerial bombardment of South Kordofan, and the Sudan government's shameless expulsion of the Head of Office for Coordination of Humanitarian Affairs in Sudan (OCHA).[14]

An altogether bigger war, however, was continuing in Darfur, a region in the west of the Republic of Sudan, with a population of six million and a land area equal to that of France. Despite the fact that most Darfuris are Muslim, and Arabic is a language common to many, conflict had been endemic in the region since the 1980s and 1990s.[15] Violence was at first localized, and the cause, or at least the prompt, was climatic: repeated seasons of drought and famine. Some Darfuri tribes, notably the Fur, Daju, Berti and Massalit, inhabiting western Darfur, on the border with Chad, are agriculturalists, living sedentary lives. Others, such as the Zaghawa in the north, and the Baqqara in the south, are nomadic cattle and camel herders. There is also a degree of 'racial' differentiation, the agriculturalists being predominantly of the 'black' African phenotype while most (but not all) of the nomadic tribes have more 'Arab' features. As their livestock was threatened by the increasing aridity of the grasslands, the nomadic tribes began raiding the farmlands for their water resources and vegetation. When the farming communities mobilized an armed movement, the Darfur Liberation Front, to resist them, Arab militias, notably the notorious mounted *Janjaweed*, intensified their attacks on villages. At first Khartoum denied that it was involved in the conflict, but government forces, recognizable by their troops' uniforms, their military vehicles and aircraft, were clearly present in the region supporting the *Janjaweed*. In early 2003, the Darfur rebels attacked a government military garrison in the town of Gulu, killing 195 soldiers, and the conflict escalated to outright war. The 'pattern of destruction' inflicted on Darfuri civilians by government forces was described by Robert Collins as follows:

> The men were killed, often mutilated, the women raped, and the children sometimes abducted. The village was burnt, the livestock seized, the fields torched, and the infrastructure – wells, irrigation works, schools, clinics – methodically destroyed in a systematic scheme to drive the African population from their ancestral holdings. Ethnic cleansing to the *Janjaweed* meant clearing the land for Arab colonization.[16]

Eric Reeves estimated in 2005 that more than a million children had been killed, raped, wounded, displaced and traumatized in the Darfur conflict, and he wrote that 'the suffering and destruction of children in Darfur is an obscenity beyond reckoning, beyond redemption, beyond forgiveness'.[17] In 2007 an African Union/United Nations 'hybrid mission' was established in Darfur, but there was little to show for it. Violence continued unaffected by the division of Sudan in 2011, reaching a new peak in 2013, when more than half a million more people were displaced – to join the two and a half million already in camps in Darfur and Chad.

The Darfur conflict had social, political and international dimensions too. Many 'black' Darfuris were profoundly alienated from the increasingly Islamist and Arab-supremacist Sudanese state, while the state for its part refused the demands of the Justice and Equality Movement, as the Darfuri defenders now called themselves, for greater political representation in Khartoum. The international community insistently called for a ceasefire and humanitarian aid, and a United Nations Disaster and Assessment Coordination Team was deployed to Darfur. The UN Security Council imposed an arms embargo on all entities operating in the region (with the inexcusable exception of the government of Sudan).[18] Eventually, belatedly, the international community began talking of 'war crimes and crimes against humanity' being committed by the Sudanese government. By mid-2004 the words 'ethnic cleansing' and 'genocide' were being voiced. UN Secretary-General Kofi Annan, on a trip to Sudan, asked 'have we learned nothing from Rwanda?' and stated that 'whatever the language we use

Many Darfuris have been driven to seek refuge in neighbouring countries. These drawings are by Darfuri children in a camp in Chad, remembering their experiences of the conflict they fled. They were gathered by Anna Schmitt during a visit to the camp on behalf of the NGO Waging Peace.

to describe atrocities in Darfur ... the international community cannot stand idle'.[19] In March 2005, after hearing a report of a UN Commission of Inquiry into potential crimes against humanity in Darfur, the Security Council (at last) voted for Sudan's leaders to be referred to the International Criminal Court (ICC). The ICC's Chief Prosecutor accepted grounds for a formal investigation, and the process now began to roll slowly towards the moment in March 2009 when Omar al-Bashir, along with four of his ministers, would be indicted on five counts of crimes against humanity (murder, extermination, forcible transfer, torture and rape) and two counts of war crimes (pillaging and intentionally directing attacks against civilians). A warrant was issued for their arrest. A trial has never taken place, however, and al-Bashir continues secure in the presidency of Sudan.

The wars on the periphery of Sudan have also been felt in Khartoum. The peoples of South Kordofan, Blue Nile and Darfur have sympathizers and supporters throughout the state, even among some of the Arab types of the dominant ethnicity, and in the capital city many students and intellectuals fiercely oppose the al-Bashir regime. The NCP, and its predecessor the NIF, have been in control for a quarter of a century. Elections, when they have occasionally been held, have been blatantly unfree and unfair, so that the NCP's power has never been democratically sourced. Opposition parties and trade unions have been neutered, and the much-feared National Intelligence and Security Service (NISS) has its spies everywhere, monitoring and curbing journalists and the media, and dealing ruthlessly with dissenters. Thousands of individuals have been seized and 'disappeared' into prisons known as 'ghost houses', in which extreme forms of torture are known to be used in interrogation.[20] The principal rebel armed groups fighting the Sudanese state in Darfur, Kordofan and Blue Nile have latterly joined forces in an alliance they call the Sudan Revolutionary Front. Its aim is ambitious: the complete overthrow of the NCF/al-Bashir regime, a separation of religion and state, and the redistribution of wealth from the domineering centre to the oppressed peripheral regions. The response of the state has been to redouble its repression, for which it has been fiercely criticized by international organizations. In May 2016, 39 international NGOs and individuals wrote an open letter to the UN Human Rights Council in concern about the excessive use of force by the Sudanese authorities.[21]

THE CONDITION OF WOMEN IN SUDAN

Here we should pause for a moment and wonder: how were women faring in this violent history? Digging into the texts, and painfully aware of the constraints on Sudanese women today, I was surprised to learn that women were active in the movement to end colonial rule way back in the 1940s, and that they founded a Sudanese Women's Union (SWU) in 1952, four years before the British withdrew. By 1955 the SWU was publishing a magazine, *Sawt al-Marra* (*The Women's Voice*), addressing controversial questions such as the right of women to choose their marriage partners. The SWU collaborated closely with progressive political parties and trade unions, pressing on them issues of equal pay and pensions, education for women and maternity leave. In the late colonial period not a few women were working in paid employment, often in clerical or nursing jobs, but also in teaching and other professions. Each time it returned, military dictatorship was a set-back for women, and many participated in the civilian uprisings for democracy in 1964 and subsequently.

When introducing *sharia* law in September 1983, the regime banned the SWU and arrested its leaders. Nonetheless a women's peace movement, the Peace Mothers Society, soon emerged, and forged a partnership with women's organizations in the south in calling for an end to the civil war. In 1989 when the NIF seized power, almost half the women employed in the public sector lost their jobs, and more than a hundred women's voluntary groups and societies, and the women's sections of opposition parties, were closed down. In 1990, al-Bashir pronounced on the deportment of 'the ideal Sudanese woman', and the following year issued a government order for all women to wear the *hijab*. Women who refused to follow the new dress rules, continued to work with unrelated men in employment or failed to observe the terms of the 1991 Public Order Act were subject to arrest, flogging and long terms of imprisonment in Omdurman Women's Prison.[22] Even today, the *sharia* regime of the Republic of Sudan continues seriously to undermine women's status, deprive them of their rights and diminish their ability to participate meaningfully in public life, according to recent reports by rights-defending organizations.[23]

In the 'African' south of Sudan, the familial system of the ancient pre-Christian and pre-Islamic society was profoundly patriarchal and subordinating of women. These practices lived on adaptively, despite the influx of missionaries and *imams*, so that even now they shape expectations and norms. Traditionally, marriage is less an individual matter than an institution involving whole families, demarcating and tying together kinship groups. Marriage proposals are instigated by the man, or his family, who approach the woman's father for permission. A bride price, often a considerable sum in cash or cattle, must be paid to the woman's family. As Orly Stern puts it, 'lives are structured around cows, marriage and children: cows give you marriage, marriage gives you children'. In such a society, clearly, remaining single is not an option for women. 'Unmarried women are scorned and not taken seriously, and are considered lowly by society.' To be a second and subsequent wife is far better than to be no wife at all.[24]

The two long periods of north–south war between 1958 and 2005 had profound effects on women in the south. As men went to the bush with the armies and militias, women were obliged to take on family responsibilities that had previously been those of their fathers, husbands, brothers and sons. They also found themselves in demand as teachers in schools, and as untrained nursing aids in clinics and hospitals. Especially from 1983, many joined the armed forces, some as soldiers, others in support roles as carers, cooks and porters. This augmentation of the women's role due to war had an 'up' side – it gave many a new confidence and a perspective on gender change.[25] The Interim Constitution for South Sudan proposed under the Comprehensive Peace Agreement of 2005 contained several optimistic provisions. South Sudanese women would get equal pay for equal work; equal participation in public life; an end to 'harmful customs' undermining women's dignity, and the right to own property and share in family estates. The constitution also stipulated that 25 per cent of political seats across all levels of government would be reserved for women. The interim government set up a Ministry of Gender, Social Welfare and Religious Affairs to 'mainstream' gender throughout the new institutions. The words augured well for the future, and the South Sudan Women's Association was meanwhile working hard to empower women, while keeping a sceptical eye on realities and judging outcomes against promises. But, as independence day dawned, Asha Arabi would write, 'Patriarchy remains prominent in South Sudan … Men dominate the economic, social and political sphere, benefitting from advantageous treatment at almost every level to the disadvantage of their female counterparts.'[26]

In the eyes of the world, the Sudans have been, like their neighbour the Democratic Republic of the Congo, notorious for the scarcely believable amount of rape and other physical abuse of women and children perpetrated by all sides in their prolonged armed conflicts. (It should also be recorded that men, especially young men and boys, are frequently raped. The perpetrators however, as in the rape of females, are male.) In the north, the crimes committed in the war in Darfur, mainly by men of the Sudan Armed Forces and their proxies the *Janjaweed* cavalries, included many of a sexual nature. The Coalition for International Justice and the US State Department's Atrocities Documentation Project reported, on the basis of more than a thousand interviews with Darfuris conducted in refugee camps in Chad, the nature of the atrocities committed at the peak of the war in mid-2004. Here are some of their findings. Women of all ages, from the very old to the youngest girl, were subject to gang rape, sometimes for days on end. The penetration was both vaginal and anal, sometimes with objects, and in some cases while the survivors were stripped naked and pinned down in spread-eagle restraint. Rape frequently ended in death. Many pregnant women had their stomachs cut open and the foetus removed and brutalized. Babies too had their stomachs sliced. Women's breasts were slashed, babies killed by beating them against trees and on the ground. Few women victims would report the attacks, for were they to do so they were likely to have the blame turned on themselves, as guilty of *zena*, or adultery, and punished by death. The government and *Janjaweed* forces also raped men and boys in Darfur, and mutilated many by castration. All these actions were accompanied by racializing insults: you 'blacks', you 'slaves'.[27] More recently the British NGO, Waging Peace, has published a report based on testimony from 77 survivors of rape in Darfur over the preceding ten-year period, dedicating it to women survivors, as a tribute to their strength and courage. They found that 82 per cent of the stories recounted involved multiple rapists. Three-quarters of the women they interviewed had not reported the assault, either to police or the UN Mission in Darfur (UNAMID), despite many of the attacks having occurred in UNAMID camps.[28] Kelly Askin suggests that sexual violence in Darfur should be seen as committed both opportunistically and strategically. It is 'men as men', exerting their will over 'available' creatures, while for the military and political command it serves the purpose of demoralizing and destroying the targeted ethnic group. The strategists energetically prevent observation and reporting of their war crimes by blocking peacekeepers and other internationals and journalists from reaching Darfur to investigate and report.[29]

Back in the power centre, in Khartoum, the police and guards of the security state also deploy the weapon of sexual violence. Here the National Intelligence and Security Service uses sexual slander to threaten and rape to punish women activists opposing the regime and women human rights defenders.[30] Meanwhile, in the new state of South Sudan, according to a recent report by the UN High Commissioner for Human Rights, sexual violence continues relentlessly. The forces of rivals Salva Kiir and Riek Machar engage massively in rape, sometimes followed by murder by hanging, dismemberment and burning alive.[31] The untold hundreds of thousands of women that have fled with their children across South Sudan's borders to seek refuge in camps in Ethiopia, Kenya, Uganda and the Congo continue to experience sexual violence, both inside the camps and when leaving their confines to forage for firewood and water.[32]

FLIGHT FROM 'FRAGILE STATES'

The Fragile States Index maintained by the US think tank Fund for Peace shows that, in the year 2015, South Sudan was the most extreme case of a 'fragile state', topping the top-four countries of the world on 'very high alert'. The Republic of Sudan was little better, standing in fourth place but nonetheless on very high alert.[33] One aspect of Sudan's fragility is a huge number of IDPs – people who have been forced to leave their homes while remaining within the borders of the country. The International Displacement Monitoring Centre calculated in 2009 that with almost five million internally displaced, the (still-unified) Sudan was 'the country with the highest number of IDPs in the world, together with Colombia'.[34] It has also experienced the flight of huge numbers of its people to other countries in search of security, a home and a livelihood. Accurate diaspora statistics for any country are notoriously difficult to establish, and those that exist seldom separate refugees from economic migrants. Estimates suggest, however, that Sudanese refugees and asylum seekers abroad may well number one-third of a million.

Many of those who fled the violence in the Sudans have been trapped, and many still remain, in the limbo of refugee camps across the border in neighbouring countries, principally Chad, Uganda, Eritrea and Ethiopia. Sudanese in this 'near abroad' were thought to number around 635,000 in 2006, falling to around 390,000 in 2009. By comparison the numbers of Sudanese refugees reaching distant countries, such as the USA, Italy, the Netherlands and the UK, have been much smaller. There were estimated to be 9,100 Sudan-born people resident in the UK in the year 2000, falling to 3,400 in the year 2006. A hint of the shifts in numbers can be found in the statistics of asylum applications to the UK. The figure for 'applications received' from people originating in Sudan peaked in 2004 at 1,205, falling to a low of 217 in 2009, but rising again in 2015 to a figure of 2,918. In these years an average of 70 per cent of applications were granted.[35] Figures published by the Refugee Council suggest that 2015 marked a recent high point for Sudan, with 528 Sudanese individuals making asylum applications in the last quarter of the year, an increase of 17 per cent on the same quarter the previous year. And Sudan had a higher percentage of its applications granted than any other country: 835 out of 993 decisions made, with only 156 refusals.[36] To put this in perspective, however, we need to note that in 2015, a peak year for flight from Sudan in all directions, the combined countries of the world apparently gave asylum to no less than 744,000 Sudanese and 641,000 South Sudanese.[37]

How many Sudanese are there in London? It is difficult to be sure. The 2011 census data for 'foreign-born' residents show London to have just under 7,000, of whom almost exactly 4,000 were living in Inner London boroughs and 3,000 in Outer London boroughs. The figures of course don't differentiate Sudanese from South Sudanese, because partition would only occur that year. Besides, as we know, the figures for those who are foreign-born always omit the families they have generated since arriving in the UK. An International Organization of Migration mapping exercise in 2006 suggested a figure of between 10,000 and 25,000 Sudanese Londoners. Due to the government's practice of 'dispersal' for asylum seekers since the 1999 Immigration Act, other sizeable communities of several thousand Sudanese have built up in Brighton, Manchester and cities in the East Midlands and Scotland.[38]

I began my search for Sudanese life in London by looking for their community organizations. Over the three years I've been writing this book, there have been multiple occasions as the chapters progressed when I've gone out on to the London streets in search of associations, clubs and advice centres of different incoming communities: Kurds, Somalis and so on. I go armed with a list of organizations culled from the web, to locate the street addresses given for each, and hopefully to meet someone who can put me in touch with the members of their community. It has been an experience common to most of these forays that one address after another I find shut and boarded up. Or the given house number turns out to be some shop or business that has nothing to do with such a community association, and whose present occupants have no idea where it can have relocated – if it exists at all.

However, on the very first afternoon I began chasing 'Sudan' around the streets of North London, I struck lucky. On the outer edge of the Borough of Camden, not far from the boundary with Brent, I came across a community centre of which the door readily swung open. Inside were signs of lively activity. And yes, here, among other things, was the Sudan Women's Association. Or rather – what had been founded in 1991 under that name and had more recently become the South Sudan Women's Skills Development Group (SSWSDG). Here I met the energetic Elizabeth Ajith, its coordinator for the last ten years and my first contact with the Sudanese community in London. Elizabeth not only works but also lives in Camden, in the neighbour-hood of Somerstown, near St Pancras. Naturally, it was to Camden Council that the Sudan Women's Association first turned for funding.

SETTLING IN CAMDEN

Elizabeth's Sudanese Women's Association received a generous response from Camden Council, as well as grants from various trusts to whom they also applied for support. Their annual funding from these multiple sources often exceeded £40,000 a year. It was this that enabled them to pay considerable annual rent for a permanent office and weekly meeting space at the multipurpose Abbey Community Centre out in the north-west of the borough, in Belsize Road. Their programmes have been impressive, including top-up courses in English, maths and science for school-age children; English as a second language for adults; 'mother tongue' courses in Dinka, Madi and Luo; artwork and dance projects; business start-up skills; mental health awareness; and introductions to different religious faiths. Sewing and knitting classes have been staple activities that continue today. Education about eradicating female genital mutilation has been important, because this remains a widespread practice in South Sudan. But there had been fun days too, with trips to Kew, Brighton and other places of interest. Increasingly, the SSWSDG has aimed to support the council's 'cohesion and integration' policies, which has involved opening up some of their activities to individuals from a diverse range of different cultural groups in the neighbourhood. Elizabeth herself has carried out a research project on the 'self-identity' differences of first- and second-generation South Sudanese migrants, in which she found the youngsters much more inclined than their parents to identify as British.[39] 'To be honest,' said one, 'I strongly feel I belong to Camden Town. The place you feel accepted is where you belong.'

As I dug deeper into the life of the South Sudan Women's Skills Development Group, I wondered more and more: yes, but where are the *Sudanese* Londoners now, the women from Khartoum, Darfur, Kordofan? On the web, Googling 'Sudan/London', I came across an organization called Waging Peace. Despite its rather global pacifist title, Waging Peace turned out to be strongly focused on supportive work among those in flight from war in the Sudans, whose plight concerns them deeply. A committed team of women activists, I found they had fostered the creation of a group calling itself the Sudan Women's Group in London. And this turned out to be the very thing I had been seeking, a gathering of women from the Republic of Sudan, originating in Khartoum and the northern peripheries – Darfur, Nuba Mountains, Blue Nile. Waging Peace arranged a meeting for me with some members of this group, from whom I learned that their first idea had been to obtain an office and meeting space alongside Elizabeth's project at the Abbey Community Centre in Camden. However, there had been no space available, and currently the group was meeting here and there, as and when, while continuing to search for a permanent home in Camden or nearby. Their aim, I was told by one of their members, is for further 'coexistence', i.e. enabling people to live between

Above: Elizabeth Ajith, founder of the Sudan Women's Association, in the London Borough of Camden.

Opposite: Marwa Kessinger and her children join a demonstration against the Sudan government's bombing of Nuba people.

their culture of origin and culture of re-homing. They wish to retain their Nuba, Darfuri or Sudanese identity and cultural 'goods', but at the same time to be fully present in London and in British society. They help each other balance 'being here' with 'being from there'. It's a skill that they want to foster in their London-born children, who, they hope, will be fluent in both English and Arabic.

A little later I came across another Sudanese initiative in Camden, with a rather similar philosophy. Sudan Children in Need is coordinated by Khadiga Khogali, who came to the UK in 2000 from Khartoum where she had lived and studied as one of a family well known and persecuted as critics and opponents of the al-Bashir regime. Since settling in London she'd been thinking a good deal about the importance of fostering the link between the generations of migrants here, in particular the relationship, so often under stress, between children and their parents. She found some others in the nearby Sudanese community thinking in a similar way, and they sat down together and exchanged ideas as to how this relationship might be fostered. Khadiga was at that time living in Cromer Street, in King's Cross. She often found herself walking past a door bearing the logo of the King's Cross Community Development Trust. One day, five or six years ago, she stopped and rang the bell, curious to know more about them and their mission. The response was beyond anything she could have hoped for. The Trust helped the group set up a non-profit company and register as a charity; gave them training and loaned a room for meetings; and went on to show them how to win grants from charitable funders. Today the Sudan Children in Need committee meets on a monthly basis. Their current project is to provide activities that strengthen the relationships between parents and their children – such as Arabic classes for the youngsters. Both fathers and mothers are involved, along with their children. The meetings are held in a neighbourhood hall in Argyll Street, or in individuals' homes. In the early days, some South Sudanese families were involved in the group, but after independence in mid-2011, Khadiga says, many of these went back to Sudan. In this way Sudan Children in Need became, not in principle but in practice, a northern, i.e. Sudanese, group.

The next and last Sudanese voluntary organization that showed up on my radar was barely an organization at all, simply called the Asylum Clinic. The initiative of a couple of committed activists,

Asma Salah and Gasim Ibrahim, it proved to be a challenging project involving outreach to newly arrived asylum seekers from Sudan aimed at drawing them to a weekly meeting where they would find friendship and practical advice. The project was offering inclusion to some very isolated and distressed young men, sharing information with them to help them achieve documentation and start to turn mere existence into a positive process of settlement. Gasim and Asma told me that in developing their Asylum Clinic they had been encountering a painful tension that appeared to be political in nature. They were trying to engage the support and resources of some of the long-settled Sudanese in London for the benefit of their present-day incoming asylum seekers, reduced to penury and a chaotic lifestyle by the devastation they had fled, the rigours of their journey and their isolation here. They had been disappointed to find some (though not all) of these well-established individuals unsympathetic to the newcomers. Discussing this phenomenon, we surmised it to be at root a difference of generation now taking shape as a class difference: those who had migrated from Sudan several decades ago had not in the main been refugees seeking asylum. Many would have been secure individuals, in tune with the regime, coming to Europe to get higher education, professional status or a rewarding job. In their eyes, these newcomers in flight from war were an unwelcome presence, threatening to the established community, lowering standards and no doubt profoundly out of tune with the authorities of the homeland. They made it clear to Asma and Gasim that they believed their young protégés were 'on the make'. They suspected their hard-luck stories were 'cooked up' for the purpose of achieving asylum and the right to remain in the UK. Given the great diversity of ethnicity, war-history and political positioning in their country of origin, it's perhaps not too surprising that some bitterness like this continues to be expressed in the diaspora. The International Organization of Migration, in the course of a 'mapping' exercise among the Sudanese communities in London, found them to be 'highly politicised, fragmented and dispersed … as a reflection of the reality of conflict and civil strife in Sudan'.[40]

CAMDEN: PARTNERING VOLUNTARY ORGANIZATIONS

What kind of support was Camden Council providing for the needy families who over the last three decades had arrived by one route or another from the Sudans? Elizabeth Ajith was warm in her gratitude to Kiran Patel, Grants Officer in the council's Communities and Third Sector Team, who had given advice and support from way back in 1992, when the Sudan Women's Association first saw the light of day. The first thing I learned from Kiran is that the council has no better idea than the rest of us just how many Sudanese, south and north, are resident in the borough. The census' 'foreign-born' data put it at quite a modest number: 375. There are no Sudanese councillors or senior officers who might have direct links to the community to substantiate this. Only one thing is for sure, Kiran says: borough borders don't really 'work' in matters of cultural communities, anyway. People travel. You may fund an organization or an event as being local to Camden, but it has to be on the understanding that the beneficiaries are likely to turn up from far and near. Being so scattered, they all the more need support, she adds. She often advises them to seek Lottery funding, which is not bounded by borough.

Guided by Kiran I did my homework on Camden's demography as revealed in *The Camden Plan: 2012–2017*.[41] Economic inequality is a primary feature. While average income in Camden is actually little different from that of London as a whole, that figure is derived by averaging income in some neighbourhoods with very poor populations (such as Somerstown) with that of others that are seriously well-to-do (such as St John's Wood and Hampstead). A second important feature of Camden is ethno-cultural diversity. Rather than possessing one dominant minority rivalling white British residents, as Tower Hamlets has its Bangladeshis, it has a veritable mixity in terms of country of origin, and in terms of the census's 'race' categories, with a sizeable BAME community including many 'white other' from European and New Commonwealth countries. The borough has a huge annual 'churn' in its population. Even more than Hounslow, which sees one-fifth of its population arrive in or depart from the borough every year, in the case of Camden fully one-third are on the move – an astonishing number. Of course Camden has been experiencing, just like other councils, dire cuts in government funding, and like them is faced with the dilemma: how to achieve ever-more ambitious goals with ever-diminishing resources. The plan's answer is to save money by enlisting 'partners' ('we can't do this alone'), and building their 'resilience' ('help people gain the ability to do it for themselves'). Heard that somewhere before? This all-important strategic relationship the borough aspires to establish with the voluntary sector is set out in a separate document.[42] There are, apparently, an astonishing 2,500 voluntary organizations in Camden, and a highly engaged population: one-quarter of all adult residents say they are regularly giving time to help others.[43] So far, so good. The council's voluntary sector strategy is to be more collaborative with these many voluntary sector organizations and to help them achieve a sustainable income. One approach to the latter is to set up particularized 'streams' of funding for their support, such as the Equalities and Cohesion Fund, and, committed ahead as far as 2024, a Strategic Partnership Fund for neighbourhoods and equalities.

Local authority funds for outward spending are of two kinds, known as 'non-discretionary' and 'discretionary'. Non-discretionary funding is that which is paid out to charities or other organizations to enable them to provide services on behalf of the council. Discretionary funds are for grants to neighbourhood or other groups, including, in this case of Camden, the SSWSDG. Back in the 1990s, Kiran's Third Sector Team allocated discretionary funding under the guidance of a Grants Sub-Committee. Refugees, especially unaccompanied children, tended to be identified as a group in special need. In this light, the Sudanese Women's Association, as it then was, had been invited to apply. Kiran explained that

the key thing was, and still is, Camden's approach which we call a 'funder-plus' approach. What this means is that you don't just give a grant to an organization, but actually go on thereafter to support its development. We must help them to acquire skills, enable them to 'hold' the organization and achieve stability. You might, as a beneficiary, get a grant for a specific purpose. But then we would ask you, 'What else do you need to do now to succeed?' Always in Camden we have had this ethos of 'funding-plus'.

It would be the Grants Officer, such as Kiran, who would support the beneficiary organizations thereafter. In any one annual cycle of funding, she would spend half a year on capacity-building with them, and a further half a year monitoring their progress. Today in the Communities and Third Sector Team they have staff explicitly titled Outcome Development Officers, to help groups achieve their goals.

In a manner similar to some of the local councils we have seen heretofore, Camden pins its discretionary funding on to an equality impact assessment, under the Equality Act of 2010. They find it particularly helpful in getting funding to women's organizations, since gender is a key dimension of the Act. All this worthy intent, however, is hostage to 'the cuts'. Kiran stressed just how the government's austerity budgets have driven down available funds. 'It's extreme', she said. The council as a whole had lost 25 per cent of its budget over the last five years and in a further five years the overall loss would be 50 per cent. And it was discretionary grants in particular that were feeling the pinch – their budget was down to little over £5 million a year. Although that figure represents a drop in funding from previous years, it is nonetheless something of an achievement. The council points out that 'a number of other boroughs either intend to, or already have, cut the vast majority of direct investment in the voluntary sector', so this commitment by Camden represents 'one of the largest local authority investments in the voluntary and community sector in the country'.[44] It may well make the difference between a future wherein the Abbey Community Centre and its tenants, such as the SSWSDG, close down for lack of funding support, or continue to survive and thrive.

OUT OF THE SOUTH: FROM EQUATORIA TO CAMDEN

In the following pages I will tell the stories of four women, as they told them to me. I've chosen them to illustrate (though of course they can never fully represent) the experiences of Sudanese in three different conflict zones: the south (before separation); Darfur; and the Nuba Mountains.

First, meet Grace Oliver. I was introduced to Grace by Elizabeth Ajith, who knows her as a regular member of the SSWSDG, where she goes every Saturday, enjoying the company and making use of the sewing and knitting machines. Grace was born in 1954, and was thus, when we met, in her early sixties. She is of the Bari tribe, and her place of birth was Kajo Keji, a town in Equatoria, in the far south of South Sudan, close to the Ugandan border. Grace's father was employed in the police force where she remembers it was his task to sound a horn to make public announcements. But at a certain age he returned to the village to take up the role of village chief. As appropriate for a man of such status, he had five wives, and 29 or 30 children in all. Grace's mother, Unice, was his third wife, and she had six children – five girls and one boy. Grace was number two. She did not attend primary school because at that time it was government policy, by decree of the autocratic President Ibrahim Abboud, not to provide schooling for children below the age of seven years. But Grace did in fact learn to read and write in her mother tongue, Bari, thanks to the local church (Church of England) where she was active in the choir.

Grace's home was not far from Torit, the town where, in 1956, a mutiny of southern soldiers occurred as independence approached. When this fighting broke out, Grace was still a young child of three or four. She herself can't remember, but it's part of the family's memory that at this moment all the village chiefs of the region, including her father, were called to a meeting in Yei, a town to the west of Kajo Keji. Here the 'Arabs', i.e. forces of the newly independent country, opened fire and shot them, killing all except her father who escaped across the border to Uganda. But there the Ugandan police broke both his wrists. Grace says, 'We had lost him. We asked people to search for him. Someone learned where he was – it was in a town called Arua. Someone went there and brought him home.' This was the time of the insurgency against northern domination by Joseph Lagu's Anyanya. This Grace does recall – how they were armed only with *pangas* (machetes), with scarcely a gun between them. Grace's father was a keen supporter of this resistance movement and would encourage people to donate food in their support. 'On one occasion,' Grace recalls,

the government forces were drawing near to us, but they were separated from us by a big river. My uncle said 'Don't run! Keep down and pray to God for rain so that the river will flood and stop the Arabs from reaching us!' So we prayed. And the water level in the river rose up so that it was in flood. The army couldn't cross. No rain was falling near to us, but our prayers had been heard. It had been raining far away upstream!

Grace was married in 1969 at the age of 15 to a boy of the same age. They were married in the village church. It was not a marriage arranged by the family – these young things chose each other. For some years in her married life Grace was in paid employment as a clerk. Her husband was in business – he had a shop in Yei, where they lived and raised a family of six children. But home, business, lifestyle and childhood were all doomed. Extreme violence came to Yei in the 1980s, during the second period of civil war. The town was destroyed by government forces. The schoolchildren, including Grace's six youngsters, ran into the bush to escape the soldiers. There was to be no return. They fled far and wide. The government forces in Yei seized everyone connected to the resistance. Grace's husband's brother was a brigadier in the SPLA. Knowing Grace to be related to the rebels in this way, they took her and locked her up. She was imprisoned with a group of 15 or more people, in a northern army barracks (Grace calls it the 'Arab' army). At a certain moment a security man kicked open the door and started to shoot into the room. Only four adults and some children survived, Grace and one of her daughters among them. Their bodies, Grace says, were drenched in blood.

In 1994, while the north–south war was still raging, and with ten years yet to pass before the Peace Accord would be in sight, Grace decided to leave Sudan and take refuge in Egypt. Her husband wished to remain in Yei. She wouldn't see him again, for he died only a few years later, still a relatively young man. Their children had been scattered into the bush in the attack on the town and Grace had lost hope of seeing them again. So she set off alone, travelling first to Khartoum, then to Cairo. Here she registered as a refugee with the UN and gained some funding support that helped her to pay her rent. She remained there for six years, one of thousands of Sudanese migrants and refugees in Cairo, paying the price for escape from violence by living a provisional and unsatisfactory life.[45]

From Egypt, strangely, Grace's first move 'to the West' was a flight to Cuba. This can only really be put down to the vagaries of people smugglers on whom Grace, like all refugees who lack resources, relied for the fixing of documentation and flights. Grace had really wanted to go to Canada. She found that life was not at all easy in Cuba. She was saying to herself, 'Let me go back to Africa!' But eventually another smuggler-assisted move brought the possibility of going back across the Atlantic to the UK. Her plane arrived in Gatwick. The UK border officials at the airport gave her a hard time. 'I had a blue passport: they could see I was from Sudan', Grace recounts:

The woman official said, 'Follow me!' and led me here and there, up and down, with my heavy luggage. She told me I must return to Uganda. I said 'No way! Human rights will protect me. If you push me I will kill myself and you will be responsible!' The woman took me to an immigration office where I was held until night time. They took samples of my blood, they examined my body, checking my health in every way.

The officials asked Grace, 'Do you know anyone in the UK?' She told them she had had a brother here. He had died, but his wife and children remained. The officer took their address and contacted them, and they came and picked her up from Gatwick Airport. They took her to their home in High Barnet, and kept her with them for four months. Grace was accepted into the UK as an asylum seeker, eventually given 'leave to remain', and six years later obtained citizenship and a British passport. After many moves from one lodging to another, she now lives in a block of flats behind the busy street market of Queens Crescent in Camden. She lives frugally on her £125 a week Employment and Support Allowance. Today she walks slowly and uses a stick, due to painful arthritis in her back and legs. But, just as when she was a child in South Sudan, she takes an active part in the life of the local Church of England congregation. She tells me she is concerned about the decline in Christian belief in Britain today. In the extraordinary and heartening way that war-scattered people so often manage to do, Grace has re-established contact with her offspring. And war-scattered is the word for it: they are living in Canada, Australia and Botswana. Only one is back in Sudan.

ESCAPE FROM THE NORTH: WAR, CHANCE AND CHOICE

Through Grace's story I've been able to show some of the bitter history of one armed conflict, that between the north and south of her country, that lives on in the memories of some Sudanese women residing today in Camden. Now I want to turn to two women, a generation or more younger than Grace, whose personal histories hold memories of the western war: the bitter and seemingly unending strife over Darfur. Placing side by side the stories these two women tell will enable me to illustrate how a war such as this, taking place in a given region and destroying the well-being of those who live there, is also waged as a civil struggle in and among the politically alert and engaged population elsewhere in Sudan, and particularly in the capital city. First I'll introduce you to Fatima, who is native to Darfur. And then go on to tell the story of Amina, born in Khartoum, where she grew to maturity strongly opposing the militaristic and religious oppression inflicted on Darfur by the al-Bashir regime. Because neither woman wishes to be identifiable, they've chosen pseudonyms here. For the same reason, we have together contrived to change certain personal details, while taking care not to undermine the essential veracity of the stories.

Fatima is a woman of Darfuri origin, now in her thirties, born and brought up in one of the principal towns of the region. At the time of her birth, Nimeiri had already seized power in Sudan's second coup, but his uncompromising military rule and imposition of strict *sharia* law had not yet penetrated Darfur and she looks back with fond memories on her childhood. 'It was very happy', she says. 'We played outside without danger, we would walk or run to and from school, go often to the market. It was peaceful, there was food, we had resources. There was a hospital.' Fatima attended both primary and secondary school in her home town. Then she passed an entrance exam that took her away to university in Khartoum. City life came as a shock. She says, 'There were people begging on the street and in the market – it made me sad to see such poverty. In Darfur people supported each other. You gave freely to help people poorer than yourself, to prevent hardship.' Within the university she found 'relationships between the students were OK'. Nonetheless, they had to be cautious. They were wary of speaking freely to each other in places, such as cafés, where they might be overheard and reported to the authorities. And out in the city, beyond the university walls, there were scary tensions:

> There were various political parties, whose adherents would speak badly of each other. They would fight each other, beat each other up. It was not as bad then as it is now, but even at that time you couldn't protest. You would be beaten, arrested or even killed. We saw what was happening, especially to the boys. So we kept well out of it.

For this reason Fatima didn't want to stay in Khartoum when her studies were complete. Her degree in hand, she went back to find employment in her home city and live once more with her mother and younger siblings. But she was struck by the differences she found there. The cost of living was higher, there were food shortages and supplies were not coming in from the villages. Three years later, the fragile peace was disrupted by a *Janjaweed* attack on neighbouring villages:

> One day we saw people running into the city, coming from the countryside, on foot, on donkeys, carrying bundles on their heads, children trailing behind. If I close my eyes, I can still see it. It was such a shock. They were in flight. Something had happened. But what? At first war didn't cross my mind. I thought maybe there had been a fire.

Life now became miserable. There was increasing violence and robbery, because more local men acquired weapons, at first for self-defence. The guns increased insecurity. A person would fear to come out of a bank with money, or to show a mobile phone.

I asked Fatima, 'Did people understand at that time that the government was backing the *Janjaweed* to do this?' 'Not for sure,' she said, 'but they would guess. The *Janjaweed* are just nomads. Where would they get weapons and horses from? Someone had to be behind them. We assumed it was the government.' The economic situation had been going downhill in Darfur. Education and health services were in decline, so people had been complaining. And the government's response was to say, 'These Darfuris are black Africans. They are not real Sudanese. The real Sudanese are Arabs. Let's drive these people out of the country. Sudan is *our* country.' Now, Fatima concurred, she and her family and community recognized themselves as black Africans. But they were all, she says, also practising and believing Muslims. True, the strict *sharia* law being imposed by the regime felt unnatural to them. They wished to practise Islam in their own way, the way that felt comfortable to them. For Fatima, 'It should be a choice, not something forced upon you. It should come from your heart and your beliefs.' But the attitude of the government was to say of the 'black' Darfuris, without good reason in Fatima's view, 'They'll abandon Islam, they'll become Christians. Get rid of the black Africans.'

Now some of those 'black' Africans did indeed begin to talk of leaving the country. Fatima went on:

> It was men who started to leave first. They were most at risk in the violence. And there were no jobs for them, with the economy down. They couldn't keep their families. Even educated men could no longer get employment. If you were from Darfur, even if you had an education, you couldn't get work in Khartoum. So thousands of Darfuri men began to leave. Boys can go. It was less easy for a girl to leave the family.

Fatima's husband was one of those who left. He reached the UK, where, to cut a very long and painful story short, Fatima would eventually follow, gaining entry on grounds of family reunion. She would start a new life here, making a home and raising a family, not a million miles from where Amina had already settled.

Amina's life, like Fatima's, was turned upside down by the war in Darfur, but her engagement in the strife was due not to contingency but to political choice. Unlike Fatima, she was not Darfuri born and bred, nor had she ever lived there. She and her family were denizens of Khartoum. 'Arab', they would have been termed by some Sudanese. But Amina would never identify herself this way. After all, she explained to me emphatically, 'The so-called "Arabs" of northern Sudan have destroyed the nation! People in power like to think of themselves as Arabs because they are in thrall to Qatar and Saudi Arabia. They are playing a game of money and power.' Amina's mother was a teacher, and so Amina had obtained an excellent schooling, after which university was a natural progression. But along with a higher education in the sciences, the University of Khartoum endowed her with political values and opinions that made her a strong opponent of the al-Bashir regime. During her final year, in 2002, when the conflict in Darfur was intensifying, Amina and her classmates set up an activist organization of Darfuris and their supporters in the university. It was a risky move, bringing them under the scrutiny of the National Intelligence and Security Services. Amina was already suspect due to the fact that her highly qualified and high-profile father had never hidden his opposition to the Islamism and militarism of the regime. His ideas had long-since resulted in his dismissal from government employment. Now hers would cost Amina her freedom, and threaten her life.

One day she was seized by the security services. She was held for days and interrogated with great brutality. She does not know where she was imprisoned, nor for how long, nor who her interrogators were. She says, 'Some wore masks. They just require you to accept their ideas. Then they pass you to the psychopathic ones.' She was subjected for days to torture that included multiple and wounding rapes. The trauma has had the effect of erasing large tracts of memory from this period, although she does recall at one point being in an obstetrics hospital. Who took her there? She has no idea. She remembers several moments in a lorry. Eventually, again without any clear recollection of how she travelled there, she found herself in Port Sudan on the Red Sea coast. What she came to understand is that her escape from NISS and from Khartoum was being engineered by a kindly and politically motivated individual, with resources and influence, committed to helping activists in trouble such as she. This unknown helper appears, first, to have paid for a boat fare to enable her to travel from Port Sudan to – where? A foreign port. Amina doesn't even know which, because when the ship docked she was deep in the hold, its doors were locked, and the next thing she knew the ship was back in motion. After a further voyage she was released and disembarked – back in Port Sudan. She returned to Khartoum, defeated.

Amina's second attempt to migrate was successful, however. The same good-hearted supporter furnished her with a fake British passport bearing an identity photo of a woman not unlike herself, wearing a headscarf. He engaged a people smuggler, paying him half his fee, together with the money for airline tickets. He was to travel with Amina on a flight out of the country, sitting beside her as her 'husband'. The plane eventually arrived at London Heathrow Airport. The fake passport did its job – the 'couple' passed without hindrance through immigration. The smuggler then took Amina out of the airport, where they were met by another unknown man – who arrived with a second instalment of cash to pay the smuggler for his work. This new stranger sat Amina down for a coffee and told her, 'Now you are in the UK, you have to go to a government department called the Home Office and apply for asylum.' He said, 'It's better I don't come with you – I might be suspected of people smuggling.' He instructed her how to get there, gave her a little cash, and left her to it. And so Amina found her way, as directed, to the Home Office in Croydon where she experienced, like thousands before and thousands since, a queue and some questions; another queue, more questions – and (a story too long to detail) was eventually released into, set adrift in, British society. We can only imagine her, back then in 2004, stepping out into the chill air of autumn, taking a deep breath, and setting out alone to find a lodging, a living, a life as an 'asylum seeker'. As Fatima, propelled into exile by the same war, would do later, she began the process of re-homing as a North Londoner.

My final story is that of Marwa, to whom I was introduced by a mutual friend in Camden. Marwa's family originates in the Nuba Mountains of South Kordofan state. They are thus, like Fatima and Amina, citizens of 'rump' Sudan, the Republic of Sudan in its new form. The Nuba people, with their dark skin as mentioned above, are despised and inferiorized by the Sudanese Arab elite as 'black' and 'African'. They have a distinctive and rich ethnicity and culture and, like the Darfuris, a long history of resisting domination and repression from the centre. The 1990s saw intense localized warfare between the Sudanese armed forces and the resident southern rebel force, the Sudan People's Liberation Movement-North. A ceasefire in 2002, and the Comprehensive Peace Agreement of 2005, reduced the levels of death and injury. But when, in 2011, an independent South Sudan was created, the Nuba Mountain people were infuriated at being left out of it, stuck north of a now international border at the mercy of a state that wished them dead. They are still in rebellion, and even today suffer government bombing raids that kill many civilians.

Marwa's maternal and paternal grandparents were all born and lived their lives in the Nuba Mountains. It was the next generation, Marwa's mother Bagara and father Ahmed, who made the move to Khartoum. Life in the capital was made feasible by her father's achievement of a school education, and subsequent professional qualification in accounting for business management. But he didn't leave behind his Nuba identity in this move – nor did he wish to do so. In a voluntary capacity, using his management skills, he actively helped Nuban people improve their economic chances by setting up small businesses. He was meanwhile quite open about his political commitment to opposing the al-Bashir regime. As a result, in 2006 he was dismissed from his management job in a major government institution in Khartoum. This, Marwa says, was pure discrimination. 'People in Khartoum couldn't tolerate his kind of activity. Everything to do with the Nuba is provocative to the Khartoum regime. They say, "The Nubans are against us. We shouldn't have anything to do with them".' At this point in his career, Marwa's father had little choice but to become self-employed. He set up in business on his own account, choosing to relocate for this purpose to the southern region, where he could continue his voluntary work among the many Nuban refugees there. He was instrumental in setting up the Nuba Mountain Bank in Juba, the Southern capital, and obtaining approval for it from the Central Bank.

Marwa was born in Khartoum towards the end of the 1970s and is thus now, as I meet her, in her late thirties. Due to her father's income she and her five siblings had been able to get a full education. Socially, however, it hadn't been easy for them in the capital. The school classes were culturally and 'racially' mixed. The majority were 'Arabs'. Children from Darfur and the Nuba Mountains were routinely called 'thieves' and 'blacks'. The teachers varied, she remembers now. Some were even-handed and respectful, others prejudiced and abusive. Marwa stuck it out, however, got good results, and went on to university where she studied accountancy. During her early twenties, in the course of her pro-Nuban activities in Khartoum, she was introduced to Jaily, a Nuban man who was looking for a wife. A few years later Jaily was driven by the attentions of the Sudanese authorities to flee the country, and he obtained asylum in Holland. In 2003 they decided to get married, to which Marwa's parents readily agreed. Jaily was by now well settled in Rotterdam, where his education as a mechanical engineer had enabled him to step into a good job, and he now had EU documentation. Her family were sad to see Marwa go, but they couldn't help but be relieved that she would escape a hazardous future in Khartoum.

Not long after arriving in Rotterdam, Marwa became pregnant – but sadly this baby did not survive to term. Subsequent attempts were successful, though, and soon the couple had two children, Ahmed and Jasmin. After the birth of Jasmin, Marwa began to feel she wanted to focus on study and work, and for this she believed a move onwards to the UK would give her more opportunity. Jaily however was happy in his job and didn't want to relocate. So in 2008, when Ahmed was three years old and Jasmin 18 months, Marwa upped sticks and came to London. Here the main problem she met was finding affordable, healthy and permanent housing for the three of them. She recounts dismaying stories of uncooperative council housing departments and ruthless, mean landlords that cost her eight years in temporary and insecure accommodation. At one point she was reduced to pawning her only remaining wealth, a few gold bracelets, just to stay in a hotel for three weeks.

Today she is settled at last in a council property to which she has a secure tenancy, and her children are settled and doing well in their schools. Marwa herself has restarted her studies: for a full and recognized accountancy qualification that will enable her to practise in the UK. Eventually, she would very much like to bring her father and mother to London, for her father, now in his late sixties, continues to be a visible opponent of the regime. Only three weeks ago, she told me during an interview in early 2016, another Nuban activist was shot dead in Khartoum. Her father is continually urged by his friends, for his own safety, to join the ruling party. But he refuses. Here in London, although the Sudanese government are believed to spy on the London Nuban community, Marwa, like her father and mother, is not afraid to persist in her defence of the Nuba and her defiance of the regime. We stood together outside the Sudanese Embassy, where she and her two children held placards of protest, while other Nuban Londoners, dressed in traditional horned helmets and grass skirts, danced and shouted: 'Stop bombing the Nuba Mountains! Send al-Bashir to the International Criminal Court!'[46]

6

Syrian War, Migration Crisis and 'Refugees Welcome' in Lambeth

In the foregoing chapters we've seen four instances of armed strife that flared during the last two and a half decades – in Turkey, Somalia, Sri Lanka and the Sudan – and the resulting flight of many thousands of refugees, some drawn to the UK, and particularly to London. We've seen how the British government progressively toughened its reception regime and tightened its border controls during this period to reduce the number of successful asylum applications, and how purposefully it has worked to deflect those who succeed in entering the country away from the capital to less popular regions. We've seen how, notwithstanding, Greater London has received and settled many refugees in these 25 years, swelling its existing migrant communities and adding to the capital's ethno-cultural diversity. We've looked at the various approaches of four selected borough councils – Hackney, Tower Hamlets, Hounslow and Camden – to meet the challenge of integration and cohesion in and among their ever-more mixed populations. And, borough by borough, we've translated demographic statistics into human realities, tracing the stories of particular women incomers – the violence that cost them their homes, perilous journeys of migration, exhausting processes of border-transit and legalization, and the practical and emotional challenges of re-homing. These incidents occurred in the recent past. But in this concluding chapter I step fully into the present (it is February 2017 as I write these words), and into what's being termed a 'migration crisis' bigger than any experienced since the Second World War.

As this new year begins, hundreds of thousands of refugees are gathered along the Mediterranean littoral at the southern borders of European countries hoping to find safety and acceptance in the countries of the European Union and beyond. At a minimum there are 363,348, because this is the number of refugees actually registered in the course of 2016, almost equally divided between Greece and Italy, with smaller numbers arriving on the shores of Cyprus, Malta and Spain.[1] They come from many countries of the Middle East, Asia and Africa. For example, 11 per cent of the Mediterranean arrivals in Europe during 2016 came from Afghanistan, 7 per cent from Iraq and 5 per cent from Eritrea. But the biggest proportion of these sea-borne asylum seekers, 22 per cent of the total, originated in Syria – displaced by a civil war that began in 2011, has made international refugees of possibly five million people and shows no sign of ending.[2] I plan to begin, therefore, by looking at the origins and trajectory of the Syrian conflict, the popular uprising, Assad's violent response, the militarization of fragmented opposition forces and the part being played by international and regional actors. I'll also sketch the ever-evolving humanitarian crisis in the Syrian population that's driving the exodus, and move on to give some sense of the magnitude of the migration currently afflicting neighbouring countries, watched with alarm by regional and more distant states. All this, however, is a prelude to examining recent developments in the UK where the government's policy has been to 'help them stay over there', and in London where divisions have deepened between an impassioned movement of support for refugees and a determined and increasingly vocal resistance to accepting even a small number for resettlement. And here I will end by describing community activism and local governance concerning asylum seekers and refugees in one London borough, Lambeth, as it implemented a policy of 'welcome'.

SYRIA: SITE OF IMPERIAL RIVALRIES

The national border of the contemporary Syrian Arab Republic delineates an area that is just a fragment of a historic region known as Sham, or Greater Syria, which spread across lands that are today called Lebanon, Israel/Palestine, Jordan and part of Turkey.[3] From the sixteenth century CE the region was governed from Constantinople (today's Istanbul) as part of the Ottoman Empire. The empire gradually contracted in the eighteenth and nineteenth centuries, so that, as the twentieth century dawned, Sham had become one of its few remaining

Arab territories. When Britain, France and Russia confronted Germany and Austro-Hungary in the Great War of 1914–18, the Ottoman Empire cast its lot with the latter. This brought devastating conflict to Greater Syria where both Britain and France deployed armed forces. Even while they engaged as partners in the Triple Alliance to achieve a military victory over the Central Powers, these rivals were already competing with each other to secure post-war imperial ascendancy in the lands of the doomed Ottoman Empire. Representatives of the French and British governments met secretly midway through the war and signed an agreement on the post-war carve-up. The Sykes–Picot Agreement as the plan became known, after the two diplomats who engineered it, while tactfully speaking of the creation of independent Arab states at the war's end, contained a clause declaring that 'France and Great Britain shall be allowed to establish such direct or indirect administration or control as they desire'. France's intention was to obtain a mandate over what we now know as Lebanon, Syria, parts of northern Iraq and the Hatay province of Turkey, while a British Mandate would be imposed on Jordan, Palestine and the remainder of Iraq. The plan had no regard to pre-existing political, economic or cultural ties. For example, it separated the Kurds from each other across four national borders.

There were two particular interests shaping Britain's hand in the negotiations. One was control of regions promising petroleum, including Kirkuk and Mosul in Iraq. The second was to secure influence over Palestine so as to be able to foster the creation there of a 'homeland' for Jews of the worldwide diaspora, as promised to the Zionist movement in 1917 by British Foreign Secretary Lord Balfour. The Treaties of Sèvres, signed in 1920, and of Lausanne in 1924, formalized the Sykes–Picot plan and drew new borders between Syria and Iraq, adjacent states bordering a post-imperial Republic of Turkey to the north. The French and British Mandates were authorized by the newly created League of Nations, with a specific promise of eventual independence. Party to these negotiations was the Emir Faisal, a powerful Hashemite Arab leader and close ally of the British during the war. Faisal was the energetic promoter of a secular pan-Arab nationalism across the region of Greater Syria. Though he had pleaded for a united Arab state, he cooperated with the Treaty and in 1920 became King of Syria under the French Mandate, and subsequently

King of Iraq under the British. Within the new Syrian national boundary the majority of the population was Arab, and Sunni Muslim by religion, but there were long-established communities of Christians and of Druze and Alawi, sects on the Islamic Shi'a fringe. Having been promised independence as the reward for joining the fight against the Ottomans, many now felt badly cheated by its postponement. In 1925 there was a massive revolt against the French presence, to which the response was a bombardment of Damascus by the French air force that killed many civilians. The French did little to make themselves welcome thereafter. They scarcely invested in transport and infrastructure, and were negligent of education and social development. But it took another world war to shake them out of Syria. An election in 1943 returned the National Party under Shukri al-Quwatli. He gave an ultimatum to the French, who thenceforth began transferring governance to Syrian control. In May 1945, a few weeks after Syria, with Egypt and others in the region, sent a purposeful pan-Arab nationalist message to the world by forming the Arab League, the French launched a retributive attack, again bombing Damascus and shelling the Syrian parliament building. But there was no averting the end of the Mandate, and by the end of 1946 the last French soldier had gone. Syria and Lebanon became members of the newly created United Nations.

The country remained at war, however, both in the region, supporting the resistance of Palestinians to displacement by the Jewish state of Israel on its creation in 1948, and within its own borders, as governments replaced each other in a succession of military coups over the next two decades. As to party politics, there was a short-lived communist party and for some years a right-wing nationalist party, but the most significant political force was the Arab Ba'ath Party, founded in 1940, with an Arab nationalist bent but a powerful leftwards thrust towards socialism. It would grow to have unmatched significance in the remaining decades of the twentieth century. The Ba'ath were briefly eclipsed after 1958 when Syria joined Egypt in a United Arab Republic, the initiative of Gamal Abdel Nasser. When they recovered power in 1963, it was by means of a military coup. The democratic principles on which the Ba'ath party had been founded by Michel Aflaq and Salah-al-Din al-Bitar – freedom of speech and belief, socialism and a healthy disrespect for ruling elites – were henceforth challenged by a right-wing tendency, returning political authority from the Sunni majority of Syria to its historically privileged Christian, Alawite and Druze minorities.

In November 1970 the Ba'athist Minister of Defence, Hafez al-Assad, an Alawite, seized the presidency of Syria and would hold on to it until his death in the year 2000 when he was replaced by his son, the current President Bashar al-Assad. Hafez's regime is described by historian John McHugo as having possessed 'a heart that was made of lead'.[4] On the one hand he ended the decades of instability, brought electricity and piped water to the villages and greatly increased literacy. But he favoured Christians and Alawites at the expense of the three-quarters of the population that were Sunni Muslims and relatively poor. He built up the powerful and unaccountable security force, the *mukhabarat*, which was always ready to torture and murder his opponents, whether Islamic extremists or moderates such as the Muslim Brotherhood. When an Islamist uprising broke out in the city of Hama in 1982, Assad shelled civilian areas of the city, killing an estimated 10,000 in a month of fighting. Externally, he allied his greatly strengthened military with those of other Arab states in an attack on Israel in 1973 (the Yom Kippur War), a costly engagement in which he failed to recover the Golan Heights seized by Israel in 1967 and exposed Damascus to Israeli shelling. He subsequently intervened extensively in the Lebanon conflict between 1975 and 1992.

Bashar al-Assad was only 34 when he succeeded his father by means of an unopposed referendum in the year 2000. He proved to be a more contradictory character. Thus he began his rule by releasing several hundred political prisoners, but a year later had replaced them in the jails with the arrest of more opposition members of parliament and other political activists. He gave girls a modern education, reflecting the secular values of the Ba'ath, yet agreed to their wearing the *hijab* in school. He pleaded for dialogue and encouraged democracy – upsetting the *mukhabarat* by promotion of a free press and civil society. But the region was entering a period of turmoil – the Second Intifada broke out in Israel, the 9/11 terror attack of 2001 provoked the USA into military engagement in Afghanistan, and the Western attack on Saddam Hussein's Iraq would follow.

The international balance of power, disrupted by the collapse of the Soviet Union in 1991, was subtly changing. Bashar fostered a relationship with the new Russia. Strongly opposing the US invasion of Iraq, he maintained a certain distance from the USA, which hit back with a trade embargo. What he and his administration could not foresee was the wave of rebellion that was about to sweep through the Middle East and North African (MENA) region.

THE ARAB SPRING AND ASSAD'S WAR

On 17 December 2010, a street vendor in Tunisia immolated himself. Let's remember him by name: Mohammad Bouazizi. Though his suicide was a response to the hard conditions of his own life – oppressive treatment by officialdom – the event resonated among many ordinary Tunisians, especially workers, traders and shopkeepers, students and intellectuals, suffering under the military dictatorship of President Zine El Abidine Ben Ali. Mass demonstrations resulted in the fall of his regime within a month. The spark lit by Bouazizi flared into mass non-violent uprisings, first in Algeria, Oman, Yemen, Bahrain and Egypt, then as 2011 progressed, throughout the MENA region and down into some African states. Many of the demonstrators were driven by economic distress – poverty, lack of employment. But the aspiration to democracy and human rights was unmistakeable. A significant theme among the slogans was a frankly revolutionary one: 'the people want to bring down the regime'.

The Arab Spring came to Syria in March. When the first good-humoured and non-violent street mobilizations gave way to more emphatic protests they were prompted by an incident in the southern town of Der'aa. Some children showed their feelings by scrawling graffiti on their school walls calling for the ousting of Assad. They were arrested, interrogated and tortured by the *mukhabarat*. Parents and supporters demonstrated for their release. When some were shot dead, 20,000 replaced them on the streets. Protests quickly spread to Damascus, Homs, Idlib, Qamishli and elsewhere. The demands of the uprising included an independent judiciary, a free press, equal rights and an end to arbitrary arrest and torture – in short, democratization. Assad responded, on the one hand, by seeking dialogue and making concessions: lifting the state of emergency which had been in place since his father's day; belatedly enfranchising the Kurds. On the other hand, he met protests with tanks and bullets.

In the summer months of 2011, as deaths were reaching the thousands, Assad's opponents organized, like him, in dual mode. In political mode, at a meeting in October in Istanbul, diverse civilian oppositional groups came together in a Syrian National Council (SNC) that stated its aim to be toppling Assad within six months and replacing him by a multi-party democracy. A year later the SNC would join others in a more inclusive National Coalition for Syrian and Opposition Forces (shortened to SOC). In armed mode, some personnel began defecting from the state military and announced the formation of a Free Syrian Army which would use force to overthrow the regime. In the following year spontaneous local militias proliferated, especially among the less-privileged Sunni majority in the population, swelling an increasingly militarized movement. Jihadist elements joined the action, the most significant being Jabhat al-Nusra (the Al-Nusra Front), an Al-Qaeda affiliate. Meanwhile, across the border in Iraq, the fundamentalist and viciously violent Islamic State of Iraq (IS) was fostering this development, and would before long send well-armed units westwards into Syria, engaging directly with Assad's forces. In March 2013, soon after it seized the northern city of Raqqa, IS leader, Abu Bakr al-Baghdadi, announced a change of name to Islamic State of Iraq and Sham (ISIS, in Arabic Da'esh), reflecting the extension into Syria of what now aspired to be a 'caliphate' of unlimited scope. During the next twelve months, despite his increasing use of air power, Assad lost control of substantial areas of the north and east of the country. Even major parts of the cities of Aleppo and Homs, and certain suburbs of Damascus, became embattled. The regime dramatically escalated the aerial bombardment of cities.

There are some highly contradictory alignments in Syria's civil war. As ISIS and ISIS-inspired terrorists, increasingly from 2014, engaged in murderous attacks in European cities, they seemed to be intended to invite a direct military response against the Islamist forces operating on the ground in the Middle East. This has led to the extraordinary anomaly, confusing to many observers, that the Western powers are battling both the Syrian regime and that regime's most feared enemies. Turkey is caught up in a similar contradiction. While President Recep Tayyip Erdoğan and the ruling AKP party are strong opponents of Assad, Turkey's armed forces are simultaneously attacking some of the Syrian regime's enemies, namely the (democratic but militarized)

Kurdish insurgents of the self-proclaimed entity of Rojava, just across Turkey's southern border in north Syria. The Turkish government presumes, incorrectly, that they are indistinguishable from the Kurdistan Workers' Party (the PKK), which has long pursued an armed insurgency against the Turkish state. Internally, too, the war has seen increasing division and mistrust both within and between the armed opposition, set on nothing short of a military victory, and the civilian opposition coalition that seeks the support of international actors in pursuit of a negotiated peace.

Meanwhile, surrounding states were taking sides in the conflict, each with its own agenda. Some were aligned on the Sunni/Shi'a axis. Though the various uprisings of the Arab Spring had not featured sectarianism, Syria now seemed caught up in a proxy intra-Muslim war between Sunni and Shi'a tendencies. Assad was joined by formidable Shi'a allies: the Hezbollah militia of Lebanon and, of particular international significance, the Islamic Republic of Iran. The Sunni-dominant trio of Saudi Arabia, Turkey and Qatar came together in support of the rebels – although cautiously distancing themselves from the *jihadists*. It was also in some sense a struggle along the axis of secularism–fundamentalism, by way of religious moderation in the shape of the Muslim Brotherhood. In February 2014, in an article in the *Independent*, Patrick Cockburn suggested that Assad's opposition was 'fighting its own civil war within the civil war. The ferocious Islamic State of Iraq and the Levant holds territory to the east and their opponents to the west of Aleppo, while they battle for control of supply lines to Turkey'.[5]

Looked at from another angle, the conflict also began to seem like a proxy 'Cold War'. In the wider world, while the Western powers were increasingly aligned against Assad's growing violence, Syria had the support of Russia and China. By September 2015, Russia had established a 'forward air operating base' with 28 planes at Khmeimim in north-west Syria, and had flown 6,000 sorties within four months.[6] As to international institutions, they seemed impotent. A gathering of international notables in Geneva in June 2012, initiated by Kofi Annan, the United Nations special peace envoy to Syria, issued a communiqué on the need for a transitional government. The UN General Assembly passed a resolution by 137 votes to twelve for Assad to resign, but Russia and China, soon afterwards, vetoed a similar resolution in the Security Council. They would certainly have done the same had any members later sought UN endorsement of armed intervention. A UN-backed conference in early 2014, termed 'Geneva II', brought the sides together ineffectually. 'Geneva III', at the start of 2016, faltered due to the lack of enthusiasm on both sides for any kind of negotiated compromise. The opposition used the platform to call for the world's military support, but none of the major international actors had any appetite for sending in troops or planes. Even when, back in August 2013, Assad deployed sarin nerve gas, killing 1,300 residents of a Damascus suburb, the British Parliament had voted against military intervention, and the US administration had felt unable, in the event, to fulfil its threat to punish any use of chemical weapons. Both administrations remembered all too well the chaos resulting from the Western powers' ill-judged attack on Gaddafi's Libya in 2011 and, before that, on Saddam Hussein's Iraq. Only with Donald Trump's election as US President in late 2016 would this caution end.

THE DESTRUCTION OF A POPULATION

By then, an appalled world was watching on its TV screens the almost total destruction by bombing of rebel-held areas of Aleppo, Syria's largest city and the commercial and industrial capital of the country. It is estimated that up to half a million inhabitants may have died under the masonry pulverized by Assad's barrel bombs.[7] His strategy, in Aleppo as elsewhere, appears to involve the deliberate targeting of medical and other humanitarian initiatives.

As we turn the corner into a new year, 2017, and Syria wobbles between extremes of violence and sporadic ceasefires, we might pause to calculate the effect of the last six years on Syria's population. A simple, stunning statistic speaks more than words about the deterioration in the quality of life. Average life expectancy in Syria has fallen by 20 years. In 2010 a Syrian could reasonably have expected to live to be 76. By the end of 2015, she or he was lucky to be alive at 56. At that point, of an original population of around 22 million, a quarter of a million had died in the conflict. Six and a half million had become IDPs, driven from their homes but as yet remaining within the country. Flight into the cities came first. The population of Damascus, which was two million before the war, had reached five million.[8] Then camps and collective centres began to be set up – now accommodating

1.7 million. The displacement from home is explained by fear of death and injury, but also by sheer necessity – small businesses and sources of self-employment were being destroyed, and well over a million housing units had been damaged in the fighting, while almost half a million were total ruins.[9]

The international agencies were not leaving the world in ignorance about the situation. It was known that 13.5 million Syrians were in need of humanitarian assistance, eleven million were in need of health assistance (half or more of public hospitals and health centres had closed or become only partly functional), 5.7 million youngsters were out of school and malnutrition was affecting 8.7 million.[10] International aid agencies were doing their best to mitigate the destitution but were encountering serious impediments. One was the unpredictability of the evolving violence: 160 non-state armed groups were fighting the government and allied armies and militias, in constantly changing allegiances, in a war whose battle lines were continually shifting. Where humanitarian initiatives were within the reach of the guns, shells and rockets of either side, staff were at risk of death, injury and kidnapping. Another was logistical: the closure of borders and destruction of communication links caused many bureaucratic hurdles. And there was a severe lack of funds. The Syria office of the United Nations High Commissioner for Refugees, for example, was receiving only 43 per cent of its known funding requirement.[11]

Given the conditions affecting the internally displaced, it's unsurprising that approaching five million Syrians have 'chosen' to cross Syrian borders and seek safety elsewhere.[12] The majority are distributed across neighbouring states. Currently, early in 2017, five million are registered in the four countries of Lebanon, Jordan, Iraq and Turkey – more than a million of them in Lebanon alone. Ten per cent are in camps, the remainder spread through the burdened population.[13] It is particularly notable that many have been sufficiently desperate to take the opposite route to that taken by ISIS fighters, seeking refuge in Iraq, notwithstanding its ongoing war.[14] For some refugees the departure from Syria is a second border crossing. An estimated 1.5 million of these 'Syrians' were not born here, but had come to settle in the country to escape conflicts in their own countries. They included 85,000 Palestinians uprooted by Israel's oppression, 400,000 Lebanese displaced by the conflict between Israel and Hezbollah in 2006 and possibly a million who fled the US-led coalition's invasion and occupation of Iraq.[15]

EFFECT OF THE WAR ON WOMEN

Syrian society is predominantly patriarchal, and women experience inequality, injustice and insecurity, even without war. Confinement to a domestic life under the control of husbands and fathers is common, so that women's economic dependency is the norm. Girls are frequently married before the age of 18, and often to partners they do not choose. Pregnancy and childbirth are added health risks for women. War and displacement have exacerbated these problems, with health facilities in the battered towns and villages severely reduced or non-existent. Husbands and fathers, their sense of personal authority damaged by loss of their accustomed status in the household and local economy, often take their frustration out on women and children in domestic violence. Combatants use rape of enemy women as a weapon of war, but women are especially vulnerable to rape, by 'friend' and enemy alike, on the road or in camp conditions. Many displaced households are headed by women so that they have become breadwinners for children, the disabled and the elderly. While, as we've seen elsewhere, this can be empowering, giving women more freedom and teaching them new skills, the stress of income-generation, on top of the burden of care, can be overwhelming. Many women are driven to prostitution for a livelihood. Daughters are given away in 'marriage' ever younger, either for cash or to protect them from injury, death or 'despoliation'. Mental health problems are widespread among women: fear, depression, loss of hope.[16] Many women in the course of time have ceased to be 'internally displaced' and become 'refugees'. Of those entering the four neighbouring states of Lebanon, Jordan, Turkey and Iraq it is believed that around 50 per cent are women and 25 per cent children and adolescents. In 2014 the charity Humanity in Action sponsored research on women refugees' health needs in those three countries, and found them to be very similar to those of the female IDP population within Syria.[17]

Nonetheless, many observers urge that we should not lose sight of the fact that women are social actors too. They've not participated greatly in the armed forces in Syria. Rather, they've been prominent in humanitarian work. Because it has been so difficult for international organizations to operate effectively amid the fighting, local organizations have formed to make help available to the displaced population. Many are run by women. So women are present in large numbers among the population in the impoverished villages, towns and cities, and among those displaced to camps, not only as recipients of aid but as givers: activists, professionals and volunteers. As Zerene Haddad puts it, in an article in *Forced Migration Review*, there is a 'new social dynamic' and women are 'transforming themselves into agents of change'.[18] The process is being fostered by the United Nations agency UN Women, which has been working actively for women's specific needs and vulnerabilities to be built into the humanitarian response to the war, and seeking to ensure the inclusion of women's representative organizations in peace initiatives.[19]

MIGRATION'S CHALLENGE TO
TRANSNATIONAL GOVERNANCE

Undoubtedly most of the men and women fleeing the war in Syria, with children or without, have done so in the hope of getting through the neighbouring states to reach Europe and beyond, to create a sustainable life and possibly to come back in due course to a peaceful, restored Syria. Between Syria and that desired haven lie thousands of miles of road and track, the Mediterranean Sea, numerous borders and controls, security and military regimes, and varieties of helper/ smuggler, agent/extortionist, bodyguard/thief. To plan and prepare for, let alone to survive and complete, such a journey needs resources – several thousand pounds-worth of available cash to pay/bribe people and to buy a ticket on a bus or train when luck brings one into view. So the five million individuals that have left Syria since 2011 as refugees have, though ragged and shoe-worn, been mainly of the business world: shopkeepers, property owners, the educated middle class.

For the first four years of the conflict, Syrians mainly made their way south through Jordan to Egypt or Libya and joined thousands of other migrants coming west and north from the impoverished and war-torn countries of Africa. There they gathered at certain known points along the Mediterranean shore, negotiated with agents or smugglers (call them which you will) and waited, in appalling conditions, often for months, to be granted the possibility of risking their lives in a small boat on the open sea. In 2011, 64,000 migrants are believed to have reached the Italian shore this way. In 2014, the figure was almost three times that, at 170,000, and by now a third of the travellers were Syrians. There were at least 3,200 deaths by drowning on the way. The patrols of the EU border security system, Frontex, achieved little reduction in the numbers leaving shore, and a short-lived Italian rescue boat exercise, Mare Nostrum, could reach only a few of the many shipwrecks.

Then, in the summer of 2015, when the civil conflict in Libya was increasing the perils of that route, Syrians awoke to the possibility of travelling north across the Turkish border and west to the Aegean coast, and there buying a passage in a small boat, often no more than an inflatable dinghy, across the few miles of sea that separates Turkey from its nearest offshore Greek islands. Photos began reaching the world's media of men, women and children splashing thankfully on to the beaches of Kos and Lesbos, discarding orange life-vests – while others in the water behind them were drowning in full sight of land. At least 500 drowned in this crossing during 2015. The survivors (an estimated half million during that year alone) were brought ashore, sheltered and fed, by generous islanders and by volunteers who responded to these scenes by gathering from far and wide. The Syrians on this route had different co-migrants from those who had shared boats with them from North Africa. They were largely from Iraq, Afghanistan and Pakistan, countries still made perilous by armed violence.

Landing on Greek shores, placing their sodden feet on Europe's soil, was a mighty step. But it was one that brought into view many more steps ahead. Most Syrians wanted to reach the economically developed countries of north and western Europe. At first the Greek authorities just waved them through, as the Italians had done before them, ignoring the EU admission rules. The delays in transiting Greece grew longer, however, sometimes the result of officialdom, sometimes due to illness or accident, sometimes to lack of transport or resources. Eventually the refugees would start a long trek north to the ill-defined Macedonian border, and beyond, through the Balkan states towards Hungary. During 2015 and early 2016, hundreds of thousands were travelling slowly, arduously, along these northbound or deviating roads, tracks and train lines. I warmly recommend Patrick Kingsley's book *The New Odyssey: The Story of Europe's Refugee Crisis*, which has the merit of supplying useful facts and figures, but doing so through the intimate stories of scores of migrants, smugglers, agents and other actors at a particular juncture in this sustained drama.[20] As the *Guardian* newspaper's migration correspondent, Kingsley travelled and talked with the refugees, hung out with them in their sheds and shelters, shared food and crossed borders with them. Until, that is, the fences began to be built between European countries. On 10 March 2016, while 3,000 migrants a day were still landing on Greek beaches, an EU spokesman announced that the northward 'corridor' was to be closed. Macedonia, Croatia and Slovenia were following Hungary's lead and shutting their borders.

European politics was by now in turmoil. Angela Merkel, Germany's Chancellor, had taken a courageous lead in the early months of the crisis, opening Germany to 200,000 incomers in 2014, then 800,000 in 2015, accepting even those who had been fingerprinted elsewhere before arrival. She started work on forging a common policy to share refugees equitably and generously around the EU. Sweden was responsive, so was Denmark. But other EU member states were not persuaded, and domestic criticism of Merkel's policies soon grew. Sceptics were unconvinced that these were all 'genuine refugees', rather than 'economic migrants'. (The fact is of course that any one of them may well be both things at once.) There were disturbances involving asylum seekers on the streets of Berlin and Munich. There were deadly Islamist terror attacks in Brussels, Paris, Nice and elsewhere, which many blamed on terrorists evading security at slack borders among the crowds of refugees. Right-wing, nationalist, anti-immigrant rhetoric was causing alarm among democrats in many countries. Even Denmark and Sweden began to step back, tightening the entry requirements in response to anti-immigrant feeling among their nationals. In March 2016 the EU signed a deal with Turkey – at that moment thought to be hosting three million refugees – that they would receive back Syrian refugees from Greece, if, for every one taken in, another residing in Turkey would be received and settled in the EU. Meantime, the bombardment of Aleppo by the Syrian regime and its Russian allies and the activity of Islamist militias in northern Syria were continuing to drive Syrians north to the Turkish border, along which the Turkish government was midway through construction of a defensive wall.[21]

THE UK's RESPONSE TO THE MIGRATION CRISIS

It was not until September 2015 that the EU achieved a deal to share refugees more equitably between member states. The agreement was for 120,000 to be taken from the crowded countries of first entry and distributed among the signatory countries. Germany and France would take more than others. The Czech Republic, Hungary, Romania and Slovakia would take none at all. Forty thousand refugees would be dispersed immediately, the remainder over two years. The agreed figure of 160,000 (a total that included 40,000 agreed previously) was, in fact, scarcely a generous number. It amounted to 0.022 per cent of the EU's population of 743 million, a miserable figure given that Germany alone had by now taken in a million (1 per cent of Germany's population). The UK, however, did not sign up to the deal at all, its refusal legitimated by its non-membership of the Schengen border-free area.[22]

Prime Minister David Cameron's distancing of the UK from the anguishing political and practical dilemma of other countries was in a way unsurprising. A ound the time of the general election that brought him to Downing Street in May 2010, there had been growing popular anxiety in some parts of the electorate, fired up by the United Kingdom Independence Party and other nationalist elements, about high levels of immigration to the UK. He had responded to this mood by making a pledge ('no ifs, no buts', he said) to reduce net immigration to the 'tens of thousands', understood to mean a target maximum of 100,000 a year. Five years on, the statistics were showing that net immigration, far from falling, was growing fast. Indeed, it would reach a record high in the year 2015 of 330,000, over three times his original target.[23] Meanwhile the Syrian conflict was intensifying and the plight of Syrian refugees, and of the countries sheltering them, was forcing a showdown in the UK, both among the public and politicians, between hard-headedness and shamed compassion.

Anticipating the EU quota deal, and opting out in advance, in early September 2015 David Cameron dragged himself upright, took a deep breath, and announced in parliament that Britain would 'live up to its moral responsibility' by resettling 20,000 Syrian refugees by 2020.[24,25] This was taken to mean 4,000 a year for five years, but Cameron stressed that the pace of transfer would depend on the speed with which the UNHCR identified appropriate refugees and how quickly Britain's local councils could 'process' them. It was a tiny number, given the scale of the problem. And this was no gesture of EU solidarity. He specified that they would be brought, *not* from countries of the EU or their beleaguered southern borders, but from UN-run camps in the countries bordering Syria. This was consistent with the UK government's often reiterated policy of giving aid in support of humanitarian projects in the Middle East as an alternative to spending funds on refugees in Europe. This was ostensibly to place the UK's aid where the situation was most volatile. But the implicit aim was clear: to keep the refugees from setting out on the westward road. Some months later, in February 2016, persisting in this approach, the Prime Minister announced his intention to double the UK's annual contribution to aid for the region, to £2.3 billion for the coming year.[26]

Another way the immigration issue was impinging on the awareness of the British public in 2015 was through news stories of migrants who had independently crossed France to the English Channel ports, and were risking their lives attempting to smuggle themselves to the UK by means of the Channel Tunnel rail link or by hiding in lorries bound for the ferries. In the last week of July more than 4,000 were reported to have attempted to enter the Tunnel, most of them unsuccessfully.[27] As winter approached there was dismay at the dire conditions in the camps near Calais where thousands, mainly but not only male, pre-dominantly young and even very young, were shacking up in flimsy tents, in bitter weather, awaiting their chance to penetrate this hardest of all borders. Refugee-support activists and volunteers went in growing numbers to take food, clothing and shelter, and brought back stories of what was coming to be known as the Calais 'Jungle'.

A clause in the European Union 'Dublin Agreement' (EU Regulation No.604 of 2013 to be precise) specifies that the first EU state in which a refugee sets foot and where, in theory, he or she should be finger-printed and registered, must be the one to consider a claim for asylum. It makes a clear exception in cases of family reunion: an unaccom-panied minor has an overriding right to be admitted to a country in which he or she has close relatives already settled. In January 2016 the

Home Office Minister for Immigration announced that Britain would take in more unaccompanied children under this 'Dublin' rule. A sum of £10 million would be invested in the project, and this time, at last, it was agreed they could come from among refugees already on the European continent, selected with the help of UNHCR as 'exceptional cases' from the 24,000 unaccompanied refugee children believed to be currently in Europe.[28]

There was still reluctance to bring youngsters from the Calais Jungle, however, notwithstanding the public agitation about the appalling conditions in the camp and the injuries and deaths occurring among the lorry-jumpers. Decisive action was taken by Labour peer, Lord Alf Dubs, who had himself been a child refugee, brought to Britain in the 1930s on the *Kindertransport* from Nazi Germany. In the House of Lords he tabled an amendment to the Immigration Act of 2016 that 'the Secretary of State must, as soon as possible, make arrangements to relocate three thousand unaccompanied asylum-seeking children who are in European countries to the United Kingdom'. They should be distinct from and in addition to Cameron's pledged 20,000 families envisaged under what was now being termed the Syrian Vulnerable Persons Relocation Scheme (SVPRS). Significantly, distinguishing the initiative from that concerning the Dublin Rules, the 'Dubs Amendment' did *not* specify that unaccompanied minors must have relatives in the UK. In moving the motion he said:

Is it not a terrible thought that in Europe, at this time and in this year, with all the sophistication and humanitarian instincts that we are supposed to have, there are children adrift, vulnerable and in danger and that very little is being done to help them? We cannot stand by … there are many signs that the British people want to help and see this as our collective British responsibility.[29]

Dubs' Amendment passed through the House of Lords but was at first narrowly rejected in the House of Commons. He then watered it down, taking out the startling figure of 3,000 children, and instead committing the government to do no more than resettle 'a specified number' of youngsters in consultation with local councils.[30] On 11 May he finally got a 'yes' vote in the House of Commons. The government was painfully slow to implement the policy, however. By September the French authorities were dismantling the Jungle and dispersing 10,000 asylum seekers arbitrarily around France in fleets of buses. Among them were an estimated 1,300 unaccompanied children, 500 of whom were believed to be eligible for resettlement in the UK under the Dublin Regulation. Yet since the start of the year the UK had admitted only 140 children under 'Dublin', and by the end of November 2016 little more than 100 under 'Dubs' . London borough councils were meanwhile pressing the government to come good on providing the funding that would enable them to accept more children.[31]

Things were moving very slowly too on the targeted 20,000 SVPRS arrivals. Between October 2015 and March 2016 only 1,602 individuals were admitted and resettled. Of the 33 London boroughs only four (Camden, Islington, Barnet and Kingston upon Thames) had accepted any.[32] Meantime refugees from all over the world, not Syria alone, were clamouring at the door. New asylum applications in the UK rose by 30 per cent, to 41,563, in the twelve months to March 2016, the fifth successive year they had risen.[33] In September, the Prime Minister spoke at a United Nations General Assembly reiterating the UK's 'fending off' position: member states should help more refugees stay in the first country they reach; distinguish better between those fleeing war and those fleeing poverty; and give countries more licence to protect their borders by force or with a fence.[34]

A CITIZENS' MOVEMENT OF WELCOME TO REFUGEES

Back in 2015, on 2 September, photographs appeared in many newspapers of the body of a young boy washed up on a Turkish beach. A policeman is seen tenderly carrying away the little corpse, later identified as three-year-old 'Aylan' or 'Alan' Kurdi, a Syrian Kurd, drowned with his mother and brother attempting the crossing to Greece in an overloaded rubber dinghy. The image galvanized movements across the world in support of assistance to refugees. In London, on 12 September, an estimated 100,000 people gathered for a demonstration organized by the campaigning group Solidarity with Refugees.[35] The *Observer* reported:

young and old, British, Syrian and other nationalities – [they] snaked down Pall Mall and Whitehall on Saturday, many carrying placards and chanting 'Say it loud and say it clear; refugees are welcome here', and pausing outside Downing Street to boo, with some shouting: 'David Cameron, Shame on you'. There were dozens of similar rallies around the country, in Belfast, Glasgow, Cardiff, Brighton, Manchester, York, Edinburgh and other cities and towns.[36]

This was the public mood to which David Cameron responded, as mentioned above, in making his pledge to bring 20,000 Syrian refugees to Britain by 2020.

The emerging movement was given a good deal of its shape and coordination by Citizens UK, a civil society organization of national scope, first established in London in the late 1990s. They call themselves 'the home of community organizing in the UK', and apply the classic methodology of Saul Alinsky, the pioneer US community activist of the mid-twentieth century. It was just prior to the September 2015 events, in the summer months of 2015, that George Gabriel took on the role of principal organizer of the 'refugee' aspect of Citizens UK's activity. In an interview, 18 months later, he told me: 'The idea of Citizens UK is assembling power to challenge power.' They are, he says, an enduring network of organizations, meeting regularly, defining issues of concern and using community organizing as a methodology to act on them. They have a team of paid, professional community organizers busy fostering the creation of other such alliances. Refugees had actually been on Citizens UK's agenda since 2001. Their very first action had been in Croydon, around Lunar House, the Home Office unit where new arrivals go when applying for asylum. It is a huge building, which used to have a draughty open area beneath it where asylum seekers were obliged to queue in the perishing cold. A campaign led by Croydon Citizens in 2006–8 was successful in getting the Home Office to build a warm reception centre at Lunar House. Nationally, in 2006, Citizens UK ran an Independent Asylum Commission, a two-year nationwide 'listening' exercise that produced 184 recommendations for change. Citizens UK took this as a mandate to work nationwide on issues of asylum and refuge. In 2010 they mounted a major campaign, culminating in an Assembly at Central Hall Westminster, which succeeded in getting the government to end the detention of child refugees – as in the case of Yarl's Wood (see

Chapter 4). They went on to run a 'civic capacity' programme to build the effectiveness of migrant communities' own organizations.

In recent years Citizens UK has created two major 'projects', as they call them, concerned with refugees and asylum seekers. Each exists at national level but has expression in their regional 'chapters', which include Citizens groups in North, South, East and West London. The first of the two projects is called 'Refugees Welcome', and it's under this that they pursue their campaigning for the implementation of the Home Office's SVPRS, the reception of vulnerable Syrian refugee families. The second is 'Safe Passage', and this frames their campaign for the reception of unaccompanied asylum-seeking children from Europe.

The Refugees Welcome project moved fast. Between September 2015 and January 2016, George tells me, they set up a website, encouraged into existence 90 Refugees Welcome local groups, and trained 1,309 organizers. In December 2015 they convened the National Refugees Welcome Board to support these widespread initiatives. They produced a campaign pack to guide and instruct local councils on how to sign up to the Syrian Vulnerable Persons Resettlement Scheme. They also worked closely with those local authorities who did so, helping them operationalize their schemes. Citizens UK, besides, joined in a second big national demonstration mounted, a year after the first, by Solidarity with Refugees. The movement was by now gaining the support of a growing list of organizations, some specific like Support Refugees, the Refugee Council, Refugee Action and Help Refugees, others general like the Red Cross, Oxfam and Médecins Sans Frontières.

Safe Passage, the second refugee-focused project of Citizens UK, responds to the scandal of the Calais camp, described above, campaigning for the UK to receive unaccompanied asylum-seeking children (UASCs) – that is, under-eighteens. It was soon after George took on his AS&R (asylum seekers and refugees) role at Citizens UK that the Calais Solidarity movement began to gather momentum. He tells me:

We went to Calais in September 2015 and were shocked by what we saw. There were so many children there who were clearly eligible under Dublin Rules: they had family in the UK. We took lawyers. We examined individual cases. Till then, the government scheme to bring children to Britain under 'Dublin' just wasn't working. We took and won a court case, and a year later achieved the first transfers under this family reunion rule.

Meanwhile, Alf Dubs was pressing forward his amendment to the Immigration Act, as described above, to bring in children *not* eligible under 'Dublin'. The French government were starting to demolish the Calais camp. Citizens UK set about mobilizing local authorities in Britain to receive both 'Dublin' and 'Dubs' unaccompanied asylum-seeking children. 'We were doing good, full-scale, head-on case work in this', George says. 'In effect we were doing the government's work for it. *They* should have been bringing the children in. But still kids were dying under lorries in a last-ditch attempt to get across the Channel before they were dispersed.' In the course of 2016, 'Dubs', with the support of Citizens UK and other organizations, achieved the entry of 200 young people, far short of Lord Dubs' hoped-for 3,000. But a start.

THE COUNTER-MOVEMENT: 'CLOSE THE BORDER'

Meanwhile, the right-wing media were energetically countering the Refugees Welcome movement with a vocalization of anti-immigrant and anti-refugee sentiment. The *Telegraph* is a good example. On 3 September 2015, just after the Aylan Kurdi story broke, the 'Telegraph View' columnist wrote, 'The slogan "refugees welcome" may make Twitter users feel better about themselves – but as a policy it risks condemning more families like Aylan's to a potentially fatal choice.' The piece termed the Prime Minister's policy of helping refugees to stay put in camps in the Middle East a 'rational and moral position'. It argued that the EU should reconsider the 'Schengen' agreement for freedom of movement within Europe.[37] The *Daily Mail* and the *Sun* were also hard at work on the 'not welcome' theme. Writing for both of them, as well as broadcasting on the radio station LBC (Leading Britain's Conversation),[38] was Katie Hopkins. An article in the US *Huffington Post* on 18 April 2015 was headlined 'Katie Hopkins wrote this in *The Sun* about migrants and now everyone is really angry'.[39] Here are some of the quotes they lifted from her articles: 'Make no mistake, these migrants are like cockroaches'; 'I don't care. Show me pictures of coffins, show me bodies floating in water, play violins and show me skinny people looking sad. I still don't care'; 'Bring on the gunships, force migrants back to their shores and burn the boats'. Predictably, when the world was grieving over Aylan Kurdi some time later, her response was to condemn Kurdi's father for having sent off his wife and sons to drown in the Mediterranean.[40] In the autumn of 2016, as unaccompanied minors began arriving from Calais, Hopkins was among the several journalists who wrote of these 'so-called children', pointing suspiciously to their fledgling beards.

In the political field, it was the United Kingdom Independence Party (UKIP), founded in 1993, that orchestrated the anti-migrant campaign. Led by Nigel Farage, it was in full swing on this theme by 2014, and gaining ever-more traction with voters.[41] Characteristic of its agenda was a huge poster showing a queue of migrants and titled 'Breaking point! The EU has failed us'.[42] It caused uproar among Refugees Welcome supporters, but it was in tune with the changing mood and shifted UKIP from the fringe of British politics to centre stage in the impulse for the national referendum on EU membership, held on 23 June 2016. The slogans of the opposing sides in the referendum were 'Britain Stronger in Europe', endorsed by David Cameron and George Osborne of the Conservatives, and 'Vote Leave', headed by Conservative Mayor of London Boris Johnson, with Nigel Farage and UKIP at his shoulder. The victory of the 'leave' camp, narrow though it was at 51.9 per cent of the vote, gained authenticity from the high turnout in the referendum – almost 72 per cent of the electorate. It was soon clear that the decision would neither be reversed nor qualified.

Though the process of withdrawing the UK from the European Union would take years, the Brexit vote had a number of immediate and startling effects. The value of the pound against the US dollar fell to its lowest point in 31 years. Prime Minister David Cameron resigned, to be succeeded by Home Secretary Theresa May. The Labour Party was plunged into a leadership election. And 'hate crime', that is 'racially' or religiously aggravated offences, rose in the week after the poll by 58 per cent.[43] The most troubling effect for the Refugees Welcome movement was that the Brexit vote was widely understood to have been an expression of one particular factor in Britain's EU membership: the freedom it had given for three million EU citizens to live and work in Britain in recent years. Now the country and its politicians fell to arguing whether 'making Britain English-speaking again' by expelling all the Poles, Romanians, Portuguese and others, as some Brexiteers wanted, would bring about the collapse of the National Health Service, agriculture and the building trade for lack of labour power. The matter of refugees was swept up into the 'border' issue featured by the Brexit campaign. They became, if they had not already been, simply the least-wanted 'foreigners' of all. When Theresa May, in her keynote speech in the Commons on 17 January 2017, made the recovery of full control of the UK border her 'red line' in the impending negotiations with the EU, this spoke as clearly to the masses in the eastern Mediter-ranean and the campers at Calais, as it did to European workers.

As Britain reeled from the June referendum, the USA was preoccupied with the competing Democrat and Republican Party campaigns for the presidential election, due on 8 November, which it soon became clear was going to pit Hillary Clinton against Donald Trump. When Trump's nationalist, racist and border-controlling posture prevailed, it gave a boost to the British extreme right. Nigel Farage went to visit Trump just six days after his election victory.[44] Prime Minister Theresa May, suppressing any doubts she may have had, crossed the Atlantic less than a week after Trump's inauguration, to be the first foreign head of state filmed at the President's side. She deemed the reaffirmation of the UK–US 'special relationship' to be crucially important now that Britain was distancing itself from Europe.[45] A few days later Farage was back State-side again, seen alongside Trump, receiving a rapturous welcome from the Conservative Political Action Conference. Each declared himself the long-term fan of the other. When Trump introduced his ban on entry from selected Muslim-majority countries, the media reported that Nigel Farage and Katie Hopkins 'back Trump's #MuslimBan and want the same for Britain'.[46]

The troubling swing to what was being termed the 'alt-right', a nationalist and nativist populism, manifest in Trump and Farage, was not limited to the USA and the UK. It was becoming evident in several European countries, including Hungary, Austria, the Netherlands and France. Even Angela Merkel's bold early welcome to refugees was causing an organized political backlash in the shape of the party Alternative for Germany. Right-wing extremists, such as Marine Le Pen in France and Geert Wilders in the Netherlands, looked increas-ingly likely to win forthcoming presidential elections. Both were hinting at referenda on withdrawing from the EU. The change of mood was being formulated in different ways and different words, but always with disquiet. In an article in the *Spectator*, John O'Sullivan suggested that in the West power had been shifting for a generation or more away from elected and accountable bodies, including parliaments, to semi-independent bureaucratic agencies such as the courts of justice, and to transnational bodies.[47] He and others were saying that 'majoritarian democracy' was mutating into 'post-democracy'. A *Newsweek* columnist wrote that 'what both Trump and Brexit have demonstrated is that a promise of unfettered independence for a nation, and cultural or racial homogeneity for its people, can prove extremely compelling … Centrists must find a way to make the opposite case better – or find themselves drowning beneath it'.[48]

POSITIVE RESPONSE:
THE LONDON BOROUGH OF LAMBETH

The Refugees Welcome movement of 2015 and 2016 inspired many people in London. It seemed possible once again, after the dismal years involving forcible 'dispersal' of asylum seekers out of the capital, to cherish London's diversity and celebrate its reputation as a place of settlement for successive waves of migrants. The movement was particularly coherent in boroughs where Citizens UK had an active local group. Lambeth, just south of the River Thames, is one of them. Along with Southwark and Wandsworth, to either side, and with Croydon, Lewisham and Greenwich, further east and south, it is part of the South London Citizens regional group. Each of the boroughs too has its local group. Lambeth Citizens is fairly typical, with a team comprising leaders from 21 member organizations.

It was in 2014 that a feeling began to intensify among certain activist individuals and groups in Lambeth that 'this refugee crisis is bad and getting worse: we must do something about it'. Action got under way, tentatively at first, in response to the daily dramas in the Mediterranean. An early initiative was taken by Rabbi Janet Darley, of the South London Liberal Synagogue, someone who has remained at the centre of Lambeth Refugees Welcome activity ever since. The annual Jewish festival of Sukkot, the Feast of Tabernacles, falls at harvest time, in the month of September or October. In 2014, with Rabbi Janet's encouragement, the synagogue, along with other organizations from

Lambeth Citizens, decided to mark Sukkot with an event signalling the plight of refugees. They built and decorated a traditional Sukkot 'tent' in Windrush Square, in the centre of Brixton. The choice of this location was meaningful. The square takes its name from the SS *Empire Windrush*, the ship that in 1948 brought the first significant group of Caribbean migrants to London, many of whom settled in Brixton.

A Sukkot tent, Rabbi Janet told me, is a temporary timber-frame structure, symbolizing 'the fragility of life'. In this case it was intended to be a reminder of what Syria had been before the war that broke out in 2011, and what had been lost. Syrian refugees were people who until recently had homes, jobs and education. Abruptly, they were on the road, they had nothing. She sought the involvement in the Sukkot event of leaders of the two other important faith groups in Lambeth – some imams came along, and priests from several Christian denominations that have churches or chapels in the borough. Together they used the occasion as a springboard for a subsequent meeting with Deputy Leader of the Council, Councillor Paul McGlone, at which they pressed for Lambeth Council to tell the Home Office that it was willing to receive refugees. But they were disappointed by Councillor McGlone's response. Though he recognized that some action was needed, he met their request to open Lambeth to refugees with a firm 'no'. The practical problems were too great, he said, particularly finding low-cost accommodation and places in local schools. If the activists were dejected, they did not think of giving up. They knew from experience that the council needs time to think about problems and how to resolve them. Rabbi Janet, and her close ally Barbara Wilson, an active member of the congregation of Corpus Christi Roman Catholic Church on Brixton Hill, stuck with it.

September 2015, a year later, was a turning point. It was on 2 September that the media carried photographs of the drowned child, Aylan Kurdi. As you will recall, this touched feelings country-wide and sparked activism for refugees, including the national march in London. The feeling was reflected too in the government's commitment to accept 20,000 refugee families under the Syrian Vulnerable Persons Resettlement Scheme. The following month, Rabbi Janet's synagogue and Lambeth Citizens repeated the Sukkot event. More attended this time. And a few weeks later, as after the first 'tent', a meeting was elicited with Councillor McGlone. This time the synagogue involved an impressive group of advocates: several Christian leaders, an imam, and a representative from the synagogue attended, together with primary and secondary school teachers and some of their pupils. This time, too, they had more with which to persuade Councillor McGlone. They told him they had mobilized a number of landlords willing to provide accommodation to families at lower-than-market rents, affordable with Housing Benefit. They could name schools with the capacity to offer places to Syrian children. They had lined up volunteers ready to teach English. One of the primary school children, a particularly articulate seven-year-old girl from Saint John's Primary School in Angell Town, took the floor at the meeting and addressed Councillor McGlone directly, saying: 'We're not as poor as they are. I just *don't understand* why we can't help them.' Many people had the feeling that it was this child's intervention that caused the Deputy Leader to change his position from 'no we can't' to 'yes we will'. Lambeth Council thereupon committed itself to taking 20 Syrian families under the now operational Home Office SVPRS, for which support was promised from central government. What's more, three families were added to the programme, to be taken from a separate government intake of refugees from the Middle East and North Africa, termed the 'Vulnerable Children's Resettlement Scheme'. This would bring Lambeth's commitment to 23 families in all – possibly 100 or more individuals. The council informed the Home Office of its decision, and the programme began to roll. The first family arrived in April 2016. As I close this chapter, in April 2017, ten families are settling in, the rest are still to come.

Simultaneously, one other refugee project was running in Lambeth, and another was about to start. Most striking to the public was the matter of UASCs, young people widely publicized as adrift in and around the Channel ports and other parts of Europe. As we've seen, George Gabriel, newly arrived at Citizens UK to take responsibility for AS&R work, began putting energy into this issue in the autumn of 2015. In creating the Safe Passage project he was prompted and helped by Rabbi Janet Darley of the South London Liberal Synagogue and the Bishop of Croydon. Several groups of Lambeth residents travelled out to the Calais Jungle and brought back distressing news. An early instance was a delegation of activists of Stand Up to Racism and Lambeth Trades Council, who set off from Windrush Square on 17

October, in a convoy carrying humanitarian aid. They came back and reported to a public meeting at Brixton's Karibu Centre.

In the spring of 2016 a group of 40 Lambeth Citizens and other activists, including leaders from Jewish, Muslim and Christian faith groups, and Councillor Paul McGlone, crossed the Channel to the Calais camps. They were deeply impressed and depressed by what they found there. As a result, on 18 May, Lambeth Council informed ministers it would be willing to receive a number of UASCs under the Dublin Rules and the Dubs Amendment, becoming one of the earliest councils to do so. While awaiting government action, Lambeth acted independently to bring in some young people under a 'National Transfer Scheme'. Some came from Kent, the county adjacent to the Channel crossings and burdened with many spontaneous arrivals. On 14 October 2016, pressure on the government was applied at a candle-lit vigil outside Brixton Underground station and a procession to Windrush Square, at which there were readings of messages from the Jungle. A national demonstration in Parliament Square followed a few days later. And then at last things started to move. In late October, just as the French authorities were about to demolish the Calais camp, a large batch of youngsters was brought to the UK. Forty arrived each day for a week, met by welcoming crowds of South London Citizens volunteers at Lunar House. From this intake Lambeth acquired ten more UASCs. Some (those coming under 'Dublin') were reunited with their family members resident in the borough; others (under 'Dubs') were fully cared for and placed in foster homes. Today, in April 2017, the number of UASCs for which Lambeth Council has taken responsibility has risen to 36, and the council has indicated that it is willing to take more 'Dubs' children, certainly up to the limit set by government of 0.07 per cent of a borough's under-18 population, which in Lambeth's case would amount to 43.

The third refugee initiative engaging Lambeth Citizens in 2015 and 2016 was less publicized, but potentially far-reaching. Sometimes termed 'Full Sponsorship', sometimes 'Direct Sponsorship' or 'Community Sponsorship', it was a project whereby, dependant on government and local authority approval, but independent of financial support from either national or local authorities, refugee families might be received by community or other civil society organizations that showed themselves ready to bear the costs and be competent to carry through the resettlement.[49] One of the first civil society groups to undertake a Sponsorship was the Church of England, in the person of the Archbishop of Canterbury, a notable resident of Lambeth Borough. Justin Welby offered to accommodate a refugee family in a house within the grounds of Lambeth Palace. Community Sponsorship is a scheme that demands a great deal of its participants, yet gradually other civil society organizations are showing interest in taking part, so that Sponsorship may, as time goes by, swell the number of refugees that find a home in Lambeth.

INTERFAITH COOPERATION

There are some remarkable features about Lambeth Refugees Welcome and Safe Passage activism. Three in particular strike me. First, as will already have become evident, there is an impressive cooperation between faith groups, within a secular framework afforded by Citizens UK. Second, there is a striking mobilization of schools and school pupils. And third, action is being achieved by means of a sustained inter-sectoral *partnership* involving civil society organizations, charities, council employees and local political leaders.

'Religion', in the present historical conjuncture, signals not peace and cooperation but rather hatred and strife. In the contemporary war zone of the Middle East, from which many of today's refugees have come, enmity between religions, and between sects within religions, is a major source of violence. The overthrow of the Muslim Ottoman Empire by Christian Western Powers in the course of the First World War disturbed the peace for long after the war itself ended. The insertion of a Jewish state of Israel into the region in the 1940s, at the expense of the Palestinian people, most of them Muslims but a substantial minority Christians, is a continuing cause of oppression and violence. Rivalry between Sunni and Shia Islam is a factor in the current wars in the region, including the Syrian conflict. In Syria itself, there are significant divisions between the majority Sunni and the minority Shia Muslims, including Bashar al-Assad's sect, the Alawi, and between these and Druze and Christian minorities. So how is it that in the context of the current refugee crisis, in Lambeth and elsewhere, people and communities of Jewish, Muslim and Christian faiths are able to work together so constructively to 'welcome refugees'?

The South London Liberal Synagogue, Rabbi Janet told me, has a long history of interfaith work. Indeed, it was precisely because of its good track record in this that she applied for the job of rabbi there. No sooner had she arrived in post than she realized that Lambeth's Roman Catholic church, Corpus Christi, was also strongly supportive both of interfaith cooperation and of work for refugees. She quickly bonded with Barbara Wilson, motivator of a 'justice and peace' group in Corpus Christi's congregation, in the context of several early Lambeth Citizens campaigns. As the Citizens Refugees Welcome group got going they met and began to work closely with a third woman, of a different Christian denomination. She was Mother Ellen Eames, associate priest at Saint John the Divine, a Church of England church in Vassall Road, whom we shall meet again in a moment in connection with schools. They found themselves able to work comfortably too with the leaders of both Sunni and Shia Muslim communities in Lambeth. The Sunni South London Islamic Centre and Mosque were situated just around the corner from the synagogue, with which it had long had a positive relationship. The Hyderi Islamic Centre in Streatham, focus for the Shia community, chaired by the cooperative Dr Sarfraz Jeraj, had a young and outgoing imam and a number of active women in its ambit.

Janet, Barbara and Ellen all told me, from their varied experience, that the basis on which adherents of these several faith groups can work together without tension is a certain similarity of belief in the three Abrahamic traditions. The Torah, the Bible and the Koran all stress the importance of hospitality, of 'welcoming the stranger', and a duty of care for 'the widow and the orphan'. And, Barbara added, 'In Citizens, we don't actually sit down and talk through doctrinal differences. We come together for action. When you work together on something, on an issue or project that resonates strongly with your beliefs, that's when interfaith partnership becomes possible.' She pointed out that, in any case, 'these values are widely owned outside the context of religious belief. They are basic tenets of morality for humanists, agnostics and atheists too.' And that indeed is what enables the monotheist groups to work together within a clearly secular framework furnished on the one hand by the Lambeth Council and on the other by Lambeth Citizens, which of course includes non-religious member organizations such as a 'think tank', the New Economics Foundation; a youth group called the Advocacy Academy; a GP's surgery; and a residents' association. When I asked Leader of the Council, Councillor Lib Peck, about the significance of the religious groups in the Refugees Welcome movement, she told me:

> For me, it doesn't have to be about faith at all. As an agnostic-going-on-atheist, what I hear from the refugees is a cry for humanity. You don't need to believe in a god to want to respond to that. I think it places a responsibility to do something. However, the participation of religious leaders in the movement does add strength. It demonstrates to a wider constituency the importance of welcoming different peoples. And draws on the faith communities for practical support and funding.

INVENTING THE 'REFUGEES WELCOME SCHOOL'

Ellen Eames, ordained in the Church of England seven years ago at the age of 27, is 35 today. She worked for a while as a curate before coming to Lambeth to take the full-time job of Chaplain at Saint Gabriel's College, a Church of England secondary comprehensive school in the parish of Saint John the Divine. 'Mother Ellen', as she is known here, is not engaged to teach, but rather to conduct worship and play a pastoral role among pupils and their families. Alongside the school's Principal and Deputy Head, she's a member of Saint Gabriel's 'senior leadership team'. Included in her job description is 'outreach', activity beyond the school walls. Engagement in the community is a matter of school ethos. 'The aim,' she says, 'is to help the school develop a sense of service.' One way through which Mother Ellen guides the school, and Saint John's Church too, along an 'integrative' path is by engaging and representing both bodies in South London and Lambeth Citizens. This locates them immediately in the desired interfaith context – as active partners of the Liberal Synagogue, the Hyderi Islamic Centre and the Roman Catholic Church.

A new school year began just a few days after Aylan Kurdi's photograph appeared in the media. Ellen thought, 'it's a good time for a new initiative'. She met with James Asfa, community organizer of South London and Lambeth Citizens, and together they took a step that would lead to a veritable 'Refugee Schools Movement'. It's a normal feature of Saint Gabriel's secondary school that there is a voluntary group of pupils who are keen to engage in social and community projects. James and Ellen brought them together now and asked them to 'think about something they would like to change'. Ellen says:

> We threw out a range of possible topics: Something to do with money, maybe? With housing? With refugees? What else? The first to speak was a pupil of Polish origin. She said, 'They're all important. But the most important of all is refugees.' Many other pupils agreed with her. So this was their choice. They were ready for it. They were seeing so many photos of people crowded in boats, in camps.

Ellen and James then asked the pupil group to imagine 'what would characterize a Refugee Welcome school'. The students eventually came forward with three features. First, everyone in the school would be well informed about the refugee crisis, have a grasp of the facts. So the first task would be one of teaching and learning. Second, a Refugees Welcome School would have in place a good welcoming process. There must be pupils ready to 'buddy' each newcomer on arrival, to help them link up with others of their identity group and to integrate with 'other others' in the school. As part of this, volunteers must be on hand to teach English as an additional language. Third, such a school would have a programme of action. To become a Refugees Welcome School, which is what the group now decided they wished for Saint Gabriel's, they would have to go public and undertake campaigning. Membership of Citizens UK would enable this.

So the action began. First, in October, some of the pupils joined the demonstration outside the Houses of Parliament calling for the government to act on its commitment to accept 20,000 Syrian refugees, by bringing in the first 1,000 to the UK by Christmas. One of them took the microphone and made an impressive speech about what Saint Gabriel's was planning for refugees expected in Lambeth. 'If we were in the situation of the Syrian refugees, we would want help from people like us,' she said, 'that's why we're here.' Very soon after this, after months of inaction, Prime Minister David Cameron announced that the first 1,000 Syrian refugee families accepted under SVPRS would indeed arrive before Christmas. 'This was so important for the students', Ellen said. 'They cheered when they heard it on the news.'

Opposite: Top, Refugees Welcome activism flourished in the London Borough of Lambeth. Bottom, campaigning for implementation of the Dubs Amendment.

Above: Mother Ellen Eames and students of St Gabriel's College, Camberwell.
Photo: source unknown.

Right: Joud, in his Lambeth home. See page 209.
Photo: Katie Barlow.

A second significant event for the school was the meeting described above following the second Sukkot tent, organized to appeal to Deputy Leader, Councillor Paul McGlone, to accept some of these Syrian families. To this Ellen took two Saint Gabriel's students, active in the school's Refugees Welcome group. 'We sat in a circle,' Ellen recalls, 'and addressed the Deputy Leader, and each one introduced herself, said why we'd come. The students – both Ghanaian, around 14 years old – they were fantastic.' Strengthened by the successful outcome of this event, Saint Gabriel's decided to share their project more widely. First, they carried the message to the younger students in their own school, using the Christmas service in Saint John the Divine church to teach them about the refugee crisis, speaking of the Holy Family in Bethlehem as having been refugees in flight. They helped create a web-page. In Refugee Week, June 2016, Saint Gabriel's pupils hosted a conference in their school hall of students from 25 schools, predominantly regional but some from a distance. 'So our idea of being a Refugees Welcome School has flowered. It's grown bigger than our school, engaged others far afield in the action. It's encouraged Citizens UK too to look for more partnership with educational organizations', Mother Ellen says.

Once refugee families, after what seemed an age, started arriving in Lambeth, the nature of the pupils' activity changed. The first families to be received were invited to a welcome party, at Saint Gabriel's College, hosted by the students. The refugee family housed by the Archbishop at Lambeth Palace were invited along as well. Everyone brought dishes of appropriate food to share. One of the students, a girl of Palestinian origin with fluent Arabic, gave a speech of welcome. There were balloons and a children's entertainer. Ellen says, 'It was so much fun. The Syrian and the local children were running around together, you couldn't tell who was who!' When a further batch of refugees arrived, Lambeth Citizens organized a second welcome party, this time in the Church of the Holy Spirit in Clapham, in which Saint Gabriel's students helped.

The most encouraging aspect of Saint Gabriel's experience as a pioneer of the Refugees Welcome School movement has been the full support they've received from staff and parents. The absence of negativity about children engaging in a movement that has undeniable political elements is no doubt mainly due to the composition of the school's intake. It may be a 'voluntary aided' Church of England school, but its 500 pupils are representative of the diversity that is Lambeth. Not only Christians, they have many faiths and 50 languages of origin between them. Mother Ellen says, 'You don't have to be a refugee to come from a war zone. A lot of our children come from troubled places. So really nobody in the school can fail to see the point of Refugees Welcome.'

GETTING DOWN TO WORK

Looking back to Chapter 1, where I ended by speculating on how London borough councils were handling the day-to-day residual responsibility for asylum seekers and refugees left to them after the 'dispersal' policy was introduced, you may recall that I found something of an absence. Few councils, so far as I could see, had prominent, advertised points of contact, fully integrated into borough and related public services. Rather, I deduced that AS&R needing advice, help and support were left to rely on their wits in locating it, digging it out and patching it together. So I was interested to see who among Lambeth Council's officers, once their elected councillors had taken the plunge and invited vulnerable Syrian and other Middle Eastern refugee families to come and re-home here, was briefed to pick up the responsibility of receiving and settling them. I couldn't have guessed who I'd find: a person with the obscure initials 'NRPF' on his office door, and with a passion for the task with which he'd just been landed.

Dr Simon Sandberg is the manager of a unit named 'No Recourse to Public Funds'. This is the function of dealing with people in the borough – they may number several hundred at any one time – who are subject to immigration control and for one reason or another are found to be destitute and have either children to support or high-level care needs. (Financial and other support from a local authority under the Children Act or Care Act is not counted as a 'public fund'.) They are not necessarily, or even normally, people fleeing the Middle East crisis. In Lambeth they are liable to be in the main Jamaican, Ghanaian or Nigerian migrants of varying age, some with children, who have become 'illegal' by overstaying tourist or student visas. Those financially supported by the local authority are required to live under 'an austere subsistence regime', but have sometimes opted willingly for this, seeing it as a kind of investment, confident they are likely to get UK resident status sooner or later if they persist. Simon is thus dealing quite a lot of the time with individual situations of crisis. He answers to two department chiefs, Housing Services and Children's Social Care, and calls on other council functions and departments as needed. He says, 'We are an integrated multi-agency team'. The Middle East crisis and the decision to accept Syrian families under the Home Office programmes has added a substantial new task to Simon's role.

Knowing that the management of 23 family cases was likely to involve a great deal of practical work of a type that the local authority was not accustomed to delivering, Simon contracted a substantial local charity to handle their day-to-day support. It was the Single Homeless Project (SHP), based locally in Vauxhall. They had the necessary experience and capacity and were indeed 'in the market' for more work. As the first families began to arrive in April 2016, the SHP furnished two caseworkers, two Arabic-speaking support staff, an employment coordinator and an 'English as an alternative language' specialist, as well as a scheme manager.

Simon would soon take on another responsibility too – for the unaccompanied asylum-seeking children from France, beginning to be delivered by the Home Office into Lambeth's care. Having already developed an effective connection with the Home Office over SVPRS, he was the natural choice for 'point person' in the case of the youngsters. The role is 'strategic', he explains. He does not, as in the case of the families, actually meet the incomers and carry operational responsibility for supervising the care they receive. This is the responsibility of the Looked-After Children Service. Rather he liaises with the Home Office and with officers of Lambeth services, particularly those of Children's Social Care, to arrange the young peoples' reception and ensure that their needs are assessed so that they either become fully 'looked-after children' or else in the case of 'Dublin' children, are connected or reconnected with appropriate family members here.

I had guessed in my ignorance that the caring motivation behind the welcoming of refugees into the borough would be reserved to the activists of Citizens – possibly extending to the councillors, with their Labour Party political platform. Local authority officers are not, after all, liable to go public about their passion for the job. But Simon finds his work for refugees deeply satisfying, and says so:

It's a lovely scheme to be involved with. A lot of what a local authority does for people routinely can make only a rather marginal improvement to their lives. It's different with the refugees. They're sometimes deeply traumatized when they arrive. A lot of them are survivors of terrible abuse. They're people with very serious psychological needs. The UASCs too, they've had unspeakable lives, many of them for years. All of these people are coming out of a very hostile environment and we're able to give them a high-quality package. It amounts to a real second chance. It's a small number we're able to take, but what we do is truly transformative.

I found Simon to be an activist as well as a council worker. Not with Lambeth Citizens and not directly on refugee issues, which he deemed would be inappropriate given his role in the council. But, as a Jew and an atheist, he makes donations to the South London Synagogue for humanitarian work, and is an active member of Jews for Justice for Palestinians. Of himself he says, 'I'm just someone among countless others, committed to working with vulnerable communities and concerned to do the best job I can.' But I was interested to learn that like so many people I've met in writing this book, Simon's link with 'refugee-dom' goes far back in time. His grandparents were Russians who arrived in Britain early in the twentieth century, as penniless refugees in flight from the pogroms in Eastern Europe. Indeed, as he told me this story, I was delighted to find my mind carried back to Chapter 1 and realize that Simon's grandmother and grandfather were among those determined few who found a way across the tough new border established by the earliest of Britain's immigration acts – the Act of 1905 (see page 11).

This personal orientation in the council's AS&R person put him well in step with Lambeth Citizens and their Refugees Welcome movement in the borough. As Rabbi Janet, Barbara Wilson of Corpus Christi and other Citizens made good their promise and came forward with offers of low-cost rental accommodation they had identified for the refugee families, and as Mother Ellen's school pupils set about organizing welcome parties for them not long after arrival, Simon valued their efforts and was prepared to work closely with them. He, like the councillors, was rewarded by a big bunch of flowers from Citizens and the school kids at the first welcome party. In turn he took pleasure in offering it to the mother of a disabled Syrian child.

A PARTNERSHIP OF LOCAL COMMUNITY
AND LOCAL STATE

What we are seeing here, it seems to me, is that third feature of the Lambeth experience I singled out above: the intense and productive partnership activity it has turned out to be. James Asfa, the South London and Lambeth Citizens 'professional' community organizer, sees it as four groups working together to make Refugees Welcome a policy of Lambeth Council and carry it through to implementation. This makes for a special kind of synergy. They are, first, the 21 member groups comprising Lambeth Citizens, and key individual members within them, guided by Citizens' well-theorized and developed methodology of community organization. These are the instigators. Second, there's the hardworking charity, the Single Homeless Project, fielding its care workers and linguists. The third element of the partnership is local politicians of Lambeth Council, including the Leader, Councillor Lib Peck, and Deputy Leader, Councillor Paul McGlone. They are bringing to it a local Labour Party political philosophy (up against a Conservative government at Westminster). The local democratic process involving regular elections of a representative authority and regular voting in the council and in committees ensures that decision-making on refugees reflects local opinion. Finally, there are council employees, notably Simon, of No Recourse to Public Funds, and a handful of others within the ambit of Housing and Child Social Care. Perhaps we may see the school system, activated by Mother Ellen, as part of 'council services', or add it as a fifth partner. It does after all engage the energies of a distinct group, Lambeth's schoolchildren, analytical and motivated, playing an unusually significant role.

As community activists go, those of Lambeth at the time the Refugees Welcome movement surged were exceptionally well organized. Not only was there a healthy number of organizations spread through all the major faith groups and humanist non-believers, but 21 of them would before long be working closely together in the framework of Lambeth Citizens. Membership of a local Citizens group afforded organizing method and even training. For instance, the Principal of

Saint Gabriel's school attended a Citizens training course with several local faith leaders. Lambeth Citizens, coming together in a monthly meeting to share information, devise strategy and plan implementation, was in a way not out of kilter with Lambeth Council's own cycle of meetings. And membership of Citizens UK furnished a mechanism for addressing Westminster and Whitehall.

Having 'membership' and being able to render it vocally or get it on the streets adds weight to the policy arguments you want to make to your local council. Mother Ellen says:

> Citizens UK say that community organizing is 'assembling power' for positive change. Our power is people. Schools have people. Churches have people. The membership of our school and church in Lambeth Citizens gives us a vehicle to act *with others*, and in that way to be taken seriously by those in power. It was when we turned up to meet the councillors with all those *varied* people – not just me as a vicar, not just a delegate from a mosque, but all of us together – that we had an effect. When they saw that we were all working together, that's when they changed the policy on refugees.

So numbers, diversity and togetherness, yes, these are effective, but success also calls for persistence. Barbara Wilson of Corpus Christi, who has years of experience of working to influence council policy, says:

> It's always taken time for the council to act on something we're asking for. The pattern has been that we seek a meeting with them, put the case and they listen to us. At first they'll say, 'we can't afford it'. We'll withdraw for a while, then return to the issue. Eventually they come round to our point of view, say 'yes', and implement the policy we've been asking for.

This is how, some years earlier, a Lambeth Living Wage had become council policy. Likewise in successive campaigns, measures for a safer city, for ending extortion and alleviating debt, and for affordable housing, were won.

A significant factor in the success of the Lambeth Citizens Refugees Welcome movement is that it doesn't restrict itself to demanding of the authorities a given policy, but shows itself willing to help implement it. They offered, and made good on the offer, to actually find landlords with appropriately priced accommodation to house Syrian families. They came through with donations of furniture and equipment. They undertook to welcome and befriend families on arrival, and when the policy was implemented they were as good as their word. They found foster carers for unaccompanied children even while the Home Office dragged its feet over bringing them to the borough. Rabbi Janet Darley told me:

> Our relationship with the council was so strong that at the time of the Austerity budget cuts in 2008, when they were very worried that they might be forced into severe reductions in services, we offered the efforts of the members in our voluntary groups. We coordinated the 'resilience' of the voluntary sector in relation to the council. The council trusted us. It's always been a respectful and collegial relationship. So when the issue of refugees came up we said to the council, 'It's important to us. We want to be involved. We'll work with you, in a relationship of partnership.'

This is recognized within the council too. Simon Sandberg, the officer responsible for refugees and asylum seekers, told me that 'Citizens are unique. They're very good at engaging with the authorities. It's primary for them.' And council Leader, Lib Peck, says of them: 'Citizens are an excellent local group. What I value about them is that they are both principled and pragmatic. They don't just challenge us, they are always also looking for solutions.' She says whatever the issues they've raised at different times the council have listened to them and taken their advice. On the Living Wage, for instance, Citizens had been patient. 'They realized it couldn't be implemented overnight. It was very costly after all to raise the wages of all the lowest grade council employees and workers in firms contracted to the council.' On refugees, it was never that she and other councillors didn't want to act. Indeed they felt keenly their duty to alleviate the suffering in whatever way they could. True, they had to be very cautious about the expenditure involved, for government funds were unlikely to cover the full cost. But 'Lambeth Citizens made it easier for us to move forward on it by the very practical step they took of sourcing accommodation for refugee families'.

FLAT FOR THREE: PROVISIONAL LONDONERS

The partnership described above, working to open the borough to refugees and settle them here, had its outliers and helpers. Among them were the several property owners, be they individuals or housing associations, identified by the activists as willing and able to offer suitably priced tenancies. These landlords are by no means necessarily motivated by a wish to support asylum. One of them, however, I had the luck to meet and I found, on the contrary, that she'd been in touch with refugee realities for some time.

Katie Barlow is an independent film maker. Since late 2015 she'd been documenting the refugee crisis. Alert to the headlines of war and migration, she had travelled to Calais, Dunkirk and Lesbos, interviewing and filming, and had been greatly touched by all she saw. She says, 'I felt I had to do what I could. I wanted to tell these human stories and make them known through whatever outlets I could find.' One of her films, shown on Channel 4, featured two young Afghans who crossed the Channel in container trucks.[50] But somehow she felt uneasy. 'There's always a certain awkwardness in filming. Just observing hardship – that's somehow compromising. I wanted to actually *help*.'

Back in London, Katie met a woman who asked her to contribute to an information film about the Syrian Vulnerable Persons Resettlement Scheme. As she investigated this story she picked up on the housing factor, learning just how much depended on private landlords stepping forward with offers of flats at lower-than-market rates. Some time later Katie would write a Facebook post about this, through which she reached several thousand people. Many of them responded saying they wanted to find a way to help house a refugee family. She felt this indicated that the majority of people, like herself, just 'hadn't heard about the scheme or didn't know they could help in this way', because the government had failed to advertise and promote it.

Now it just so happens that Katie herself owns a two-bedroom flat in a street-fronting block of apartments in Brixton – a property she holds on a mortgage and normally lets for an income. She had indeed just signed up a new tenant. 'What a shame, I thought! If I'd known about this sooner I would have been happy to rent to a refugee family. My mortgage is reasonable. I could afford a little drop in rent. I'm in a position to help. Not everyone is.' Then, by chance, her prospective tenant pulled out. Her flat became free! She stepped forward and offered it to the council for a Syrian family. At last she had found a practical way to help.

The family who were allocated Katie's flat, nominated for SVPRS by the United Nations Refugee Agency in the Middle East, are a couple in their twenties, Merry and Nehad, with a little boy, Joud, who is two and a half. They are Syrians from Aleppo, of the Christian (Catholic) minority, and university-educated professionals. They had not been part of the uprising against Assad. In fact, Nehad told me, they are opposed to both Assad and the insurgents, for 'both sides are killing, both are to blame'. Their flight from Syria, in other words, had not been politically driven. It was simple necessity. A bomb fell through the roof of their four-storey apartment block. They escaped unharmed, but the building was no longer habitable. Indeed, the great city of Aleppo was being reduced to rubble around them. Besides, Nehad was in danger of being enlisted into compulsory service with the national military. So, with the equivalent of $400 in hand, they took a bus to join the million or more Syrian refugees harboured by neighbouring Lebanon. In Beirut they were lucky to avoid the refugee camps. They sustained themselves by part-time, lowly jobs in fast-food outlets, earning barely enough to maintain themselves in cramped lodgings. A little later, Joud was born.

Then occurred a violent incident on the street, in which Nehad was set upon by a hostile gang of Lebanese criminals involved in a ransom scandal. He was seriously injured and left for dead, to be rescued from the roadway many hours later. Then he was taken to hospital and subjected to lengthy surgery involving, among other things, the insertion of a metal plate into his leg. The operation saved his life, but left him crippled. The couple were bankrupted by the cost of the medical care. They received some assistance from the Christian church, however, and a charitable organization took up their case and eventually prevailed upon the United Nations Refugee Agency to nominate the family, on account of Nehad's condition, for transfer to the UK under SVPRS.

I met Nehad, Merry and Joud, and also Katie, in March 2017 at the flat of which they are now tenants and she their landlady. Nehad

I learned is getting good medical care and will soon have corrective surgery on his leg at St Thomas's Hospital. Merry is very happy to be getting dental treatment. They are receiving good support from the Single Homeless Project, who met them at Heathrow and brought them to the flat and have since provided a (female) care worker and (male) Arabic interpreter. Lambeth Citizens' welcome party ensured they were quickly in touch with the Syrian families that had already arrived under SVPRS, including the Archbishop's tenants.

Once they are settled and their English has improved, Nehad hopes to obtain the accountancy work his Syrian degree fits him for, and Merry, who is qualified in banking, thinks, as Joud reaches school age, she will work towards becoming a teacher. Meanwhile, she hopes to exchange Arabic for English lessons. And she's set up a WhatsApp group with some of the other Syrian women. The family enjoy the nearby park, and Joud is delighted to have close at hand the four things he loves most in life: chicken nuggets, chips, Nutella and noodles. 'But Katie is the best thing that's happened to us in England', says Merry.

When I met Councillor Lib Peck, the Leader of Lambeth Council, I asked her whether it was difficult to reconcile the demands on resources of, on the one hand refugees, and on the other the many impoverished and poorly-housed local people. Is there not a conflict of interest leading to potential resentment if newcomers are seen to be favoured? She replied, 'There's been surprisingly little criticism of the decision to accept refugees in the borough. In fact, I can't think of a single instance, inside the council or outside. People have been incredibly welcoming.' She believes that,

> Without glossing over the deprivation of many in Lambeth and the reality of the government's public expenditure cuts, it's a population of huge diversity where 120 languages are spoken. And that's celebrated, a good energy comes from it. Council research shows the population has a lot of 'cohesion'. A high proportion of people say they 'get on well together'. So I think it's a borough that is fairly at peace with itself, and that's why people are able to welcome refugees rather than feel threatened by them.

This is borne out too, she reminded me, by the absence of any UKIP presence locally, and the fact that Lambeth returned a 78 per cent 'Remain' vote in the 2016 EU referendum, second only to Gibraltar among UK constituencies.

While Lambeth and other local councils shifted during 2016 towards acceptance of both Syrian vulnerable families and UASCs, in the spring of 2017 the government itself regressed. In February, Prime Minister Theresa May abruptly announced, without consulting local authorities, that she was forthwith cancelling the 'Dubs' scheme, thus reneging on the acceptance of an anticipated 3,000 lone children from the Calais Jungle.[51] Councillor Lib Peck and others from Lambeth joined protests at 10 Downing Street. Then on 28 March, in an ambiguous move, Amber Rudd, Secretary of State for Home Affairs, announced that the status of SVPRS families would, with retrospective effect, be changed from one of 'humanitarian protection' to that of 'refugee'. This would be beneficial in providing them with a few more entitlements, such as certain benefits, travel documents and swifter access to student support.[52] On the other hand, it would render them liable to the mean-minded regulation introduced only a few weeks earlier, that 'refugees', when their asylum status has been upgraded to 'limited leave to remain', would no longer automatically obtain UK citizenship at the end of the five-year period of leave. Instead their case would be reviewed, and if the country from which they had escaped were now deemed 'safe', they would be required to return there – and subjected to forcible deportation should they fail to go voluntarily.[53] Thus 'refugee status' will no longer mean that refugees such as Merry and Nehad can sleep peacefully in their beds and spend their days putting energy into building durable new livelihoods and long-term careers. Rather, eventual UK citizenship must remain in doubt, their re-homing insecure, and their identity as 'Londoners' no more than provisional.[54]

Notes

Unless otherwise stated, website references throughout the footnotes were last accessed in March 2017.

INTRODUCTION

1. See Cynthia Cockburn, *The Local State: Management of Cities and People* (London: Pluto Press, 1977); and *In and Against the State* (Pluto Press, 1979) co-authored by what we called 'The London Edinburgh Weekend Return Group'.
2. Cynthia Cockburn, *Brothers: Male Dominance and Technological Change* (London: Pluto Press, 1983); *Machinery of Dominance: Women, Men and Technical Know-how* (Pluto Press, 1985); and *In The Way of Women: Men's Resistance to Sex Equality in Organizations* (Basingstoke and London: Macmillan, 1991).
3. Cynthia Cockburn, *The Space Between Us: Negotiating Gender and National Identities in Conflict* (London and New York: Zed Books, 1998); *The Line: Women, Partition and the Gender Order in Cyprus* (London and New York: Zed Books, 2004); *From Where We Stand: War, Women's Activism and Feminist Analysis* (London and New York: Zed Books, 2007); and *Antimilitarism: Political and Gender Dynamics of Peace Movements* (London and New York: Palgrave Macmillan, 2012). For other titles, see my website www.cynthiacockburn.org.

CHAPTER 1

1. See Vision of Britain, website managed by the Department of Geography, University of Portsmouth, http://tinyurl.com/knqbguh
2. Migration Observatory, *London: Census Profile*. Briefing. 20 May, 2013, http://tinyurl.com/l6kf7cu
3. London Datastore. Derived from Office of National Statistics, London. Census of Population 2011. Table: London Borough Detailed Country of Birth (2011). Online at http://tinyurl.com/k7c3wv6
4. Nick Merriman (ed.), *The Peopling of London: Fifteen Thousand Years of Settlement from Overseas* (London: The Museum of London, 1993).
5. Ibid., 32.
6. Ibid.

7. Philip Marfleet, 'City of Paradox: The Refugee Experience', in P. Cardullo, R. Gupta and J. Hakim (eds), *London: City of Paradox* (London: Centre for Research on Migration, Refugees and Belonging, University of East London, 2014), 48–53.

8. Cited in ibid., 7.

9. Steve Cohen, *Standing on the Shoulders of Fascism: From Immigration Control to the Strong State* (Trent, UK and Sterling, USA: Trentham Books, 2006); and Runnymede Trust, *British Immigration Control: A Brief Guide*, authored by Paul Gordon and Francesca Klug (London: The Runnymede Trust, 1984).

10. Runnymede Trust, ibid., iii.

11. My terminology here needs explanation. I write in the understanding that 'race' is not a scientific but a social construct, and its unquestioning use is often derogatory (see Robert Miles, *Racism* (London and New York: Routledge, 1989)). I shall therefore always use 'race', and its derivatives 'racial' and 'racially', in quotation marks. In signifying matters of physical appearance I shall use the science-based concept of 'phenotype', meaning the set of observable characteristics of an individual (including skin colour and hair texture) resulting from the interaction over millennia of its genotype with the environment. An argument could be made for signalling the complex intentions of the words black, brown and coloured in the discourse described here by placing them in quotation marks – but to avoid tedious overemphasis I have chosen not to do this.

12. Runnymede Trust, *British Immigration Control*, 4.

13. Home Office, *Immigration from the Commonwealth*. Cmnd. 2739 (London: H.M. Stationery Office, 1965).

14. Steve Cohen, *Standing on the Shoulders of Fascism*, 7.

15. Zig Layton-Henry, 'Britain: From Immigration Control to Migration Management', in Wayne A. Cornelius, T. Tsuda, P. L. Martin and J. F. Hollifield, *Controlling Immigration: A Global Perspective*, 2nd edition (California: Stanford University Press, 2004), 297–338: 306.

16. Figures in this and the following paragraph derive from Office of National Statistics, London. Historical Census Tables, online at http://tinyurl. com/k7c3wv6 – I have also found London Datastore, Greater London Authority, a helpful source of Census statistics and comparisons. See, for example, 'Census 2011 Demography', http://tinyurl.com/kb9m3gu

17. Alice Bloch, 'A New Era or More of the Same? Asylum Policy in the UK', *Journal of Refugee Studies*, Vol.13, No.1, 2000, 29–42.

18. See for instance British Refugee Council and Association of London Government, *No Place to Call Home: A Report and Recommendations for London Local Authorities on the Implementation of New Legislation affecting Refugees and Asylum Seekers* (London, 1996).

19. Steve Cohen, *No-one is Illegal: Asylum and Immigration Control Past and Present* (Trent, UK, and Sterling, USA: Trentham Books, 2003); and Steve Cohen, *Standing on the Shoulders of Fascism*.

20. Zig Layton-Henry, 'Britain: From Immigration Act to Migration Management'.

21. CAMPACC, 'A Permanent State of Terror?' Published by Campaign against Criminalising Communities and the Index on Censorship (London, 2003).

22. Ibid., 21.

23. Fran Cetti, 'Asylum and the Discourse of Terror: The European "Security State"', in B. Brescher, M. Devenney and A. Winter (eds) *Discourses and Practices of Terrorism: Interrogating Terror* (London: Routledge, 2010).

24. I have drawn in the above section on the *Guardian* newspaper's web page 'A–Z of Legislation', http://tinyurl.com/kn7dx6a – in the case of the Immigration Act of 2014, I draw on the online report by Jasmine Shergill at www.turbervilles.co.uk/blog/5-things-you-need-to-know-about-the-immigration-act-2014 – accessed November 2016.

25. Orson Nava, director, *Everyday Borders*. Film (London: Centre for Research on Migration, Refugees and Belonging, University of East London, May 2015), http://tinyurl.com/hh74fd6

26. Don Flynn, 'Frontier Anxiety: Living with the Stress of the Every-day Border', *Soundings: Journal of Politics and Culture*, No.61, Winter 2016, 62–71.

27. Home Office, *Contest: The United Kingdom's Strategy for Countering Terrorism*, 3rd edition (London: H.M. Stationery Office, 2011, first published 2003).

28. Home Office, *Prevent Strategy*. Cmnd. 8092 (London: H.M. Stationery Office, June 2011, first published 2003), http://tinyurl.com/oxz5uzy

29. Local Government Association, 'Councils' Role in Preventing Extremism' (London, 2015), http://tinyurl.com/zar6747

30. Open Society Justice Initiative, 'Eroding Trust: The UK's Prevent Counter-Extremism Strategy in Health and Education' (New York and London, 2016), http://tinyurl.com/kukhrbz

31. Alan Travis, *Guardian*, 11 November 2016.

32. Vaughan Robinson, 'Dispersal Policies in the UK', in Vaughan Robinson, R. Andersson and S. Musterd (eds) *Spreading the 'Burden'? A Review of Policies to Disperse Asylum Seekers and Refugees* (Bristol: The Policy Press, 2003), 103–47.

33. Chartered Institute of Housing, 'Providing a Safe Haven: Housing Asylum Seekers and Refugees'. Policy paper (London: Chartered Institute of Housing, 2003).

34. Vaughan Robinson, 'Dispersal Policies in the UK'; and Audit Commission, 'Another Country: Implementing Dispersal Under the Immigration and Asylum Act 1999' (London: Audit Commission, 2000).

35. Audit Commission, 'A New City: Supporting Asylum Seekers and Refugees in London' (London: Audit Commission, 2000).

36. Refugee Council, www.researchasylum.org.uk/node/3167

37. Cited in Vaughan Robinson, 'Dispersal Policies in the UK', 126.

38. Pippa Crerar, *Standard Newspaper*, 29 November, 2016. See also Kate Forrester, 'London Boroughs Ask What's Next for Asylum-Seeking Children Settled in the Capital Since Calais Camp Was Dismantled', 2 December 2016, London Councils, http://tinyurl.com/js8meh3

39. Refugee Council, 'England's Forgotten Refugees: Out of the Fire Into the Frying Pan' (London: Refugee Council, 2016), http://tinyurl.com/k8gv94n

40. London Councils, 'Budget Cuts Are Unsustainable', 18 December 2015, http://tinyurl.com/k2muf5y

41. Figures published online by home.co.uk, a property search website, http://tinyurl.com/mzkufcq

42. Published online by *City A.M.*, journal and blog, http://tinyurl.com/phsr6lg

43. It is interesting to look at what this means for the five boroughs we shall be visiting in following chapters. The London Borough of Hackney had 19,715 on its waiting list; Tower Hamlets had 19,783; Hounslow 8,504; Camden an alarming 24,644; and Lambeth 18,792. From London Datastore, 2016, data furnished by the Department of Communities and Local Government, online at http://tinyurl.com/hs7lbah

44. *Building Construction Design*, 'Statistics Gathered by Think Tank New London Architecture, Reveal Frightening Extent of London Housing Crisis', 2016, http://tinyurl.com/j7vgtho

45. British Refugee Council and Association of London Government, *No Place to Call Home*.

46. London Asylum Seekers Consortium, 'A Warm Welcome? Public Services and Managing Migration in London'. Scoping Research and Introductory Report (London: LASC, 2008).

47. Home Office, *Building Cohesive Communities: A Report of the Ministerial Group on Public Order and Community Cohesion*. Chaired by John Denham (London: H.M. Stationery Office, 2001).

48. Independent Review Team, 'Community Cohesion: A Report of the Independent Review Team', chaired by Ted Cantle. Known as the 'Cantle Report' (London: Home Office, 2001).

49. Home Office, *Secure Borders, Safe Haven: Integration with Diversity in Modern Britain*. Cmnd. 5378 (London: H.M. Stationery Office, 2001), http://tinyurl.com/mw5z2ww

50. Commission on Integration and Cohesion, *Our Shared Future*. Final report (London: H.M. Stationery Office, 2007), 9, http://tinyurl.com/2at69z

51. Ibid., 10.

52. Ibid., 7.

53. Local Government Intelligence Unit, 'Connected Localism: A Blueprint for Better Public Services'. Report and essays (London, 2013), 8, http://tinyurl.com/osa95um

54. Runnymede Trust, 'Developing Community Cohesion: Understanding the Issues, Delivering Solutions'. Report of a conference (London, 2003), 5.

55. *Building Construction Design*, 'Statistics Gathered'.

56. Peter Ratcliffe, 'Community Cohesion: Reflections on a Flawed Paradigm', *Critical Social Policy*, Vol.32, No.2, 2012, 262–81.

CHAPTER 2

1. Gerard Chaliand (ed.) *A People Without a Country: The Kurds and Kurdistan* (London: Zed Books, 1993); and *The Tragedy of the Kurds* (London: Zed Books, 1994).

2. James Mellaart, *Čatal Hüyük: A Neolithic Town in Anatolia* (New York: McGraw-Hill, 1967).

3. Michael M. Gunter, *The Kurds Ascending: The Evolving Solution to the Kurdish Problem in Iraq and Turkey* (Basingstoke: Palgrave Macmillan, 2008).

4. David McDowall, *A Modern History of the Kurds* (London: I.B.Tauris, 1996).

5. Ibid., 407.

6. Ibid.; and Michael M. Gunter, *The Kurds Ascending*.

7. Abdullah Öcalan, *Democratic Confederalism*. Booklet, International Initiative Edition (London,and Cologne: Transmedia Publishing Ltd, 2011), 27, 53.

8. Michael M. Gunter, *The Kurds Ascending*.

9. Cengiz Gunes, *The Kurdish National Movement in Turkey: From Protest to Resistance* (London and New York: Routledge, 2012).

10. United Nations Office of the High Commissioner for Human Rights (UNOHCHR), *Report on the Human Rights Situation in South-East Turkey: July 2015 to December 2016*, Geneva, http://tinyurl.com/zss8g58

11. Kerim Yıldız, *The Kurds in Turkey: EU Accession and Human Rights* (London and Ann Arbor: Pluto Press, 2005).

12. This chapter was mainly written in early 2015. In the remainder of that year and during 2016 when, as we have seen, armed violence between the state and the PKK recurred, it was in the context of the intensification of the civil war in Syria, across Turkey's southern border, in which Turkish, Iraqi and Syrian Kurds have all been, in different ways and with different effects, active combatants.

13. Office of National Statistics, Home Office. Asylum Statistics. Volume 2. Table as_02: Asylum applications and initial decisions for main applicants and dependants, by country of nationality, 1979–2015. Online at http://tinyurl.com/ltzlmgg

14. Osten Wahlbeck, 'Community Work and Exile Politics: Kurdish Refugee Associations in London', *Journal of Refugee Studies*, Vol.11, No.3, 1998,

215–30; and *Kurdish Diasporas: A Comparative Study of Kurdish Refugee Communities* (Basingstoke: Macmillan, 1999).

15. Kurdish Human Rights Project, *What Impact Does UK Government Legislation and Policy have on the Kurdish Diaspora?* Report (Berlin: Berghof Peace Support, Centre for Just Peace and Democracy, 2011).

16. London Borough of Hackney, *A Place for Everyone: Hackney Council's Corporate Plan to 2018* (London: Hackney Borough Council, 2015).

17. See http://tinyurl.com/hzb5ueg

18. Roj Women's Association, *A Woman's Struggle: Using Gender Lenses to Understand the Plight of Women Human Rights Defenders in Kurdish Regions of Turkey*. Booklet (London: Roj Women's Association, 2012).

19. Anna Grabolle-Çeliker, *Kurdish Life in Contemporary Turkey: Migration, Gender and Ethnic Identity* (London: I.B.Tauris, 2013).

20. Handan Çağlayan, *Mothers, Comrades and Goddesses: Women in the Kurdish Movement and the Formation of Women's Identity* (Turkey: Iletism, 2007), informal translation of excerpts. See also Handan Çağlayan, 'From Kawa the Blacksmith to Ishtar the Goddess: Gender Constructions in Ideological-Political Discourses of the Kurdish Movement in Post-1980 Turkey: Possibilities and Limits', *European Journal of Turkish Studies*, No.14, 2012, http://tinyurl.com/heqbovk

21. Dilşah Pinar Ensari, 'At the Crossroads of Education and Politics: Kurdish Women Students in Istanbul'. MA Thesis, cultural studies (Istanbul: Sabanci University, 2012).

22. Handan Çağlayan, 'From Kawa the Blacksmith to Ishtar the Goddess'.

23. See for instance Abdullah Öcalan, *Democratic Confederalism*; and TATORT Kurdistan, *Democratic Autonomy in North Kurdistan: The Council Movement, Gender Liberation, and Ecology in Practice* (Porsgrunn, Norway: New Compass Press, 2013).

24. For example, Abdullah Öcalan, *Liberating Life: Woman's Revolution*. Booklet (Cologne: International Initiative and Mesopotamian Publishers, Neuss, 2013).

25. James Mellaart, *Çatal Hüyük*.

26. Abdullah Öcalan, *Liberating Life*.

27. Ibid., 11.

28. Gerder Lerner, *The Creation of Patriarchy* (Oxford: Oxford University Press, 1986).

29. Maria Mies, *Patriarchy and Accumulation on a World Scale* (London: Zed Books, 1986).

30. Abdullah Öcalan, *Liberating Life*, 47.

31. Ibid., 43.

32. Ibid., 27.

33. Ibid., 51.

34. Handan Çağlayan, *Mothers, Comrades and Goddesses*.

35. Komalên Jinên Kurdistan, 'Jineology Conference 2014', http://tinyurl.com/hoe7a7x

36. 'Bercem' is a pseudonym.
37. Ayar Ata, 'The Transformation of Identity within a Diaspora'. PhD thesis, international development, emergencies and refugee studies (London: London Southbank University, Weeks Centre, 2014).
38. Kurdish Human Rights Project, *What Impact*, 5.
39. TATORT Kurdistan, *Democratic Autonomy in North Kurdistan*.
40. In preparing this chapter I benefited greatly from interviews afforded me by Ali-Riza Aksoy (Hackney Refugee Forum), Estella Schmid (Peace in Kurdistan, and Campaign against Criminalizing Communities – CAMPACC), Hackney Councillor Feryal Demirci, Houzon Mahmoud, Margaret Owen (Widows for Peace), and Sonia Khan (Head of Policy, London Borough of Hackney). I would especially like to thank Suna Parlak, 'Bercem' (a pseudonym), and Turkan Budak for generously recounting, and permitting me to reproduce, aspects of their personal histories. Two other women who kindly granted me interviews asked, for reasons I fully respect, that I neither publish their accounts nor reveal their names. Ayar Ata and Ayse-Gul Altinay took time to read an early draft of this chapter and gave me helpful comments which I have gratefully taken on board – any remaining errors are my own responsibility. I warmly thank all these people for their help.

CHAPTER 3

1. Karen McVeigh, 'Somalia Famine Fears Prompt UN Call for "Immediate and Massive" Reaction', *Guardian*, 3 February 2017.
2. United Nations Office for the Coordination of Humanitarian Affairs (UNOCHA), *Somalia Humanitarian and Development Statistics*, July 2014, http://tinyurl.com/gmgfnro
3. UNDP, *Somalia's Missing Million: The Somali Diaspora and its Role in Development*, 29 August 2011, http://tinyurl.com/zwl2t54
4. UNDP, *Somalia Human Development Report 2012*, 28 September 2012, http:/tinyurl.com/9ysnbvu
5. UNDP 2012 ibid.
6. Afyare Abdi Elmi, *Understanding the Somalia Conflagration: Identity, Political Islam and Peacebuilding* (London: Pluto Press, 2010).
7. Haggar Erlich, *Islam and Christianity in the Horn of Africa: Somalia, Ethiopia, Sudan* (Boulder and London: Lynne Rienner, 2010).
8. Afyare Abdi Elmi, *Understanding the Somalia Conflagration*.
9. Ibid.; and Mary Harper, *Getting Somalia Wrong: Faith, War and Hope in a Shattered State* (London and New York: Zed Books, 2012).
10. Adam B. Lowther, *Americans and Asymmetric Conflict: Lebanon, Somalia and Afghanistan* (Westport, CT and London: Praeger Security International, 2007).

11. Lidwien Kapteijns, *Clan Cleansing in Somalia: The Ruinous Legacy of 1991* (Philadelphia: University of Pennsylvania Press, 2013).
12. Haggar Erlich, *Islam and Christianity in the Horn of Africa*; Mary Harper, *Getting Somalia Wrong*.
13. Armed Conflict Location and Event Data Project (ACLED), 'Real-Time Analysis of African Political Violence', *Conflict Trends Report*, No. 29 (August 2014), http://tinyurl.com/gmz75gr
14. Shaul Shay, *Somalia in Transition since 2006* (New Brunswick and London: Transaction Publishers, 2014).
15. Murithi Mutiga, *Guardian*, 7 April, 2015, http://tinyurl.com/jelrnpe
16. Human Rights Watch, 'The Power These Men Have Over Us', 8 September 2014, http://tinyurl.com/jz3f3qr
17. Human Rights Watch, *Dispatches*, 'Somalia – Firing Squad on the Football Field', 13 March 2014, http://tinyurl.com/zw24cdu
18. Fund for Peace, *Fragile States Index 2015* (Washington, DC: Fund for Peace, 2016), http://tinyurl.com/o9nscr6
19. David Hayes and Harun Hassan, 'Somalia between Violence and Hope', article in *Open Democracy Online Journal*, 21 July 2009, http://tinyurl.com/jah4ygc
20. Mary Harper, *Getting Somalia Wrong*, 200.
21. Rhoda M. Ibrahim, 'Women's Role in the Pastoral Economy', in Judith Gardner and Judy El Bushra (eds), *Somalia, the Untold Story: The War through the Eyes of Somali Women* (London: Pluto Press, 2004), 24–50.
22. UNDP, *Somalia Human Development Report 2012*.
23. Fowzia Musse, 'War Crimes Against Women and Girls', in Judith Gardner and Judy El Bushra (eds), *Somalia, the Untold Story*, 69–96.
24. UNOCHA, *Somalia Humanitarian and Development Statistics*.
25. Amina Mohamoud Warsame, 'Crisis or Opportunity? Somali Women Traders and the War', in Judith Gardner and Judy El Bushra (eds), *Somalia, the Untold Story*, 116–38.
26. United Nations Development Fund for Women (UNIFEM), East and Horn of Africa Regional Office, *Gender Justice in Somaliland/Somalia* (Nairobi: Rock Foundation Trust, 2005), 14, http://tinyurl.com/kwvgh4n
27. Zeynab Mohamed Hassan and Shukri Hariir Ismail, 'Women and Peace-Making in Somaliland', in Judith Gardner and Judy El Bushra (eds), *Somalia, the Untold Story*, 142–52.
28. Dekha Ibrahim, 'Women's Roles in Peace-Making in the Somali Community in North Eastern Kenya', in Judith Gardner and Judy El Bushra (eds), *Somalia, the Untold Story*, 166–74.
29. Sonya Newland, *Somalia* (London: Hachette, 2012).
30. Hala Al-Karib, 'Rebuilding Somalia', 17 December 2012. Article in *Open Democracy Online Journal*, http://tinyurl.com/jmr64xy
31. International Organization for Migration, *Mapping of the Somali Diaspora in England and Wales* (Geneva: International Organization for Migration, 2013), http://tinyurl.com/z9uj2na

32. Office of National Statistics, Home Office. *Asylum Statistics*. Volume 2. Table as_02: Asylum applications and initial decisions for main applicants and dependants, by country of nationality, 1979–2015. Online at http://tinyurl.com/ltzlmgg

33. David J. Griffiths, *Somali and Kurdish Refugees in London: New Identities in the Diaspora* (London: Ashgate, 2002), 294.

34. A good source of demographic statistics on London is London Datastore, Greater London Authority. See, for example, 'Census 2011 Demography', http://tinyurl.com/kb9m3gu

35. London Borough of Tower Hamlets, 'Ethnicity in Tower Hamlets: Analysis of 2011 Census Data', *Research Briefing Series*, No. 2013–01 (February 2013), http://tinyurl.com/lkqb2s3 – and Borough Statistics, http://tinyurl.com/lxjmll7 – http://tinyurl.com/ktg8rjo – and http://tinyurl.com/k8ttvwq

36. Farhan Hassan, Munira Musse, Jaffar Jama and Faduma Mohamed, *Mapping the Somali Diaspora in England and Wales* (Geneva: International Organization for Migration, 2013).

37. East London Alliance, 'Understanding East London's Somali Communities' (August 2010), http://tinyurl.com/zxm6m47

38. For example, London Borough of Tower Hamlets, *Strategic Plan 2015/16*, http://tinyurl.com/myj2ast – and *Strategic Plan 2016/17–2018/19*, http://tinyurl.com/ze8wdpy

39. London Centre for Social Impact, 'Action on Poverty in Tower Hamlets: A Community-Based Participation Solution', 2012, http://tinyurl.com/zk8celz

40. Karen Chouhan, Stuart Speeden and Undaleeb Qazi , *Experience of Poverty and Ethnicity in London* (York: Joseph Rowntree Foundation, 2011).

41. Alice Bloch, 'Labour Market Participation and Conditions of Employment: A Comparison of Minority Ethnic Groups and Refugees in Britain', *Sociological Research Online*, Vol.9, No.2, 2004, http://tinyurl.com/j6drbq9 – and Institute for Public Policy Research (IPPR), *Britain's Immigrants: An Economic Profile*. September 2007, http://tinyurl.com/gq69ggm

42. East London Alliance, 'Understanding East London's Somali Communities', 85.

43. M. A. Hassan, H. Lewis and S. Lukes, *No Voice, Little Choice: The Somali Housing Emergency in North and East London* (London: Karin Housing Association Ltd, 2009).

44. Patrick Wintour, *Guardian*, 4 November 2014.

45. See this official account in Press Release, 'Secretary of State Sends in Commissioners to Tower Hamlets', issued by H.M. Government on 17 December, 2014, at http://tinyurl.com/mrhnhcg

46. Rabina Khan, 'The Trouble in Tower Hamlets', article in *Red Pepper* (February–March 2015), 38–40.

47. Rajeev Syal, *Guardian*, 7 June, 2015.

48. London Borough of Tower Hamlets, *Strategic Plan 2015/16*, http://tinyurl.com/myj2ast – and *Strategic Plan 2016/17–2018/19*, http://tinyurl.com/ze8wdpy

49. See UK Government Legislation, *Equality Act 2010*, http://tinyurl.com/lzy22tv – and London Borough of Tower Hamlets, 'Single Equality Framework', http://tinyurl.com/lt4xxdc

50. David Griffiths, *Somali and Kurdish Refugees in London*, 94.

51. East London Alliance, 'Understanding East London's Somali Communities'.

52. See Trust for London, https://www.trustforlondon.org.uk/ – and Council of Somali Organisations, http://councilofsomaliorgs.com/content/reports

53. Alice Bloch, 'Labour Market Participation and Conditions of Employment'.

54. Ken Menkhaus, 'The Role and Impact of the Somali Diaspora in Peace-Building, Governance and Development', in Raj Bardouille, Muna Ndulo and Margaret Grieco (eds), *Africa's Finances: The Contribution of Remittance* (Cambridge: Cambridge Scholars Publishing, 2008), 187–202.

55. Farhan Hassan et al., *No Voice, Little Choice*, 2013.

56. Mary Harper, *Getting Somalia Wrong*, 56.

57. Mark Bradbury, *Becoming Somaliland* (London: Progressio, 2008), 73.

58. In the London Borough of Brent I found a rather different aspect of the diaspora that enabled me to see Tower Hamlets in perspective. Brent has a greater preponderance of so-called ethnic minorities than any other borough in London: they are 71 per cent of the total population – see London Borough of Brent, 'Brent's Borough Profile: Summary', 2010, http://tinyurl.com/mgmkemr

    They are well represented on the council, whose elected membership is well over half non-white. Among them are many Somalis. I had a chance to meet Harbi Farah, one of the two Somali borough councillors, who had involved himself deeply in council/community relations, both as chair of Brent Voluntary Sector Liaison Forum and Deputy Lead Member for Stronger Communities. There is, Harbi confirms, much more clan variation than in Tower Hamlets, with its dominant presence of Isaaq. The conflictual Darod and Hawiye, from south and central Somalia, and many other clans and sub-clans, have a presence in Brent. But a growing movement to end tribalism, based in Shepherds Bush in West London, and with offices in Mogadishu and Nairobi, is attracting some energetic young Somali activists and supports the trend to reduce clan identification in London and elsewhere in the diaspora – see Anti-Tribalism Movement, 'Our Work', 2015, http://theatm.org/what-we-do/our-work/

59. David Griffiths, *Somali and Kurdish Refugees in London*, 108.

60. H. Summerfield, 'Patterns of Adaptation: Somali and Bangladeshi Women in Britain', in G. Buijs (ed.), *Migrant Women: Crossing Boundaries and Changing Identities* (Oxford and Providence, RI: Berg, 1993).

61. I wish to thank warmly the following individuals for furnishing me with information, advice and encouragement in the preparation of this chapter. First, I had the privilege of interviewing four individual Somali women resident in London: Naima Aden, Ruby Smith, Idil Mohamed Ahmed and Suad Hussein. I greatly appreciated the information and encouragement received from personnel at the Ocean Somali Community Association in Tower Hamlets, namely director Abdi Hassan, and staff members Aydarus Sarman, Mohamed Adan and Khadra Sarman. Thanks also for informative conversations with Abdi Yassin (Somali Action on Youth Crime), Bethan Lant (Praxis), Harbi Farah (London Borough of Brent and Help Somalia Foundation), Mahamed Ismail (Praxis), Mustafa Ibrahim (Tower Hamlets Somali Organizations Network) and Paul Butler (Council of Somali Organizations). Thanks to Shanara Matin, Service Manager, Research and Equality Team, Corporate Strategy and Equality Service, Susan Mulligan, Adviser, Communications Department and Emily Fieran-Reed, Service Manager, in Community, Cohesion, Engagement and Commissioning, all three in Tower Hamlets Council, for devoting time to an interview about council community policies. Finally, I owe a special debt of gratitude to those who told me something of their personal histories and agreed to my recounting them in this chapter: Hinda Ali and her partner Ali Jimale, Ubah Ibrahim and Dahabo Ahmed.

CHAPTER 4

1. *Economist*, 'Sri Lanka: A War Strange as Fiction', unauthored article, 7 June 2007, http://tinyurl.com/jng4kk9

2. Sri Lanka Tourism Development Authority, *Annual Statistical Report for 2014*, http://tinyurl.com/mq6d2zo

3. K. M. Da Silva, *A History of Sri Lanka* (India: Penguin Books, revised and updated edition, 2005).

4. Tamil Information Centre, *Tamils of Sri Lanka: The Quest for Human Dignity* (London: Tamil Information Centre, 2015).

5. Index Mundi, *Sri Lanka Demographics Profile 2014*, http://tinyurl.com/89ml6lf

6. Gordon Weiss, *The Cage: The Fight for Sri Lanka and the Last Days of the Tamil Tigers* (London: Vintage Books, 2012), 22.

7. Ibid., 27.

8. Ibid., 48.

9. Tamil Information Centre, *Tamils of Sri Lanka*.

10. Samanth Subramanian, *This Divided Island: Stories from the Sri Lankan War* (London: Atlantic Books, 2014), 48.

11. Ibid., 147.

12. Tamil Information Centre, *Tamils of Sri Lanka*.

13. Gordon Weiss, *The Cage*, 4.

14. Samanth Subramanian, *This Divided Island*, 247.

15. Gordon Weiss, *The Cage*, 142.

16. Channel 4 Television, 'Sri Lanka's Killing Fields' and 'No Fire Zone'. Films, 2011 and 2012, http://tinyurl.com/kcwng26

17. United Nations Office of the High Commissioner for Human Rights (UNOHCHR), *Investigation on Sri Lanka*. Geneva, 2015, http://tinyurl.com/z7kh99j

18. See Mark Salter and Erik Solheim, 'Roadmap to Reconciliation: Four Post-Election Challenges for Sri Lanka'. *Open Democracy Online Journal*, 31 August 2015, http://tinyurl.com/klp2yes

    The hopes may proved misplaced. In February 2017 the activist international NGO Sri Lanka Campaign for Peace and Justice obtained an advance reading of the UNOHCHR's review of the government's performance on its promises, due for publication in March 2017. It found therein 'a disappointing picture: the overwhelming majority of the government of Sri Lanka's commitments remain mostly or wholly unimplemented ... Plainly, the government still has a long way to go in order to address, meaningfully and effectively, the country's recent past.' Sri Lanka Campaign, 'Broken Promise: Monitoring the Government of Sri Lanka's Commitments for Achieving Justice and Reconciliation under Resolution 30/1', http://tinyurl.com/lt8707f

19. UNDP, *Human Development Report 2014: Sustaining Human Progress – Reducing Vulnerabilities and Building Resilience* (New York: United Nations, 2015), http://tinyurl.com/kman8k3

20. Institute of Policy Studies of Sri Lanka, *Migration Profile: Sri Lanka* (Colombo, 2013), http://tinyurl.com/kjqxkk6

21. Øivind Fuglerud, *Life on the Outside: The Tamil Diaspora and Long-Distance Nationalism* (London: Pluto Press, 1999).

22. Alagaiah Navaratnarajah, *Tamil Migration to the West* (Kyoto, Japan: Ryukoku University, 2005); and Michael Peel and Mary Salinsky, *Caught in the Middle: A Study of Tamil Torture Survivors Coming to the UK from Sri Lanka* (London: Medical Foundation for the Care of Victims of Torture, 2000).

23. Sarah Wayland, 'Ethnonationalist Networks and Transnational Opportunities: The Sri Lankan Tamil Diaspora', *Review of International Studies*, Vol.30, 2004, 405–26, 417.

24. Maya Ranganathan, *Eelam Online: The Tamil Diaspora and War in Sri Lanka* (Cambridge, UK: Cambridge Scholars Publishing, 2010).

25. Camilla Orjuela, 'Distant Warriors, Distant Peace Workers? Multiple Diaspora Roles in Sri Lanka's Violent Conflict', *Global Networks*, Vol.8, No.4, 2008, 436–52.

26. Sarah Wayland, 'Ethnonationalist Networks and Transnational Opportunities', 418.

27. Selvy Thiruchandran, *Stories from the Diaspora: Tamil Women Writing* (Sri Lanka: Vijitha Yapa Publications, 2006), 24.

28. Office of National Statistics, Home Office, Web Archive, Issue 14/98, Asylum Statistics UK 1997, 21 May 1998, tables 2.2, 3.1 and 3.3, http://tinyurl.com/l45zmjm

29. Office of National Statistics, Home Office, *Asylum Statistics*, 2016, Table as_02: Asylum applications and initial decisions for main applicants and dependants, by country of nationality, http://tinyurl.com/ltzlmgg

30. Richard Plender, 'The Catch 22 in Asylum 87', *Times*, 4 March 1987.

31. Stop Deportations, '2012: A Year (or More!) of Resistance Against Deportations to Sri Lanka', *Stop Deportations*, 2012, http://tinyurl.com/l2q4llg and video at http://tinyurl.com/93k7ngn

32. Human Rights Watch, 'UK Halts Deportation of Some Tamil Asylum Seekers', *News*, 2012, at https://www/hrw.org/news/2012/10/25/uk-halts-deportation-some-tamil-asylum-seekers – accessed September 2016.

33. Human Rights Watch, 'United Kingdom: Document Containing Cases of Sri Lankan Deportees Allegedly Tortured on Return,' *News*, 2012, http://tinyurl.com/lza68d3

34. Tamil Information Centre, *Tamils of Sri Lanka*.

35. Amnesty International, 'Tamils Set for UK Deportation Following Suicide Attempt', *News*, 16 June 2011, http://tinyurl.com/mfznoer

36. Home Office, *Country Information and Guidance Sri Lanka: Tamil Separatism*, London, August 2016, http://tinyurl.com/lk73mbr

37. For a thorough-going criticism of the UK's mass-deportation practices in this period, see Corporate Watch, *Collective Expulsion: The Case Against Britain's Mass Deportation Charter Flights*, (London: Corporate Watch, 2013), http://tinyurl.com/mpt7wgc

38. Julian Borger, 'Tamil Asylum-Seekers Being Deported from UK Despite Evidence of Torture', *Guardian*, 23 September 2014, http://tinyurl.com/kxtwgew

39. Foreign Affairs Committee, *The Foreign and Commonwealth Office's Human Rights Work in 2011: Third Report of the Session 2012–13*, 11 October 2012 (London: H.M. Stationery Office); and Channel 4 Television, 'Tamil Woman Raped by Sri Lankan Soldiers to be Deported', *News*, 4 July 2014, http://tinyurl.com/kapjbtt

40. L. M. Ratnapalan, 'Memories of Ethnic Violence in Sri Lanka among Immigrant Tamils in the UK', *Ethnic and Racial Studies*, Vol.35, No.9, 2012, 1539–57.

41. Ann-Belinda Steen, *The Varieties of the Tamil Refugee Experience in Denmark and England* (Copenhagen: Minority Studies, University of Copenhagen/Danish Centre for Human Rights, 1993).

42. Ahalya Balasunderam, 'Gang-Related Violence among Young People of the Tamil Refugee Diaspora in London', *Safer Communities*, Vol.8, No.2, April 2009, 34–41.

43. A good source of demographic statistics on London is London Datastore, Greater London Authority. See, for example, 'Census 2011 Demography', http://tinyurl.com/kb9m3gu

44. Hounslow Borough Council, *Cohesion and Integration Strategy 2012–2015: Action Plan*, 2012, http://tinyurl.com/kqcrxvr

45. Hounslow Borough Council, *Emerging Communities in Hounslow and West London: Mapping and Needs Assessment.* Based on research commissioned from Middlesex University (London: Hounslow London Borough Council, Community Partnerships Unit, 2014).

46. Nirad Pragasam, 'Tigers on the Mind: An Interrogation of Conflict Diasporas and Long Distance Nationalism: A study of the Sri Lankan Tamil Diaspora in London'. PhD thesis, London School of Economics and Political Science, 2012.

47. Hounslow Borough Council, *Thriving Communities and VCSE Sector Strategy: 2015–2019* (London: Hounslow Borough Council, Community Partnerships Unit, 2015).

48. Ibid.

49. Ibid., 10.

50. Hounslow Borough Council, *Emerging Communities in Hounslow and West London.*

51. Local Government Information Unit, *Resilience in Practice* (London: Islington, 2015), http://tinyurl.com/ku7hkls

52. Hounslow Borough Council, *Thriving Communities and VCSE Sector Strategy*, 26 and 15.

53. Ibid.

54. Hounslow Borough Council, *Emerging Communities in Hounslow and West London.*

55. *London24 Online Journal*, 'Londoner of the Day: Thavarani Nagulendram', 2014 – accessed February 2016. London24 has since closed down.

56. Selvy Thiruchandran, *Stories from the Diaspora*, 79.

57. Home Office, *Controlling Our Borders: Making Migration Work for Britain. Five Year Strategy for Asylum and Immigration* (London: H.M. Stationery Office, February, 2005), http://tinyurl.com/my3qhmk

58. Amelia Gentleman, '"What crime have I committed to be held like this?": Inside Yarl's Wood', *Guardian*, 3 March 2015.

59. Refugee Council, *Detention in the Asylum System* (London: Refugee Council, September 2015).

60. Stephen Shaw, 'Report of the Inquiry into the Disturbance and Fire at Yarl's Wood Removal Centre'. Prisons and Probation Ombudsman for England and Wales. October, 2004, http://tinyurl.com/kn5vkmm

61. Black Women's Rape Action Project and Women Against Rape, 'Rape and Sexual Abuse: In Yarl's Wood Immigration Removal Centre 2005–2015', London, 2015, http://tinyurl.com/n5fluwh

62. Women for Refugee Women, 'I Am Human: Refugee Women's Experiences of Detention in the UK', London, 2015, http://tinyurl.com/mtz7kye

63. See for instance, Radhika Sanghani, 'Inside Britain's Worst Immigration Removal Centre at Christmas', *Telegraph*, 24 December 2014, http://tinyurl.com/ljl6p6d

64. Channel 4 Television, 'Yarl's Wood: Undercover in the Secretive Immigration Centre', *News*, 2 March 2015, http://tinyurl.com/mafxshj

65. H.M. Inspector of Prisons, *Report on an Unannounced Inspection of Yarl's Wood Immigration Removal Centre* (London: H.M. Inspector of Prisons, 2015), http://tinyurl.com/o92vxvg

66. Medical Justice, *A Secret Punishment: The Misuse of Segregation in Immigration Detention* (London: Medical Justice, 2015), http://tinyurl.com/mtbr25f

67. Mark Townsend, 'Yarl's Wood: UN Special Rapporteur to Censure UK Government', *Guardian*, 3 January 2015, http://tinyurl.com/lqms8u8

68. Yarl's Wood Immigration Removal Centre, 'An Independent Investigation into Concerns about Yarl's Wood Immigration Removal Centre', January 2016, http://tinyurl.com/n8ktae7

69. Diane Taylor, 'Dossier Calling for Yarl's Wood Closure Chronicles Decade of Abuse Complaints', *Guardian*, 15 June 2015, http://tinyurl.com/moly7qa

70. United Nations High Commissioner for Refugees (UNHCR), *Guidelines on International Protection: Gender-Related Persecution within the Context of Article 1A(2) of the 1951 Convention and/or its 1967 Protocol Relating to the Status of Refugees* (Geneva: UNHCR May 2002).

71. Home Office, Asylum Policy Instruction, 'Gender Identity Issues in the Asylum Claim', London, October 2006, http://tinyurl.com/m3xnojk

72. Freedom from Torture (Medical Foundation for the Care of Victims of Torture), *Tainted Peace: Torture in Sri Lanka since May 2009* (London: Freedom from Torture, 2015), http://tinyurl.com/kjpfkby
    See also Human Rights Watch, '"We will teach you a lesson": Sexual Violence against Tamils by Sri Lankan Security Forces'. Report, 2013, http://tinyurl.com/myqr2lc

73. Human Rights Watch, 'Fast-Tracked Unfairness: Detention and Denial of Women Asylum seekers in the UK'. Report, February, 2010, 9, http://tinyurl.com/lohr72d

74. Asylum Aid, 'Unsustainable: The Quality of Initial Decision-Making in Women's Asylum Claims', London, 2011, 1, http://tinyurl.com/kh2cu60

75. Women for Refugee Women, 'I Am Human'; and Inspector of Prisons, *Report on an Unannounced Inspection*.

76. Radhika Sanghani, 'Inside Britain's Worst Immigration Removal Centre at Christmas'.

77. Mark Townsend, 'Hundreds Protest to Demand Closure of Yarl's Wood Immigration Centre', *Guardian*, 6 June 2015, http://tinyurl.com/m3zzamz

78. Transitional Government of Tamil Eelam, website at www.tgteparliament.com

79. Maja Korac, *Remaking Home: Reconstructing Life, Place and Identity in Rome and Amsterdam* (New York and Oxford: Berghahn Books, 2009).

80. I am indebted to Vairamuttu Varadakumar, Secretary of the Tamil Information Centre in Kingston upon Thames, for early advice and information as I prepared to address the story of Sri Lankan Tamils in war, and in flight. My thanks to Laura James of the Community Partnerships Unit of Hounslow Council for generously affording me a long interview from which I learned much about the council's approach to policy and practice regarding the borough's ethno-cultural minorities. I would like to express deep appreciation to Thavarani Nagulendram (Rani), the founder and organizer of the Tamil Community Centre, who introduced me to the Centre's activities and shared her personal story with me. And finally, a warm thank you to Veena Mylvaganam, and 'Srisivakumar' (a pseudonym), who also recounted moving tales from their lives including experiences in detention in the UK. A special thank you to Kulasegaram Geetharthanan, who introduced me to them.

CHAPTER 5

1. The historical data in this chapter are drawn largely from two sources: James Copnall, *A Poisonous Thorn in Our Hearts: Sudan and South Sudan's Bitter and Incomplete Divorce* (London: Hurst and Company, 2014); and Jok Madut Jok, *Sudan: Race, Religion and Violence* (London: One World Publications, 2007, revised 2016).

2. Jok Madut Jok, *Sudan*, 12.

3. Andrew Natsios, *Sudan, South Sudan and Darfur: What Everyone Needs to Know* (Oxford: Oxford University Press, 2012).

4. Amnesty International, 'South Sudan: Army and Police Forces Shooting and Raping Civilians in Jonglei', *News*, 3 October 2012, http://tinyurl.com/lnttvaw

5. James Copnall, *A Poisonous Thorn in Our Hearts*, 248.

6. Amnesty International, 'Q&A: Three Years On, South Sudan is Locked in a Cycle of Violence', *News*, 8 July 2014, http://tinyurl.com/lpzgn53 – Human Rights Watch, *World Report 2015: South Sudan. Events of 2014* (New York and London: Human Rights Watch, 2015), http://tinyurl.

com/lw6b9t3 – and Oxfam International, 'From Crisis to Catastrophe', *Emergency Briefing Note* (Oxford: Oxfam, 2014).

7. Amnesty International, 'UN: South Sudan Arms Embargo Crucial after Massive Chinese Weapons Transfer', *News*, 17 July 2014, http://tinyurl.com/lljc7yu

8. Amnesty International, *Annual Report: South Sudan 2015/2016* (London: Amnesty International, 2016), http://tinyurl.com/go96ecc – see also *Annual Report: South Sudan 2016/17*, http://tinyurl.com/kf7v26u

9. Human Rights Watch, '"We can die too": Recruitment and Use of Child Soldiers in South Sudan', *Report*, 14 December 2015 (New York and London: Human Rights Watch, 2015), http://tinyurl.com/kn37zmz

10. Luke Patey, *The New Kings of Crude: China, India and the Global Struggle for Oil in Sudan and South Sudan* (London: C. Hurst & Co. Ltd, 2014).

11. Jok Maduk Jok, *Sudan*, 198.

12. Human Rights Watch, *World Report 2014: South Sudan. Events of 2013* (New York and London: Human Rights Watch, 2014), http://tinyurl.com/n3jv4s3

13. Human Rights Watch, 'Sudan: Cluster Bombs Used in Nuba Mountains', *News*, 15 April 2015, http://tinyurl.com/lrp9e69 – and Amnesty International, 'Sudan: Dire Human Rights Situation Continues'. Amnesty International submission to the UN Universal Periodic Review, May 2016, http://tinyurl.com/m7p3rrw

14. Foreign and Commonwealth Office, UK, 'Joint Statement on Aerial Bombardment in South Kordofan and De Facto Expulsion of OCHA Head', 27 May 2016, http://tinyurl.com/mtgs7er

15. For information in the following paragraphs about the Darfur conflict I am indebted in particular to three sources: Samuel Totten and Erik Markusen (eds), *Genocide in Darfur: Investigating the Atrocities in the Sudan* (New York and London: Routledge, 2006); Robert Collins, 'Disaster in Darfur: A Historical Overview', in the foregoing volume, 3–23; and Anders Hastrup, *The War in Darfur: Reclaiming Sudanese History* (London and New York: Routledge, 2013).

16. Robert Collins, 'Disaster in Darfur', 11–12.

17. Eric Reeves, 'Children within Darfur's Holocaust'. Article, 23 December 2005, in his *Sudan: Research, Analysis and Advocacy*, http://tinyurl.com/kpaxop7

18. United Nations, 'The United Nations and Darfur: Fact Sheet', *News*, 2007, http://tinyurl.com/mf8yhzu

19. Eric Reeves, 'We Have Learned Nothing from Rwanda'. Article, 3 July 2005, in his *Sudan*, http://tinyurl.com/n3298r7

20. Amnesty International, *Annual Report, 2015/16*, May 2016, http://tinyurl.com/go96ecc – and Human Rights Watch, 'Sudan: Students, Activists at Risk of Torture', *News*, 25 May 2016, http://tinyurl.com/jxcayfq

21. Human Rights Watch, 'Sudan: Wave of Opposition Arrests', *News*, 28 August 2015 (New York and London), http://tinyurl.com/m4t6h6r –

and Human Rights Watch, 'Open Letter from 39 NGOs and Individuals Concerning Excessive Use of Force by Sudanese Authorities', *News*, 3 May 2016, http://tinyurl.com/mqawldj

22. Sudan Update, *Report: Women in Sudan*, 1996. Available online at the website www.sudanupdate.org

23. Human Rights Watch, 'Good Girls Don't Protest: Repression and Abuse of Women Human Rights Defenders, Activists and Protesters in Sudan', *Report*, 23 March 2016, https://www.hrw.org/report/2016/03/23/ good-girls-don't-protest/repression-and-abuse-women-human-rights-defenders – accessed June 2016.

24. Orly Stern, '"This is how marriage happens sometimes": Women and Marriage in South Sudan', in Friederike Bubenzer and Orly Stern (eds), *Hope, Pain and Patience: The Lives of Women in South Sudan* (South Africa: Institute for Justice and Reconciliation and Jacana Media (Pty) Ltd, 2011), 1–23, 4, 7.

25. Jane Namadi, 'Taking on New Challenges: South Sudanese Women in Service Delivery', in Friederike Bubenzer and Orly Stern (eds), *Hope, Pain and Patience*, 163–91; and Lydia Stone '"We were all soldiers": Female Combatants in South Sudan's Civil War', in Friederike Bubenzer and Orly Stern (eds), *Hope, Pain and Patience*, 25–51.

26. Asha Arabi, '"In power without power": Women in Politics and Leadership', in Friederike Bubenzer and Orly Stern (eds), *Hope, Pain and Patience*, 193–213, 201.

27. Kelly Dawn Askin, 'Prosecuting Gender Crimes Committed in Darfur: Holding Leaders Accountable for Sexual Violence', in Samuel Totten and Erik Markusen (eds), *Genocide in Darfur*, 141–60.

28. Waging Peace, 'Rape in Darfur: A History of Predation', November 2015, http://wagingpeace.info/images/Rape_report_v.3b_web.pdf – accessed August 2016.

29. Kelly Dawn Askin, 'Prosecuting Gender Crimes Committed in Darfur'.

30. Human Rights Watch, 'Good Girls Don't Protest'.

31. UNHCR, United Nations Office of the High Commissioner for Human Rights, 'South Sudan: UN Report Contains "Searing" Account of Killings, Rapes and Destruction', 2016, www.ohchr.org/EN/HRBodies/HRC/ RegularSessions/Session31/Documents/A-HRC-31-CR?P-6_en.doc – accessed May 2016.

32. Godriver Wanga-Odhiambo, *Resilience in South Sudanese Women: Hope for Daughters of the Nile* (Lanham, Boulder, New York, Toronto and Plymouth, UK: Lexington Books, 2014).

33. Fund for Peace, *Fragile States Index 2015* (Washington, DC,... Fund for Peace, 2016), http://tinyurl.com/o9nscr6

34. I have drawn in this and the following paragraph on data assembled from many sources by the International Organization of Migration, London, and published in its report *Migration in Sudan: A Country Profile 2011*.

With the Sudanese Centre for Migration, Development and Population Studies (London and Khartoum, 2013), http://tinyurl.com/ma727wv

In particular I draw on Table 5: Sudanese refugees and asylum-seekers abroad, around 1 January 2009; Table 28: Sudanese population abroad by selected countries of residence, 1 January 2000–2008; and Table 34: Sudanese refugees in neighbouring countries, 2006–2009.

35. My source for these asylum figures is Office of National Statistics, Home Office. *Asylum Statistics*, Volume 2, Table as_02: Asylum applications and initial decisions for main applicants and dependants, by country of nationality, 1979–2015, http://tinyurl.com/ltzlmgg

36. Refugee Council, *Quarterly asylum statistics* (London, February 2016), http://tinyurl.com/l5w57zn

37. Red Cross, 'Refugee Facts and Figures' (London, 2016), http://tinyurl.com/jayonnp

38. International Organization of Migration, *Sudan: Mapping Exercise, London July 2006* (London, 2011), 16, http://tinyurl.com/kg8w6zb

39. Elizabeth Ajith, 'Identity and Belonging among the First and Second Generation of South Sudanese in London'. Accredited Empowerment Course, Development and Presentation of Research Skills: 2011–2013 (London: Evelyn Oldfield Unit and Africa Educational Trust, 2012).

40. International Organization of Migration, *Sudan*, 7.

41. London Borough of Camden, *The Camden Plan: 2012–2017* (London: Camden Borough Council, 2012), http://tinyurl.com/kbzqe5h

42. London Borough of Camden, *A New Strategic Relationship with the Voluntary Sector* (London: Camden Borough Council, 2015), http://tinyurl.com/k5568cee

43. London Borough of Camden, *CS Investment and Support Programme 2012–2016* (London: Camden Borough Council, 2010), http://tinyurl.com/lprrmyk

44. London Borough of Camden, *A New Strategic Relationship with the Voluntary Sector*.

45. Craig Walzer (ed.), *Out of Exile: Narratives from the Abducted and Displaced People of Sudan* (San Francisco: McSweeney's Books, 2008).

46. I would like to express my warm thanks to the several people who gave generously of their knowledge and their time to assist me with this chapter. First, I very much appreciate the welcome I received at the South Sudan Women's Skills Development Group from its Coordinator, Elizabeth Ajith, and her introduction to the group and its work. Thank you also to Khadiga Khogali, Coordinator of Sudan Children in Need, for telling me about this group's intergenerational activity. I was fortunate to meet Sonja Miley and other activists of Waging Peace, and am grateful to them for information and advice, for introducing me to members of the Sudan Women's Group, and for enabling me to reproduce one of the children's drawings (see page 141) gathered by an associate, Anna Schmitt, in the course of a project among Sudanese refugees in a camp in Chad. I

very much value the insight and experience shared by Gasim Ibrahim and Asma Salah, of the Asylum Clinic; and of Dalia Abdelrahman, a courageous activist here in London against repression in Sudan whose story I very reluctantly had to omit in the interests of word count. My warm thanks to Kiran Patel, Grants Officer in the Communities and Third Sector Team of Camden Borough Council, for her guidance concerning the council's policy and practices. Finally, and above all, I would like to thank the women who shared their life stories with me, all of which inform the chapter and some of which are recounted in some detail. They are: Akuol Parek Makar, Grace Wani Oliver, 'Fatima' and 'Amina' (pseudonyms) and Marwa Ahmed Kessinger.

CHAPTER 6

1. International Organization for Migration, the United Nations Migration agency, Switzerland, http://tinyurl.com/kftb35s

2. United Nations High Commissioner for Refugees (UNHCR), Data Portal, http://tinyurl.com/n26ppq4

3. In the ensuing two sections briefly summarizing Syria's history from the First World War to the present conflict, I draw mainly on five sources: Reese Erlich, *Inside Syria: The Backstory of Their Civil War and What the World Can Expect* (New York: Prometheus Books, 2016); Robert Fisk, Patrick Cockburn and Kim Sengupta, *Syria: Descent into the Abyss* (London: Independent Print Limited, 2015); Charles Glass, *Syria Burning: A Short History of a Catastrophe* (London: Verso, 2016); John McHugo, *Syria: A Recent History* (London: Saqi Books, 2016); and Christopher Phillips, *The Battle for Syria: International Rivalry in the New Middle East* (New Haven and London: Yale University Press, 2016).

4. John McHugo, *Syria*, 155.

5. Patrick Cockburn, article in Robert Fisk et al., *Syria*, 150.

6. Christopher Phillips, *The Battle for Syria*, 213.

7. UN envoy for Syria, Stefan de Mistura, cited a quarter of a million deaths by April 2014, rising to 400,000 by spring 2016. Violence has continued with little interruption since. Article in *Aljazeera News*, http://tinyurl.com/hr7bvam

8. Charles Glass, *Syria Burning*.

9. UNHCR, 'Syria: 2015 End of Year Report', 2015, http://tinyurl.com/qekphz

10. Ibid.

11. Ibid.

12. UNHCR Data Portal, http://tinyurl.com/n26ppq4

13. Ibid., at http://tinyurl.com/7hgo7zy

14. United Nations Development Programme, 'Alone in Iraq: Syrian Women and Girls Struggle to Survive in Iraq', http://tinyurl.com/ztj3ykr

15. John McHugo, *Syria*.

16. Phoebe Greenwood, 'Rape and Domestic Violence Follow Syrian Women into Refugee Camps', *Guardian*, 25 July 2013, http://tinyurl.com/qekphz – Zerene Haddad, 'How the Crisis is Altering Women's Roles in Syria', *Forced Migration Review*, No.47, September 2014; and Kristin Myers, 'Five Unique Challenges Facing Syrian Refugee Women', 9 March 2016. Article for the charity Concern USA, http://tinyurl.com/lngc9s2

17. Goleen Samari, 'The Response to Syrian Refugee Women's Health Needs in Lebanon, Turkey and Jordan and Recommendations for Improved Practice', Humanity in Action, http://tinyurl.com/kwy3kmd

18. Zerene Haddad, 'How the Crisis is Altering Women's Roles in Syria'.

19. UN Women, *Annual Report: 2016*, http://annualreport.unwomen.org/en/2016

20. Patrick Kingsley, *The New Odyssey: The Story of Europe's Refugee Crisis* (London: Guardian Books and Faber & Faber Ltd, 2016).

21. Sevil Erkuş, 'Turkey's Wall on Syria Border Sharply Reduces Illegal Crossings', *Hurriyet Daily News*, 25 March 2017, http://tinyurl.com/moq6c5g

22. Patrick Kingsley, *Guardian*, 10 August 2015; and Ian Traynor and Patrick Kingsley, *Guardian*, 22 September 2015.

23. Refers to the twelve months to March 2015. Alan Travis, *Guardian*, 28 August 2015.

24. Patrick Wintour, *Guardian*, 7 September 2015.

25. Prior to this initiative, in 2014 the government had established a modest 'Syrian Vulnerable Persons Programme' to accept a small number of the most vulnerable Syrian refugees, mainly women and children. During 2015, 1,194 people came into the UK under this scheme. In the same period, 2,609 Syrians made asylum applications in the UK, having made their own way across the border. See Refugee Council, *Brief Guide to Asylum* (London: Refugee Council, February 2016).

26. David Cameron, article in the *Guardian*, 4 February 2016.

27. Alan Travis, *Guardian*, 1 August, 2015.

28. Patrick Wintour, *Guardian*, 28 January 2016.

29. House of Lords, Grand Committee, Tuesday, 9 February 2016, Immigration Bill. Hansard, http://tinyurl.com/j54rt7k

30. Anushka Asthana and Karen McVeigh, *Guardian*, 26 April, 2016.

31. London Councils, 'London Boroughs Ask What's Next for Asylum-Seeking Children Settled in Capital Since Calais Camp Was Dismantled', 2 December 2016, http://tinyurl.com/js8meh3

32. Esther Addley and Helen Pidd, *Guardian*, 28 May 2016.

33. Alan Travis and Rowena Mason, *Guardian*, 27 May 2016.

34. Josh Lowe, 'Theresa May: World Must Do More to Reduce Migration', *Newsweek*, 19 September 2016, http://tinyurl.com/hx04ux4

35. Solidarity with Refugees, see their website at www.swruk.org

36. Emma Graham-Harrison and Lizzie Davies, *Observer*, 13 September 2015.

37. Unauthored article in the *Telegraph*, 3 September 2015, Telegraph View, 'The Refugees Welcome Fad Will Do More Harm Than Good', http://tinyurl.com/ngtycyv

38. See their website, www.lbc.co.uk/radio/

39. *Huffington Post*, 'Katie Hopkins Wrote This in *The Sun* About Migrants and Now Everyone Is Really Angry', 18 April 2015, http://tinyurl.com/kmnr4jr

40. *Plymouth Herald*, 'Katie Hopkins Attacks Dad of Drowned Refugee Baby Aylan Kurdi on Anniversary of His Death', 2 September 2016, http://tinyurl.com/hp4no5d

41. Alex Hunt, 'UKIP: The Story of the UK Independence Party's Rise', *BBC News* website, 21 November 2014, http://tinyurl.com/juttr36

42. Media Mole, 'Nigel Farage's Anti-EU Poster Depicting Migrants Resembles Nazi Propaganda', *New Statesman*, 16 June 2016, http://tinyurl.com/hsa7mkr

43. Jon Stone, *Independent*, 22 December, 2016, http://tinyurl.com/hs5bom4

44. Edward Helmore and Martin Pengelly, *Guardian*, 13 November 2016.

45. Heather Stewart, *Guardian*, 26 January, 2016.

46. *RT News*, 'Nigel Farage and Katie Hopkins Back Trump's #MuslimBan, Want the Same for Britain', 30 January 2017, http://tinyurl.com/qekphz

47. John O'Sullivan, 'Populism vs. Post-Democracy', *Spectator,* 31 December 2016, http://tinyurl.com/n3erpul

48. Josh Lowe, 'The Next Brexit', *Newsweek*, 23 November 2016.

49. It was a scheme pioneered by the Canadian government and adopted by the British Home Office in July 2016, see http://tinyurl.com/mk93xpw

50. Katie Barlow, 'Ahmad's Story', *Channel 4 News*, 7 June 2016, http://tinyurl.com/ktj7mc2

51. *Politics Home*, 'MPs: Evidence Lacking for Scrapping Dubs Child Refugee Scheme', 6 March 2017, http://tinyurl.com/kdd4nbb

52. Parliament UK, Minister of State, Home Office, 'Syrian Vulnerable Persons Resettlement Scheme and Vulnerable Children's Resettlement Scheme – Arrangements: Written statement – HLWS553', http://tinyurl.com/qekphz

53. Colin Yeo, 'Home Office Ends Policy of Automatic Settlement for Refugees after Five Years', 9 March 2017, online at the website freemovement.org.uk, http://tinyurl.com/z5pssfo

54. Many people helped me with this chapter. First and foremost I would like to thank George Gabriel, for teaching me about the inspiring movement called Citizens UK, and the two major projects he has fostered therein, Refugees Welcome and Safe Passage. I thank him too for introducing me to James Asfa, a key organizer in the regional South London Citizens and the local Lambeth Citizens, who in turn kindly led me to leaders of some of their most active groups. Among these, a big thank you to Rabbi Janet

Darley of the South London Liberal Synagogue, Barbara Wilson, 'justice and peace' activist in the Roman Catholic Church of Corpus Christi in Brixton, and Mother Ellen Eames, pastor of Saint Gabriel's College secondary school in Camberwell, for taking time to recount your parts in the mobilizing of a Refugees Welcome movement. I gained greatly from interviews accorded me by the Leader of Lambeth Council, Councillor Lib Peck, and Dr Simon Sandberg, Manager of the NRPF Unit associated with the Departments of Housing and Children's Social Care in the Borough Council – my warm appreciation to you both. And finally, to Hafiza, long-time Syrian resident of Lambeth; Merry and Nehad, newly-arrived SVPRS refugee family; and Katie Barlow, their Refugees Welcome landlady and documentary film-maker, a special thank you for generously sharing your stories.

Index